Birth Control

Recent Titles in the

CONTEMPORARY WORLD ISSUES
Series

Books in the **Contemporary World Issues** series address vital issues in today's society such as genetic engineering, pollution, and biodiversity. Written by professional writers, scholars, and nonacademic experts, these books are authoritative, clearly written, up-to-date, and objective. They provide a good starting point for research by high school and college students, scholars, and general readers as well as by legislators, businesspeople, activists, and others.

Each book, carefully organized and easy to use, contains an overview of the subject, a detailed chronology, biographical sketches, facts and data and/or documents and other primary source material, a forum of authoritative perspective essays, annotated lists of print and nonprint resources, and an index.

Readers of books in the Contemporary World Issues series will find the information they need in order to have a better understanding of the social, political, environmental, and economic issues facing the world today.

Birth Control

A REFERENCE HANDBOOK

David E. Newton

ABC-CLIO®

An Imprint of ABC-CLIO, LLC
Santa Barbara, California • Denver, Colorado

Library of Congress Cataloging-in-Publication Data

Names: Newton, David E., author.
Title: Birth control : a reference handbook / David E. Newton.
Other titles: Contemporary world issues.
Description: Santa Barbara : ABC-CLIO, [2020] | Series: Contemporary world issues | Includes bibliographical references and index.
Identifiers: LCCN 2019045868 (print) | LCCN 2019045869 (ebook) | ISBN 9781440872846 (hardcover ; alk. paper) | ISBN 9781440872853 (ebook)
Subjects: MESH: Contraception—history | Contraception—methods | History of Medicine | United States
Classification: LCC HQ763 (print) | LCC HQ763 (ebook) | NLM WP 11 AA1 | DDC 613.9—dc23
LC record available at https://lccn.loc.gov/2019045868
LC ebook record available at https://lccn.loc.gov/2019045869

ISBN: 978-1-4408-7284-6 (print)
      978-1-4408-7285-3 (ebook)

24 23 22 21 20   1 2 3 4 5

This book is also available as an eBook.

ABC-CLIO
An Imprint of ABC-CLIO, LLC

ABC-CLIO, LLC
147 Castilian Drive
Santa Barbara, California 93117
www.abc-clio.com

This book is printed on acid-free paper ∞

Manufactured in the United States of America

Preface

Unplanned pregnancies are a crucial fact of life in the United States and other countries of the world today. In 2011, the year for which the most recent data are available, 45 out of every 1,000 pregnancies (an estimated 2.8 million pregnancies) in the United States were unplanned. That number means that about 5 percent of reproductive-age women in the country were having an unintended pregnancy every year. Of this number, 27 percent (out of 45 percent) were unexpected pregnancies that a women or couple had hoped for "sometime later" in their lives. The other 18 percent were pregnancies that were just not wanted under any circumstance. These numbers are the highest for any developed country in the world.

The rate of unplanned pregnancies was very different for various subgroups of women: five times as great among women below the poverty rate compared to those above the poverty rate; the highest for women in the age group 15–19 years for any age group of women; twice as high for black women as for their white counterparts; and nearly twice as great for women without a high school diploma as for those with a diploma. Roughly half of all unintended pregnancies (42 percent, not counting miscarriages) end in abortion; the remaining 58 percent end in childbirth.

Methods are available, of course, to reduce the risk of unplanned pregnancy: contraceptives. In the United States today, 18 contraceptive devices and methods have been approved by the U.S. Food and Drug Administration for use by women and men. The efficacy of these options varies from

100 percent (abstinence, vasectomy, and tubal ligation) to about 75 percent (fertility awareness-based methods, spermicides, withdrawal, and vaginal sponge). Even with the accessibility of these devices and methods, however, a surprisingly low number of reproductive-age women (and their partners)—about 62 percent—actually make use of contraception during their reproductive lives.

For a variety of reasons, young adults are especially at risk for unintended pregnancies. They may not be well informed about birth control; are discouraged by parents, friends, or others from using the most effective means of contraception; or do not have easy access to contraceptive devices. Sex education that includes information about contraception is now available in a large fraction of American schools. But those programs may emphasize only one form of contraception (abstinence) or skip over the topic entirely. For a variety of reasons, then, adolescents are more limited in their access to contraception than are women and men of almost any age.

This book is designed to help remedy that situation. It provides factual information about contraception, along with a variety of tools with which readers can learn more about the topic. Chapter 1 focuses on basic issues, such as history and the nature of contraceptives themselves: how they work and how effective they are likely to be. Humans have been concerned about contraception throughout history. In the earliest days, women and men invented devices and methods that now seem more than primitive; they were sometimes harmful and even life threatening. In fact, it was not until the early 20th century that even the simplest effective contraceptive devices had been developed and brought to the marketplace. The invention of the pill in the late 1960s, for example, not only changed the nation and the world's birth control practices but also revolutionized the role of women in society.

Chapter 2 of the book deals with current issues relating to contraception. It probably goes without saying that abortion, the distribution of condoms among adolescents, the teaching of sexual abstinence in the schools, the use of birth control for population control issues, and the availability of assisted reproductive technologies have raised not only technical problems but also profound social, political, economic, and other issues of widespread popular interest. The country sometimes seems to be moving forward in resolving some of these issues but at other times appears to be mired in apparently unresolvable debates.

The remaining chapters of the book provide tools with which readers can further explore the topic of birth control. Chapter 4 provides profiles of important individuals in the history and current status of contraception. Chapter 5 consists of a selection of important court cases, laws, and other documents, as well as some relevant statistics, about contraception. Chapter 6 is an extensive annotated bibliography on the topic, and Chapter 7 offers a chronology of important events in the history of birth control. Finally, a glossary contains definitions for many of the terms used in this book, along with other terms that one might encounter in one's further research on the topic. Chapter 3 differs somewhat from these chapters in that it provides a group of essays about specific aspects of birth control that may not be discussed or are treated only very lightly, in the main text itself. The reader is also encouraged to pay special attention to the references at the conclusion of Chapters 1 and 2. These references are useful clues to other topics and more detailed treatment of subjects covered in the two chapters.

Birth Control

There is also a third type of phalangium, a hairy spider with an enormous head. When this is cut open, there are said to be found inside two little worms, which tied in deer skin as an amulet on women before sunrise, act as a contraceptive. . . . They retain this property for a year. (Piroreschi 1995, 79)

This recipe for a birth control method was first proposed by the famous Roman natural philosopher Pliny the Elder (23–79 CE). It is only one of a host of substances, devices, and methods developed to prevent pregnancy or to abort an embryo or fetus. Physicians in ancient Egypt, Greece, Rome, China, India, and other cultures knew essentially nothing about the human reproductive system. They relied on folk medicine, natural products, and their own conjectures as to how a woman could be protected from pregnancy and/or childbirth. In fact, it was not until the Renaissance that scientific experimentation began to produce reliable information about the parts of the human reproductive system and the ways in which those parts were involved in the development of an embryo, fetus, and baby. The first of those breakthroughs occurred in the late 17th century with the discovery of the sperm and egg. The role

Margaret Sanger and Fania Mindell in the Brownsville Clinic, October 1916. (Library of Congress)

played by these structures in the human body, however, was not explained until almost two centuries later. Throughout this period, researchers argued about the steps that occurred when a man impregnated a woman, producing a new human being (Clarke 2006; Cobb 2012; Cole 1930).

Birth Control: Ancient Times to the Renaissance

Prior to the rise of the earliest human civilizations in about 3500 BCE, birth control was probably a nonexistent or minor issue. Such was the case largely because natural forces tend to mitigate against successful rates of reproduction. Human reproduction tends to be a slow and relatively inefficient process. Women ovulate about once a month, the only time during which they are likely to become pregnant. Babies and young children are especially susceptible to disease and accidents, so that, especially during the earliest period of humanity, the infant death rate tended to be high. Breastfeeding, historically the most common form of nourishment for the young, tends to continue for many months or years, a period during which women are unlikely to become pregnant again. (This process is known as *lactational amenorrhea*, the inability of a woman to have menstruation while she is producing milk for her baby.) For reasons such as these, prehistoric and early historic human societies were probably more concerned about a low rate of reproduction than excessive births (Potts 1972, 2019).

Throughout the vast stretch of human history, then, physicians recommended a variety of birth control methods. These methods can be classified into three main categories: chemicals, devices, and behaviors.

Spermicides and Other Chemicals

The ancients used a wide variety of natural (and sometimes synthetic) materials designed to prevent a woman's becoming pregnant or kill and expel the embryo or fetus growing inside her. Substances of the former type are generally *spermicides* (or *spermaticides*), chemicals that destroy sperm, or *abortifacients*, chemicals that cause the expulsion of an embryo or fetus from the womb. Among the very large number of such chemicals recommended throughout the centuries are the following:

- A combination of acacia leaves (*Acacia auriculiformis*), honey, and ground dates soaked in a cotton or wool pad and inserted into the vagina. The mixture may have been somewhat effective since the acacia leaves ferment to produce lactic acid, a spermicide (Dembitsky 2008, 641).
- Pomegranate peel, chopped and mixed with water, and then applied to the vagina.
- Ghee (clarified butter), combined with honey, tree seeds, water, and, sometimes, salt, to be applied to the vagina. This concoction was especially common in Southeast Asia (Helig 1905).
- Crushed juniper berries smeared on either male or female genitalia (or both), a recipe recommended by Greek physician Pedanius Dioscorides in his classic work *De Materia Medica*.
- Olive oil or cedar oil in combination with other substances, such as honey and/or cedar resin, a recipe thought to have been created by Aristotle.
- Poultices of hemlock, pennyroyal, or other toxic herbs, prepared (hopefully) in concentrations insufficient to kill the user, but sufficient to cause an embryo or fetus to be expelled.
- Solutions of lead, mercury, and/or arsenic, all of which are toxic or very harmful to human health. Again, the challenge was to produce a combination that would destroy sperm and/or expel the embryo or fetus without seriously harming the woman who used the mixture. The recipe was especially popular among Chinese prostitutes (Zhuhong 2009).

- The silphium plant (also known as laserwort, laser, or silphion), which became extinct as a result of its overuse for contraception. The plant was apparently first discovered in about the seventh century BCE by Greek settlers to the North African province of Cyrene. The plant had so many uses for medical problems (including contraception) that it was heavily harvested and disappeared by about 100 CE. Seventeen other species in the *Silphium* genus still exist, as members of the Asteraceae family (McCarthy 1999).

- The dung from animals such as the crocodile, elephant, cow, camel, and donkey. These materials were inserted into the vagina with what may have been a spermicidal effect. These materials tend to be slightly acidic and may, therefore, be toxic to sperm. (For a good overview of contraception in ancient times, see Knowles 2012.)

Barrier Methods

The idea of using some type of physical barrier during intercourse to prevent a man's sperm from entering a woman's vagina goes back to the earliest days of human civilization. Almost every type of mechanical contraception available to women and men today—including male and female condoms, cervical caps, diaphragms, and suppositories—had an early expression long before the beginning of the modern era.

Condoms

As with any information about birth control (and many other topics), assessing the "first," the "original," or the "earliest" appearance of an object or event is very difficult to determine. According to some authorities, the first appearance of the male condom dates to about 11,000 BCE in artwork that appears to depict a man in the process of having sexual intercourse while wearing a condom (Capitan Breuil 1902). An occurrence more commonly mentioned as the first use of a condom, this one designed for use by a woman, dates to the origins of the Minoan civilization sometime after 2000 BCE. As with the earlier event, this episode is clouded in mystery and, in fact, is apparently the only mention of condoms during the ancient Greek and Roman periods (Feldblum and Rosenberg 1989). According to this story, Minos was unable to have children because his sperm contained serpents and scorpions. A woman friend made him a condom out of a goat's bladder that was inserted to his partner's vagina, thus removing the serpents and scorpions from his body. He then went on to sire eight children with his wife (Khan et al. 2013).

The use of condoms as a form of contraception apparently received little attention in ancient Greece and Rome, and for a millennium thereafter. One of the very few such references, by the Roman writer Antoninus Liberalis, mentions a female condom made from a goat's bladder (Stern 2002). Condoms available during this period were usually made out of linen; silk; oiled paper; the bladder or intestine of a lamb, sheep, or goat (or, as sometimes claimed, muscle tissue of a dead gladiator); animal horn; and tortoise shell (Marfatia, Pandya, and Mehta 2015). But they were usually intended to prevent the transmission of sexual diseases such as syphilis and gonorrhea. In fact, male condoms reached their peak of popularity in the premodern world in the early 16th century. The proximate cause of this change was the appearance and rapid spread of syphilis, pejoratively called by a variety of names—the "French disease," by the English, Italians, and Germans; the "Neapolitan disease," by the French; the "Polish disease," by the Russians; the "Christian disease," by the Turks, just to name the most common terms—to assign blame for the terrible epidemic that developed. Perhaps the most notable response to this epidemic was the invention by Italian anatomist Gabriele Falloppio (1523–1562) of a male condom made of linen soaked in a mixture of chemicals that included wine, guaiac, and mercury. Falloppio tested his device on 1,100 volunteers and found it to be highly effective at preventing the spread of syphilis. Almost nothing was known at the time, however, about possible contraceptive effects of the invention (Tsaraklis, Athanasios et al. 2017).

As the use of male condoms to prevent sexually transmitted diseases spread throughout the general population, observers began to note that that use was generally accompanied by a reduction in the birth rate, the first evidence that male condoms might have use in that arena also. In fact, in 1666, the English Birth Rate Commission, taking note of an unexpected drop in the nation's birth rate, attributed that change to an increasing use of "the condom," generally thought to be the first appearance of the modern term in print (Collier 2007, 67).

The popularity of the male condom soon produced a reaction among critics who found such use sinful and immoral. One of the first complaints of this type has been credited to the Belgian Jesuit priest Leonardus Lessius. In his 1632 book, *De Justitia et Jure. Ceterisque Virtutibus Cardinalibus Libri Quatuor* (*The Justice and Rights. Four Other Cardinal Virtues Books*), Lessius argues that the use of male condoms is sinful and immoral and, therefore, prohibited to Christians (Khan et al. 2013). Unsurprisingly, this view soon spread throughout the secular community, where the use of male condoms became associated with prostitutes, libertines, and other individuals of ill-repute. By 1717, for example, the renowned English physician Daniel Turner had begun to write against the use of male condoms since the practice encouraged men to feel safer during sex and, therefore, more inclined to have relationships with women of poor character who were likely to be infected with a sexual disease (Samuel 2005; Stevens 2017). The claim that male condom use encourages infidelity, promiscuity, prostitution, an early introduction to sexual behavior, and other forms of immoral sexual behavior hardly disappeared with the end of the Victorian era in England; indeed, it remains one of the pillars of opposition to at least some forms of male condom use throughout the world today.

Almost certainly, the most important event in the history of the condom took place in the mid-1800s with the discovery of rubber vulcanization by American inventor Charles Goodyear. Although Goodyear's name is most commonly associated with the process, his work was anticipated in some regards by a similar line of research by British inventor Thomas Hancock. By 1820, Hancock had received patents for the production of several personal and household products, such as gloves, stockings, and shoes. But his products suffered from the same problems as other products made out of natural rubber: they expanded and sometimes melted in warm weather and contracted and became brittle in cold weather.

By 1839, Goodyear had invented a method for dealing with this problem: vulcanization. Vulcanization involves the addition of small amounts of sulfur to molten rubber. When the rubber cools, it becomes a stable material that maintains its shape and other physical properties at a wide range of temperatures. By 1844, both Hancock and Goodyear had received patents for the invention of condoms made out of vulcanized rubber. The condoms were safer than traditional products, both in their barrier properties and in their tendency not to break. (The latter property meant that they could be washed and reused, not a practice that is recommended any longer! [The Chemistry of Condom Materials—From Sheep Guts to Synthetic Rubber 2018; from Penis Sheaths to Mandatory Condoms—A Journey Through Time 2019; Schwarcz 2016].)

The next stage in the development of condoms involved the use of synthetic latex. Natural latex is a milky white fluid obtained from the Pará rubber tree (*Hevea brasiliensis*). It consists primarily of an organic compound (polyisoprene) suspended in water, along with several impurities. Natural rubber is obtained by treating latex to obtain a purer product with many practical uses. In the early 1920s, researchers discovered ways of making latex by synthetic means, producing suspensions of polyisoprene or similar compounds in water. One of the first products made from synthetic latex was a new form of condoms, stronger and thinner than previous kinds of condoms, with a longer shelf-life. The first such products were made commercially available by Youngs Rubber in the United States in 1920. They were sold under the "Trojan" brand name. The first latex condoms became available in Europe in 1932, produced by the London Rubber Company (Collier 2007, Chapter 12).

Condom technology has continued to develop ever since the appearance of the latex models. The focus of most recent research has been the use of polymeric materials (plastics) in place of rubber or latex. A virtually endless range of plastics have been invented, and researchers continue to test many of these products in the design of new types of condoms. The first such product, made of polyurethane, became available from the London Rubber Company in 1994 (First Plastic Condom for Men Becomes Available Next Year 1993).

Diaphragms and Cervical Caps

Diaphragms and cervical caps are dome-shaped devices designed to fit over the cervix, thereby preventing sperm from reaching the uterus. Diaphragms and cervical caps are generally similar in shape, with the latter somewhat smaller in size than the former. The cap is generally designed, also, to fit more tightly over the cervix. Both devices are also coated with a spermicide before insertion.

Such devices have been known since time immemorial. Individuals have tried a seemingly endless number of ways of achieving this objective, using materials as diverse as oiled paper discs, algae and seaweed, sponges, tissue paper, beeswax, rubber, wool, pepper, seeds, silver, tree roots, rock salt, fruits, vegetables, and barriers made of molded opium (Wortman 1976). Some of the earliest forms of diaphragms and cervical caps were *pessaries*, made of wood, metal, leaves, or other materials. Modern diaphragms and cervical caps are very much improved forms of a pessary.

The earliest modern device made on these general principles was described in 1838 by German physician Friedrich

Wilde. Wilde called his device, perhaps the first form of a cervical cap, the "cautchuk pessarium." It was an updated version of a traditional German pessary made by covering the cervix with melted beeswax. The device had to be custom-fitted and made for each user. Wilde's device appears to have had limited usefulness as the natural rubber of which it was made rapidly hardened, and the device was no longer effective. This problem was largely resolved by the invention of vulcanization by Charles Goodyear in 1839. At that point, several inventors in the United States, Great Britain, and other countries began to develop one or another form of the cervical cap. In the United States, for example, physician and author Edward Bliss Foote designed and sold a device that he called a *womb veil*, essentially identical in form to the modern cervical cap. Foote advertised his product widely and sold it for about six dollars each (Tone 2002, Chapter 2).

The origin of the modern diaphragm is generally dated to a device developed by German physician Karl Hasse in 1882. It consisted of a latex covering held in place over the cervix by means of a coiled spring. Hasse published his work under the name "W. P. J. Mensinga" because of concerns that his invention might harm his professional reputation. For that reason, the device was generally known as the Mensinga diaphragm (Bosch 2017; there is disagreement as to the relationship of the names "Hasse" and "Mensinga," with respect as to which was his real name and which was his pseudonym). Word of Hasse's invention soon spread to other parts of Europe and the United States. It was developed most fully in the Netherlands, where physicians Aletta Jacobs and Jan Rutgers began to recommend the device for their women patients. By the mid-1910s, the diaphragm was being imported to the United States (secretly, because of the Comstock Laws) by Margaret Sanger and Mary Ware Dennett and their Voluntary Parenthood League. This action by American proponents of contraception was, in fact, one of the primary reasons that Sanger and others were eventually arrested under provisions of the Comstock Laws (Bosch

2017). For about a decade, Americans had access to the dia-phragm only as an imported product hidden in oil cans shipped from Sanger's husband's plant in Canada. Finally, in 1925, the first American diaphragm plant was established in New York by the Holland-Rantos Company (Payne 2010).

Vaginal Sponge

A vaginal sponge is a small pad made of an absorbent mate-rial soaked with a spermicide inserted into the vagina prior to intercourse. Some of the earliest references to such a contracep-tive device can be found in the Talmud, dating to sometime after 200 CE. These references mention several situations in which a sponge (a type of *mokh*) can or must be used during sexual intercourse, either prior to or after the act itself (Feld-man 1968, Chapters 9, 11, and 12). Occasional mention of similar devices can be found throughout the next 17 centuries. For example, a text written by the French physician S. A. D. Tissot in the mid-18th century contains a detailed description of the structure, composition, and use of a vaginal sponge (Tis-sot 1765).

The modern-day vaginal sponge first appeared in 1983 with the release of the Today sponge by the VLI Corporation of Irvine, California. The product was the result of a nearly 10-year research project funded by the Program for Applied Research on Fertility Regulation of the U.S. Agency for Inter-national Development. The product rapidly became one of the most popular forms of contraceptive because of its three-pronged approach: physical blocking of semen from the vagina, chemical destruction of sperm with a spermicide soaked into the sponge, and an absorbent for sperm released during ejacu-lation (New Developments in Vaginal Contraception 1984). The product was later removed from the marketplace in 1994 because of manufacturing problems. It was then reintroduced in 2005 before being discontinued and reintroduced again in the late 2000s (Singer 2009).

Procedures

Contraception can also be based on certain activities that a person can take to prevent pregnancy from occurring. One of the oldest and most common of those actions is *sexual abstinence*.

Sexual Abstinence

Sexual abstinence is a fundamental component of many religions and systems of philosophy. The underlying principle seems to be that one cannot concentrate on the glorification of gods and goddesses and the pursuit of a pure and holy life if he or she is distracted by the pleasures of the flesh. The sex drive is probably the most powerful force, after the need for air, water, and food, in human existence. Great teachers have often instructed the faithful that one must learn to put the need and desire for sexual acts in order to achieve higher and more noble goals.

Sexual abstinence can take several forms, including celibacy, continuous abstinence, and periodic abstinence. The term *celibacy* refers to a condition in which a person chooses to remain unmarried and, as generally as a consequence, renounces sexual activity throughout his or her life. Celibacy has a very long tradition in human civilization. In most (perhaps all) of earliest cultures, some select group of women and/or men were selected to devote their lives to studying the philosophical or religious principles on which a society was based and then transmitting this knowledge to the general population. In many cases, young boys were castrated without their consent in order to ensure that they would carry out such functions without secular distractions later in their lives. The earliest record of this practice dates to the 21st century BCE in the Sumerian city of Lagash. Celibacy has been a common practice ever since in many, if not most, religious organizations that require the condition in order to focus a person's life on issues beyond the everyday life of the common man and woman. In such religions, celibates may include priests, monks, nuns, hermits, anchorites, and friars (Eunich 2019; Hester 2005). For example, the Roman Catholic Church decided in a pair of rulings in 1123 and 1139 that all priests, deacons, and sub-deacons must swear to be celibate, a policy that remains in effect today (Bertram 2016).

Continuous abstinence is somewhat similar to celibacy in that an individual or couples are expected to refrain from sexual relations for extended periods of time. The Buddha required celibacy from all who would follow his teachings, abandoning wives and children, as he himself had done. But for those who were unable to become completely celibate, continuous abstinence was an acceptable alternative. The term has also had a number of other meanings, including the renunciation of both intercourse and outercourse for at least some extended period of time (The Samahita Blog 2019). It may also refer to the rejection of sexual activity for a variety of reasons, such as medical issues or separation from one's partner (Sivananda 1997).

Periodic abstinence is one of the most common forms of birth control in use around the world today. It refers to the practice of going without sexual relations for some given period of time (a few days or weeks, for example), often at very regular times. For example, during the Middle Ages, Christians were expected to abstain from sex for specified periods of time throughout the year: anywhere from 47 to 62 days at Lent, between 22 and 35 days during Advent, and as many as 13 weeks in the time surrounding Pentecost, as well as all Sundays and feast days (Brundage 2009).

One form of periodic abstinence is called *the rhythm method*, a term that refers to the process of determining the times during which a woman is most likely and least likely to become pregnant and then planning one's sexual activity based on that information. For couples hoping for a pregnancy, sexual activity would occur during a woman's ovulation; for those avoiding pregnancy, they would abstain at that time. The general principle involved in the rhythm method is now better known as *fertility awareness*.

Religious organizations have long argued over the most appropriate use of fertility awareness in planning one's sexual activities. The Roman Catholic Church, for example, has historically taught that humans should have sexual relations only during a woman's fertile period. At any other times, such relations only reflect the base nature of human life and should be avoided. One of the earliest proponents of this view was Clement of Alexandria, who wrote in 191 CE that "to have coitus other than to procreate children is to do injury to nature." This view was repeated many times over in the following centuries by leaders of the Church (The Early Church Fathers on Contraception 2005). The Church has held this position almost to the present day, with the possible modification of that view in 1994 by then-pope John Paul II. (See Frequently Asked Questions Regarding Catholic Teaching on Contraception n.d.)

Other Procedures

Several other actions are also possible to prevent pregnancy. They include outercourse; coitus interruptus and coitus reservatus; late marriage; and physical actions such as sneezing or squatting. The origin of the term *outercourse* is not well documented. According to *Merriam Webster Dictionary*, the word may have first appeared in 1986. Since that time, it has been used more often, but usually without a clearly defined meaning (Outercourse 2019; Roffman 1991). In general, the term refers to any form of non-penetrative sex, actions that do not involve entry of the penis into the vagina, rectum, and, sometimes, the mouth. Some examples of outercourse include talking about sex with another person, kissing, cuddling, massage, masturbation and mutual masturbation, intercrural sex (placement of the penis between a partner's thighs, breasts, or other body parts), tribadism (a form of lesbian sex), and frottage (the touching and/or rubbing of one part of a person's body against a part of a second person's body or a physical object).

Attitudes toward outercourse in ancient history vividly illustrate contrasting views about birth control in Christian Europe and Southeast Asia, where Hinduism, Buddhism, Jainism, and other sects predominated. In the reign of Augustine of Hippo (354–430 CE), for example, the Roman Catholic Church espoused a very sex-negative philosophy, generally disapproving of all forms of sex except those intended for procreation. At almost the same time in India, however, probably the most popular work on human sexuality was the *Kama Sutra*. This text described well over a hundred positions in which both intercourse and outercourse could be conducted. It was for centuries, and continues to be, one of the world's most famous books on "the joy of sex," procreative or otherwise (Hooper 2008; The Kama Sutra of Vatsayayana 2008).

Coitus interruptus is another form of birth control with a very long history. The term *coitus interruptus* refers to any procedure in which a male withdraws his penis from a woman's vagina prior to ejaculation. The process is intended to prevent fertilization of an ovum and, thus, to avoid pregnancy. (The method is not completely safe for this purpose, however.) Many authorities date the first mention of the practice to ancient Jewish and Christian references to an event involving a man named Onan, son of Judah, himself the founder of the Jewish tribe of Judah. Upon the death of Er, Onan's older brother, God is said to have ordered Onan to marry Er's widow, Tamar. In order to ensure the proper paternity of any future children, Onan practiced coitus interruptus with his new wife, instead "spilling his seed upon the ground." God was so angry with Onan that he killed him for his disobedience in not consummating his marriage to Tamar (Onanism 2019).

Coitus interruptus may well have had an even older history than suggested by the story of Onan. Some experts point to the teaching of the Chinese master physician Tung-hsuan about the procedure. They differ, however, as to the reasons that the master made this recommendation, as a means of birth control or a way of preserving a man's "yang." ("Yang" is one of two basic principles in Chinese philosophy, one negative, dark, and feminine (yin), and one positive, bright, and masculine (yang).) In any case, records indicate that coitus interruptus continued in use in ancient Greece and Rome, although no evidence is available as to the extent or even the precise reasons for its use (Bullough 2002). (Another very old procedure related to coitus interruptus is coitus obstructus, popular in ancient China and India. See Sex Using Tantra—II 2000.)

A similar procedure, known as *coitus reservatus*, was also popular in ancient China. It involved a man's withholding climax during sex until a woman reached orgasm. He then remained within her vagina until his erection ended. The procedure was by no means a simple one and generally required training to be successful. Historians appear to agree that the primary purpose of coitus reservatus was a religious reason, ensuring that a man would not lose significant amounts of yang, while possibly gaining some yin from the woman. When used successfully, however, coitus reservatus was obviously also a method of birth control (Bullough 2002; Gross 1981).

Any number of additional methods of birth control may have existed throughout history. Occasionally, one finds reviews of such methods that seem especially curious or bizarre. For example, one of the many techniques recommended by the Greek physician Soranus of Ephesus (98–138 CE) in his classic book, *Gynaecology*, involved having a woman make physical moves inclined to reject sperm after intercourse. She might do so by sneezing, squatting, or jumping up and down to expel the sperm. This method was mentioned several times over the following 17 centuries, by physicians of many nationalities and periods of time. It still has had its proponents even in very recent times (see, for example, Khan, Siddiqui, and Nikhat 2013; Risky Contraceptive Methods Some Women Are Forced to Use—In Pictures 2018; Wallechinsky and Wallace n.d.).

The Human Reproductive System

Since the earliest days of civilization, humans have wondered about the process of reproduction. How is it that a man and a woman can come into physical union (intercourse) with each other and, by that mechanism, produce a new human, a baby? Ancient thinkers devised a number of explanations for this amazing process, all based on the act of sexual intercourse. (They also devised several methods for preventing that event from occurring, methods of contraception, described earlier in this chapter.) The only tool available to these scholars was guessing. Untold numbers of physicians and philosophers tried to imagine the steps that occurred once a man's semen entered a woman's vagina. But they had no ways of knowing whether their ideas were correct. They only knew that the contraceptive methods they recommended sometimes worked (prevented pregnancy), but more often did not.

Quite often, acceptance of a person's explanation of reproduction depended primarily on the extent to which that person was respected by other scholars and, therefore, by the public as a whole. For example, the Greek natural philosopher Aristotle (384–322 BCE) was the first person to devise a coherent and complete description of the process of reproduction in humans and other animals. He argued that the "driving force" of reproduction resides in the male's semen. The role of the woman's body is to provide a setting in which that force can grow and develop into an embryo. (Aristotle's theory is clearly based on his more general notion that men are superior to women in almost every way.) Although largely disproved by the Roman physician Galen (130–210 CE), Aristotle's theory continued to prove widely popular among medical scholars for almost 2,000 years (Lawrence 2010).

The Rise of Scientific Embryology

A new and far more reliable method of studying reproduction did not become available until the scientific revolution, dating to about the late 16th century. Among the guiding principles adopted as part of that period was a reliance on experimentation for obtaining valid information about some particular object or event. That is, in order to determine the precise function of semen in the process of reproduction, one would first have to develop some type of experiment that would allow a researcher to observe that process, carry out the experiment, and then decide what the results of the experiment showed about the original question.

Some of the earliest successes of this approach to studying human reproduction were recorded in the two-decade period covering the 1660s and 1670s. Some of the many discoveries made during that span of time included the following:

- Reinier de Graaf (1641–1673) discovered fluid-filled sacs in the ovary that contain immature eggs. Those structures are now known as Graafian follicles (Dupont 2008).

- William Harvey (1578–1657) is best known for his research on the circulation of the blood. But he was also interested in and wrote about the process of human reproduction, discussed in his *Exercitationes De Generatione Animalium* (1651). He is recognized less for this work than for his pioneering philosophy of the role of experimentation in such research (Donaldson 2009).

- Antoine (also Anton, Antoni, or Antonie) van Leeuwenhoek (1632–1723) is largely credited with the first observation and description of human sperm, collected from his own semen. (Van Leeuwenhoek's young colleague, Johan Ham, actually anticipated, but incorrectly interpreted, his discovery [Howards 1997].)

- Marcello Malpighia (1628–1694) was praised by his colleague Lazaro Spallanzani as "the first one to think of artificially fertilizing animals." Malpighia also conducted very detailed studies on the development of chicken embryos (Adelmann 1966).

- Dutchman Jan Swammerdam (1637–1680) and Dane Niels Steno (1638–1686), students of French poymath Melchisedec Thévenot, concluded on the basis of their studies that all living animals come from eggs (Cobb 2012). (A major resource for this topic is Cobb [2007].)

Modern Embryology

Today, scientists have a relatively complete understanding of the anatomy, biochemistry, and physiology of the reproductive process.

Spermatogenesis

The term *spermatogenesis* refers to the production and development of spermatozoa, or sperm cells, in the male testis. (To follow this explanation, see an illustration of the process on the Internet, such as Mudalier 2019; Spermatogenesis 2019.) The process begins when undifferentiated stem cells in the *seminiferous tubules* of the testis undergo mitosis, producing differentiated cells known as *primary spermatocytes*. Those cells then undergo meiosis, forming first *secondary spermatocytes*, and then *spermatids*. One final change converts spermatids into spermatozoa. After they are produced, sperm travels to a structure known as the *epididymis*, where it is stored for two to three weeks. If ejaculation occurs during this time, sperm travels to the tip of the penis, from which it is ejaculated. (For a good video of this process, see Sperm Release Pathway 2019.)

Oogenesis

(To follow this explanation, see an online illustration of the process, such as Almukhtar 2018; Reproduction and Development 2019, at 19:30 of video.)

Oogenesis, the production and development of oocytes (eggs), mimics the process of spermatogenesis, but on a very different time schedule. It begins during the fetal stage when undifferentiated stem cells begin to develop and specialize as *oogonia*, or egg stem cells. At the maximum stage of development, about six million to seven million egg cells are present in the fetus's body. Those eggs then begin to degenerate until about a million remain at birth. At that point, a woman's body contains all of the egg cells it will ever produce. At birth, oogonia are converted to *primary oocytes* that are encased in primary follicles, which remain inactive until puberty. With the arrival of puberty, primary oocytes begin to change into *secondary oocytes*, and the process of ovulation begins. Ovulation occurs when the body releases eggs in a process known as *menstruation*. That process occurs on a regular basis, about once each month, until the appearance of menopause, at roughly the halfway point in a woman's life.

Neither spermatogenesis nor oogenesis is a spontaneous process, occurring on its own in the male and female genital organs. Instead, both take place because of the action of chemical messengers in the body known as *hormones*. A hormone is a chemical messenger produced in one part of the body that travels to another part of the body where it controls the function of cells and organs there. During spermatogenesis, for example, a small structure in the brain known as the hypothalamus releases a hormone called gonadotropin-releasing hormone (GnRH) to the anterior pituitary, another small structure in the brain. That hormone stimulates the pituitary gland to release two other hormones, follicle-stimulating hormone (FSH) and luteinizing hormone (LH), both of which travel to the testis and begin the process of spermatogenesis. (They also produce other effects in the testis, such as the release of testosterone, which in turn produces "masculinizing" effects in the body.)

Understanding how this process occurs makes possible, at least in theory, a new method of birth control: the male contraceptive pill. This pill would be similar in concept to the female contraceptive pill described later in the chapter. It would contain chemicals that interfere with the synthesis of sperm in the testis, thus eliminating the release of sperm during sexual intercourse. Although research is currently being conducted on this concept, no such pill has yet been discovered (The Pill for Men 2019).

The role of hormones in the female reproductive system is more complex. The first stage in that process is the same as it is in the male reproductive system: The hypothalamus releases GnRH to the anterior pituitary, stimulating the pituitary gland to release FSH and LH, both of which travel to the ovaries. There, they stimulate the development of a few dozen follicles and the eggs contained with them. Eventually, one of those follicles begins to dominate the others and releases a mature egg into the fallopian tube next to it. The egg is then fertilized or sloughed off (Molnar and Gair 2012).

That process does not complete the involvement of hormones in the reproductive process, however. As the follicles begin to mature, they also start to release other hormones, a group of hormones known as *estrogens*, and another hormone called *progesterone*. (The most common of the estrogen hormones is called *estradiol*. Progesterone belongs to a family of chemical compounds known as *progestins*.) These hormones are responsible for preparing the endometrium for implantation of a fertilized egg, for the development of typical female physical characteristics, and for the control of future FSH and LH release from the hypothalamus. Understanding the details of this process also makes possible the development of a contraceptive pill for women to control the likelihood of pregnancy. That possibility has, of course, actually been achieved in a series of experiments sometimes described as one of the most consequential discoveries in biology in the 20th century. A description of that discovery follows.

Hormonal Methods of Birth Control
Birth Control Pills

It seems likely that more than one individual in history had considered the possibility that obtaining relief from pregnancy might be as easy as simply taking a pill, not unlike taking an aspirin for a headache. Such a birth control method would protect women from the risk of pregnancy with an inexpensive and effective procedure they could conduct in the privacy of their own homes and truly become the masters (or mistresses) of their own bodies. The historical record shows, however, that the first person to put such dreams into words and concrete action was the nurse, sex educator, and birth control advocate Margaret Sanger, as early as the 1920s. Sanger was unable, however, to find a chemical manufacturer willing to take on the research needed for such a project. As one, those companies rejected the possibility of searching for a contraceptive pill because of the notoriety the work would bring to their reputations. After all, contraception overall was still thought generally to be an impolite, "dirty," even unmentionable activity in the United States.

Sanger eventually found an answer to her dream of finding a "magic pill" that would prevent contraception. That event occurred in 1950 when Sanger convinced philanthropist Katharine McCormick to donate $2 million (more than $25 million in 2019 dollars) to a research program on the contraceptive pill. McCormick had her own reasons to be interested in such a project. In 1905, she had married Stanley McCormick, heir to the International Harvester fortune. Only two years after the marriage, Stanley was diagnosed with and hospitalized for schizophrenia. Fearing that the condition was hereditary, the McCormicks decided not to have children, and Katharine was confronted with the problem of dealing with birth control for the rest of her reproductive life. Sanger's plea for research funds fell, therefore, on receptive ears (Eig 2014; Roberts 2015).

In 1951, Sanger found a company that was willing to take on research on the contraceptive pill, the Worcester Foundation for Experimental Biology (WFEB), located in Shrewsbury, Massachusetts. American biologist Gregory Goodwin Pincus had founded the company in 1944 when he was blackballed by other mainstream entities for carrying out "disreputable" research on human reproduction. After meeting Pincus at a cocktail party in 1951, Sanger discovered that he was very much interested in working on a contraceptive pill. The plan came to fruition two years later when Sanger introduced McCormick to Pincus and his colleague Min-Chueh Chang, and a deal was struck.

The work at WFEB was based on earlier findings that progesterone supplements reduce the risk of a woman's becoming pregnant. As we now know, the hormone reduces the thickness of the endometrial lining, greatly reducing the likelihood of implantation after fertilization. Pincus and Chang decided to look for a synthetic form of the hormone that could be used in a contraceptive pill. They tested more than 200 substances before settling on two synthetic analogs of progesterone, norethindrone and norethynodrel. After extensive testing of the new product, they received the Food and Drug Administration (FDA) approval for the first contraceptive pill, Enovid, on May 9, 1960. Enovid is a combined oral contraceptive pill (COCP) that contains both norethynodrel and mestranol, a compound that acts like estrogen in the body. After production in the ovaries, it travels to the hypothalamus and pituitary gland, where it reduces the production of GnRH, LH, and FSH. Today, more than 30 different kinds of FDA-approved COCPs are available to consumers (Anderson 2018a).

As enthusiastic as researchers and users were about the availability of a new birth control pill, some issues remained. Several side effects were associated with the use of the new product. Some of those side effects were disturbing, but not life-threatening: for example, headaches, nausea, bloating, mood swings, and elevated blood pressure. Others were more troubling, such as blood clots in the legs, liver disorders, gallbladder disease, and increased risk of heart attack and stroke (Smith 2018). The occurrence of these side effects encouraged some researchers to look for an alternative form of oral contraceptive. One of the most promising leads was a pill that contained synthetic analogs of progesterone. This line of research was pursued because there was some evidence that the side effects of COCP were caused by estrogen in the pills. The first product of this kind was produced in France in 1968. It was withdrawn only two years later because of a handful of studies that found disturbing side effects with this pill also. Research on the progesterone-only pill (POP), also known as the *mini pill*, continued, however, and it was reintroduced in Germany in 1971 (Gelijns 1991, 171–179). Today, the mini pill is available in a number of formulations with trade names such as Camila, Errin, Heather, Jolivette, Micronor, Nor-Q.D., Norethindrone, and Ovrette (Center for Young Women's Health 2017).

A number of factors are involved in a woman's decision as to which contraceptive pill, COCP or POP, would be best for her. Both forms of the pill are highly effective as contraceptives, and that decision is based largely on individual factors in a woman's life. For example, the use of COCP is contraindicated for women who have had a history of breast cancer, stroke, or heart disease; are breastfeeding; have diabetes-related conditions; or have unexplained uterine bleeding. The use of POP, by contrast, is contraindicated by some similar conditions, such as breast cancer or uterine bleeding, as well as those on anticonvulsive agents. A woman's personal physical and emotional feelings in favor of one or the other pill are also a determining factor on her choice of medications (Anderson 2018b; Choosing a Birth Control Pill 2019; Contraception in Early Adolescence 2011).

Emergency Contraception

Most of the history of contraceptive technology involves the use of materials and methods in use *prior to* sexual intercourse. However, materials and methods for use *after* intercourse have also been known and used for millennia. Recall that Soranus of Ephesus recommended to women that they jump up and down or behave in other physically active ways in order to expel the agency (a man's sperm) that he felt was responsible for pregnancy. The first attempt to use modern hormonal technology to prevent or interrupt pregnancy after intercourse dates to 1964 when a 13-year-old girl who had been gang-raped in Rotterdam was brought to the office of Dutch physician Ary (also Arie) Haspels. Haspels gave the girl a large dose of estrogen, and her pregnancy was terminated. Many historians point to this event as the beginning of research on *emergency contraception*, treatments that can be used to prevent or terminate pregnancy after intercourse. (The question as to whether such treatments *prevent* or *terminate* pregnancy is not an inconsequential matter of etymology. Some people say that a woman becomes pregnant as soon as fertilization has occurred, while others say that pregnancy does not occur until some later time. How these positions affect the debate over abortion is the subject of one section of Chapter 2 [Prescott 2011, 60; Sheldon 2013].)

Haspels's approach to the use of emergency contraception had one serious drawback: It was accompanied by rather severe nausea, vomiting, and menstrual bleeding. The high level of estrogen used in the treatment was undoubtedly the cause of these undesirable side effects. In an attempt to avoid these harsh side effects, a research team led by Canadian physician A. Albert Yuzpe decided to try using a postcoital method using more traditional oral contraceptive components. They reported the results of their study in 1974, setting off a line of research that has led to more than two dozen such products in the United States as of 2019. In all cases, the postcoital pills consist of a combination of estrogen and a progestin. The treatment regimen must begin within 72 hours of intercourse. It consists of two pills taken 12 hours apart. (For a list of products and more details on emergency contraception, see Emergency Contraception: History and Access 2013.) Some products are used on an "off-label" basis, that is, for uses (e.g., emergency contraception) for which they were not originally designed.

Progestin-only emergency contraceptives are also available. The active ingredient in these medications is the progestin levonorgestrel. The first and one of the most popular products, Plan B (now called Plan B One Step), was approved by the

FDA for use in the United States in 1999. Other products that are available include Next Choice One Dose, After Pill, Take Action, and My Way, as well as some that are available on an off-label basis (Levonorgestrel—Drug Summary 2019).

Alternative Forms of Hormonal Birth Control

Hormonal contraceptives also come in forms other than an oral pill, including patches, rings, inserts, shots, and intrauterine devices (IUDs). All of these devices work in essentially the same way as an oral contraceptive pill. They release hormones into the body where they act to reduce ovulation and development of the structure of the endometrial lining, thereby preventing pregnancy.

- The hormonal patch is a 4 centimeter by 4 centimeter plastic patch similar in appearance to a Band-Aid that can be applied to the upper arm, abdomen, buttocks, or upper torso. It contains a combination of synthetic estrogen and progestin that is absorbed through the skin. It must be replaced about once every week to retain its effectiveness. As of 2019, only one FDA-approved patch, Xulane, is available for sale in the United States (Birth Control Patch 2019).

- A hormonal ring is a device inserted into the vagina and left there for a month. It is made of a flexible, colorless, transparent plastic with an outer diameter of about 4 centimeters and a thickness of about 4 millimeters. Only one device of this type, the NuvaRing, is currently approved for use in the United States. A woman can control whether she will or will not continue having menstrual periods by adopting one of two possible insertion schedules (How Do I Use a NuvaRing 2019).

- The only contraceptive implant currently available in the United States, Nexplanon, consists of a thin plastic rod about 4 centimeters long and 2 millimeters in diameter. It contains 68 milligrams of the synthetic progestin etonogestrel, along with a small amount of barium sulfate. The latter compound is opaque to X-rays, so that implantation can be checked by that means to make sure it has been implanted correctly. The rod is implanted in the upper arm and can be left in place for up to three years (Nexplanon 2019). Nexplanon is a type of contraceptive device known as a *long-acting reversible contraceptive*, or LARC. The other type of LARC currently available is the IUD. LARCs are so-called because they are left in place in the body for long periods of time and can be removed at any point a user chooses to do so (Long-Acting Reversible Contraception: Intrauterine Device and Implant 2018).

• A hormonal contraceptive shot is an injection of a medroxy-progesterone acetate, a derivative of progesterone. The compound produces the usual contraceptive actions of preventing development of follicles (and, therefore, ovulation) and thinning of the endometrial lining. The shot is effective for a period of about three months, after which a repeat injection can occur (Stacey 2019).

Long-Term Effects of Hormonal Contraceptives

As with almost any drug, the active components of oral contraceptive pills are associated with a variety of adverse effects. Some of those effects are relatively mild, with few or no long-term consequences. These effects include (but are not limited to) nausea; vomiting; abdominal cramps and bloating; vaginal bleeding or spotting; change in menstrual flow; amenorrhea; temporary infertility after discontinuation of treatment; edema; breast tenderness, enlargement, secretion, or other changes; change in weight; migraine; rash; depression; vaginal candidiasis; and intolerance to contact lenses. For women who take the pill for extended periods of time, more serious adverse events have been identified. These include hypertension (high blood pressure); myocardial infarction (heart attack); gallbladder disease; hepatic tumors (benign tumors of the liver); pulmonary embolism, cerebral thrombosis, thrombophlebitis, or arterial thromboembolism (blood clot in the lungs, brain, veins, or arteries); and cerebral hemorrhage (bleeding inside the brain) (Loestrin® 21 2013).

Data about other possible adverse events associated with use of the pill are inconclusive. For example, one of the issues most often mentioned in this regard is the risk of cancer posed by women who use oral contraceptives. The risk factor differs substantially depending on the type of cancer involved and may be positive or negative. That is, the use of the pill may actually decrease a woman's risk for some types of cancer, such as colon, endometrial, or ovarian cancer, but increase her risk for other types of cancer, such as breast or cervical cancer. In either case, the risk factor may be quite small, sometimes less than 10 percent (Oral Contraceptives and Cancer Risk 2018). The effects of oral contraceptives on the whole range of health problems have been assessed by one of the nation's most reliable sources of information on health issues, the Mayo Clinic. That source has concluded that

> healthy women who do not smoke cigarettes have almost no chance of having a severe side effect from taking oral contraceptives. For most women, more problems occur because of pregnancy than will occur from taking oral contraceptives. (Estrogen and Progestin Oral Contraceptives [Oral Route] 2019)

One concern about the use of oral contraceptives is the risk posed to women who smoke. Smoking increases the risk of almost all adverse events, sometimes by a significant degree. Among women smokers in the age group 15–34 years, the risk of cardiovascular disease is about five times as great as that of nonsmokers in the same age group (3.3 per 100,000 to 0.65 100,000). That risk is also observed in older smokers: 29.4 per

100,000 smokers in age group 35–44 compared to 6.21 non-smokers in that age group (Kroon 2007).

Intrauterine Devices

An IUD is a small (usually) T-shaped device inserted into a woman's uterus to prevent pregnancy. The device tends to be about 30 millimeters in length across the top of the T and a bit longer on the vertical leg of the device. The first IUD was invented in about 1909 by German physician Richard Richter, who used silkworm gut encased in celluloid for his device. Richter's IUD never became very popular, and researchers searched over the next half century to find the best shapes and materials from which to make an IUD (Margulies 1975).

Two types of IUDs are available: copper and hormonal. The copper IUD is made of a T-shaped plastic base around which is wrapped a copper wire. The copper in the device acts as a spermicide, preventing fertilization of the egg (Nelson and Massoudi 2016). As of 2019, only one copper IUD had been approved for use in the United States, Paragard. It is said to remain effective as a contraceptive for up to 10 years (Paragard 2019).

A second type of IUD acts by releasing small amounts of the hormone levonorgestrel every day. As with oral contraceptives, levonorgestrel acts in a variety of ways to prevent fertilization and implantation: by killing sperm that enters the vagina; by increasing the viscosity of cervical mucus; and by preventing the endometrium from thickening and, thus, preventing the implantation of the fertilized egg. Four hormonal IUDs are available for use in the United States: Mirena, Kyleena, Liletta, and Skyla. A major difference among the four is the length of time over which they work effectively in the body, from about three years for Skyla up to five to seven years for the other products (IUD 2019).

The popularity of IUDs has changed significantly over the past half-century. When first introduced, they impressed many women with their apparent safety, long-term effectiveness, and efficiency of contraception. The percentage of contraceptive users who chose an IUD for protection rose from about 250,000, or 1 percent of that population in 1965 to 2.5 million users (10 percent of the population of users) in 1970. At that point, however, reports of health risks associated with one specific type of IUD, called the Dalkon Shield, caused many users to have second thoughts about that device and, in fact, IUDs in general. The number of IUD users began to fall off, reaching a low of about 250,000 (1 percent of all contraceptive users) in 1995. As the design and safety of IUDs has improved since that time, the number of users has once again increased, reaching more than 38 million (12 percent of all users) in 2014 (the last year for which data are available) (Kavanaugh and Jerman 2018; Secura 2013).

Abortion

The topic of abortion is one of the most contentious issues in all of birth control, indeed, in all of social debate in the United States today. The debate begins over the best definition of the term *abortion*. Both medical and everyday definitions are used for the term. And many versions of each type of definition are available. According to one medical dictionary, an abortion is the "expulsion from the uterus of an embryo or fetus before viability (20 weeks' gestation [18 weeks after fertilization] or fetal weight less than 500 g)." A distinction can also be made between abortion and premature birth, an event that occurs after the stage of viability, but before 37 weeks' gestation (Abortion 2019). An abortion that occurs naturally is also called a *spontaneous abortion* or *miscarriage*. Miscarriage is the most common risk factor in pregnancy. Anywhere from 13 to 26 percent of miscarriages occur among women who are not even aware that they are pregnant. That number remains high (8 to 20 percent) among women who are up to 20 weeks' pregnant (Tulandi and Al-Fozan 2019). These numbers vary considerably depending on a number of factors, including a woman's age and previous history of pregnancy. The number of natural abortions in the United States is roughly 13 times as great as the number of induced abortions, 19 percent to 1.5 percent respectively (Induced Abortion in the United States 2018).

Surgical Abortions

The most common form of induced abortion during the first trimester (first three months) of pregnancy is vacuum aspiration. In this procedure, a thin tube is passed into the uterus, and a mild vacuum is applied through the tube, expelling contents of the uterus. The procedure is safe, simple, and quick. It can be done in a doctor's office and usually takes about 15 minutes (Vacuum Aspiration for Abortion 2018). The most common procedure used during the second trimester is called *dilation and curettage* (or *evacuation*), also called *D&C* or *D&E*. In this procedure, the vagina is dilated (opened more widely), and a special surgical instrument called a *curette* is inserted to remove tissue from the uterus. The procedure is normally done in a hospital on a same-day basis and takes about a half hour (Dilation and Evacuation [D&E] 2018). Induced abortions during the third trimester are generally illegal in the United States and are performed under only very special conditions.

Medical Abortions

A second general type of abortion is called *medical* (or *medication*) *abortion*. In this procedure, some type of chemical is used to interrupt the normal stages of pregnancy, causing the fertilized egg to be expelled. (One of the best general sources of information on this topic is Foster [2005].) The first such compound to be discovered was mifepristone, first synthesized in 1980 by French chemist Georges Teutsch, working at the Roussel-Uclaf chemical works. The compound later became better known as RU486, for the name of the company plus the number of the trials in which it was discovered (#38,486).

As the properties of mifepristone were investigated, researchers found that it disrupted the function of the receptor to which progesterone binds in the body. This discovery opened up the possibility of using the compound as a disrupter of embryo development because the action of progesterone is a critical step in that process. By September of 1988, clinical trials of RU486 as an abortifacient had been completed, and the compound had been approved for public sale. Within a matter of days, a majority of Roussel-Uclaf executives and board of directors voted to discontinue the sale of the pill for ethical reasons, a decision that was also overturned in a matter of days by the French government. The reason for the government's action was that it believed the pill to be a safe, simple method of doing abortions during the early weeks of pregnancy. The debate over the use of RU486 (now better known as mifepristone or Mifeprex) continued for more than 20 years in the United States and other nations, eventually resulting in approval of the drug's use by the FDA in 2000 (Hogan 2000; Jones and Lopez 2014, 427–429).

Since the discovery and approval of mifepristone, two other abortifacient drugs have been developed, methotrexate (MTX) and misoprostol (Cytotec). MTX was first synthesized in the late 1940s and approved for use in the United States by the FDA in August 1959. It was originally developed for several types of cancer, including leukemia, lymphoma, osteosarcomas, trophoblastic neoplasms, and breast, head, neck, lung, and bladder cancers, as well as a host of other conditions, including rheumatoid arthritis, juvenile dermatomyositis, psoriasis, psoriatic arthritis, lupus, sarcoidosis, Crohn's disease, eczema, and vasculitis. As of 2019, methotrexate has not been approved by the FDA as an abortifacient. It is, however, used on an off-label basis in combination with misoprostol. Methotrexate works by interfering with the production of DNA that results in the inability of the fertilized egg to implant properly in the endometrial lining. The side effects associated with the use are serious enough, however, to limit its uses to locations or conditions in which the more popular misoprostol is not available (Creinin 2004; Methotrexate [MTX] for Early Abortion 2014). Methotrexate is, however, used more commonly in connection with misoprostol. A common regimen involves an injection of methotrexate followed by an injection of misoprostol three to seven days later (Medical Management of First-Trimester Abortion 2016).

The most common type of medical abortion involves an initial dose of mifepristone taken orally, followed 24 to 48 hours later by a dose of misoprostol, taken orally, under the tongue, beside the cheek, or vaginally (Medical Management of First-Trimester Abortion 2016, Table 2).

Abortions in History

The history of abortion is so long and complex that it can hardly be treated adequately even in a book many times the size of this one. All we can offer here is a brief overview of that extensive and intricate story. It begins, as with contraception, in the earliest history of human civilization. The earliest laws of which we have any record often mention abortion and/or miscarriage. In general, they provide punishments for any person causing the loss of a fetus, whether accidentally or intentionally. For example, the Assyrian Code of Laws, dating to about 1500 BCE, provides penalties for any man who strikes a woman, causing her to abort a fetus. The punishment consists of a fine that varies depending on the social status of the individuals involved. If a woman aborts a fetus by her own action, she is sentenced to death by impalement and prevented from being buried, a particularly severe penalty in the culture of the time. Even if she died during an abortion, her body was to be treated in the same way. Similar provisions are mentioned in other laws of prehistoric societies in the Near East and Southeast Asia (Damian 2010 [India]; Fuller 1994 and Jastrow 1921 [Near East]; Fox 2018 [China]; Riddle 1992 [Egypt]).

Of special interest to many readers may be the mention of abortion in the Bible. Generally speaking, there is little or no mention of abortion itself in the book or in the teachings of Jesus specifically. Since the word itself appears not to even have existed at the time, this omission is perhaps understandable. Opponents of abortion throughout history and still today argue that their stand is supported by a general overview of the Bible and Jesus's teachings, rather than any specific condemnation of the act.

The most common reference mentioned by scholars is a passage in the book of Exodus, 21:22–23. That passage reflects the view of many early civilizations, as noted earlier, that at least some types of abortion are immoral and/or illegal and must be punished. As it occurs in the King James version of the bible, the passage reads:

> If men strive, and hurt a woman with child, so that her fruit depart from her, and yet no mischief follow: he shall be surely punished, according as the woman's husband will lay upon him; and he shall pay as the judges determine. And if any mischief follow, then thou shalt give life for life.

That selection and the more general tone of disapproval that many theologians find in the Bible are more than adequate for them to condemn the practice on religious grounds, but are somewhat thin and unconvincing to others who fail to find concrete objections to abortion in Christian history (Fuller 1994; Luo 2005; What Does the Bible Say about Abortion? n.d.).

And yet, strong prohibitions against abortion have existed throughout history. In the Roman Catholic Church, for example, one of the earliest written statements about the practice dates to about 70 CE. The second book of the Didache says that "the second commandment of the teaching: Thou shalt do no murder. . . . Thou shallt not procure abortion, nor commit infantacide" (The Didache 2011). That teaching has been repeated many times throughout the Church's history, most recently in Pope Paul VI encyclical *Humanae Vitae* from 1968: "We are obliged once more to declare that the direct interruption of the generative process already begun and, above all, all direct abortion, even for therapeutic reasons, are to be absolutely excluded as lawful means of regulating the number of children" (Paul VI 1968, section 14).

Attitudes about abortion differ considerably among the other religions of the world, ranging from strong prohibitions that may include severe punishment to relatively modest disapproval that may involve few, if any, penalties (Abortion and Religion 2011; Maguire 2009).

Perhaps the single most crucial question in discussions about abortion is when human life begins. If one agrees that the reproductive process begins with fertilization of the egg (conception) and moves through a series of episodes in which the fertilized egg grows and develops into an embryo and then a fetus, and is eventually born, the question is at what point in that long process is the fertilized egg no longer a collection of cells or nonliving tissue within the womb and is, instead, a living human being. That point in time is sometimes called *ensoulment*, a moment at which a soul enters the collection of cells, forming a human being. Another common term used for this event is *quickening*, a somewhat-ambiguous term that refers to the time at which a woman can actually feel a fetus moving in her body. Among ordinary women and men, decisions about abortion were often based on the question as to whether or not quickening had occurred. If it had, abortions were usually prohibited; if it had not, no penalty was assessed for an abortion (Austin 2003).

A long list of philosophers, theologians, scientists, and other thinkers have attempted to answer this question. For example, the founder of Greek medicine, Hippocrates, believed that ensoulment accorded at conception, and the life began as soon as the egg was fertilized. A later writer, the Greek physician Porphyry (c. 234–c. 305 CE) took the most extreme opposite position, that life does not begin until childbirth. Yet another view was expressed by the famous Greek natural philosopher Aristotle, who thought that the male embryo "came alive" on the 40th day of development, and the female embryo, on the 90th day (the difference reflecting Aristotle's view of the natural inferiority of women) (Horrocks 2014; Wear 2014). The debate as to when life actually begins has continued throughout history and remains a key point of contention in the battle over abortion in today's world. (See further discussion of this issue in Chapter 2.)

Abortion law and practice in the early United States varied considerably from colony to colony, largely dependent on the European origin of settlers in each. In British settlements, law and practice tended to follow English custom, with abortion prior to quickening permitted, but disallowed once quickening had occurred. In colonies with French settlers, abortion was likely to be illegal, although not uncommonly performed. The most severe laws and penalties were those in settlements with large proportions of Spanish and Portuguese immigrants (Acevedo 1979).

During the period from colonial times to the end of the Civil War, public opinion tended to oppose the practice of abortion, although very few laws banning the practice existed. Laws that were imposed were often difficult to enforce, and safe and effective abortions remained available to most women. By some estimates, as many as a fifth of all pregnancies during that period ended in abortion (Mohr 1978, 76). That pattern began to change in the late 1860s, with most states adopting laws prohibiting abortion, with the primary objective of the protection of women's health rather than the survival of the fetus (Dellapenna 2006). An important force in this revised view of abortion was the American Medical Association, which took the position that abortion was largely a crime, rather than a legitimate medical issue (Reagan 2008). By the beginning of the 20th century, abortion had become illegal (except for special cases, such as rape or health of the mother) in every state. It remained so until the most pivotal court case in the history of abortion in America, *Roe v. Wade*, was decided in 1973. As a result of that decision, all state laws criminalizing abortion during the first trimester were nullified. (For a detailed description of *Roe* and its effects on abortion law in the United States, see Hull and Hoffer [2010].)

Sterilization

One of the most effective means of birth control is sterilization. For women, sterilization is accomplished either by tubal ligation ("tying one's tubes) or by a hysterectomy (removal of all or part of the uterus). For men, sterilization is achieved by a vasectomy. A vasectomy is a procedure by which the tubes through which semen and sperm travel from the testes to the urinary tract, the *vas deferens*, are cut and then sealed off. (For an illustration of the procedure, see https://www.mayoclinic .org/tests-procedures/vasectomy/about/pac-20384580.) This process prevents expulsion of sperm during ejaculation, making fertilization of an egg impossible. Tubal ligation involves cuts in the Fallopian tubes, through which eggs travel from ovaries to the uterus. (For an illustration of the procedure, see https://www.youtube.com/watch?v=EotpnXLXmrM&app=de sktop.) In the absence of an egg in the Fallopian tubes, fertilization cannot occur (Sterilization 2019).

Both female and male sterilization procedures or methods have been used for several purposes throughout history. For example, kings and other members of the royalty sometimes castrated boys to work as eunuchs in their harems. Castration is a more extreme form of sterilization than vasectomy that involves total removal of a male's testes (or, in the case of a female, her ovaries). A castrated male never develops secondary sexual characteristics such as body hair, a low-pitched voice, and sexual desires. They were ideal, therefore, for watching over the women in a man's harem. Men were also castrated in early history to sing with high-pitched voices in religious and secular ceremonies. The last *castrato* to have performed such music was

Alessandro Moreschi, a member of the Sistine Chapel choir, who died in 1922.

Male (as well as female) sterilization has also been used for medical reasons of questionable repute. For example, at the end of the 19th century, some physicians began to use vasectomies as a way of treating physical and mental illness. They believed that cutting just one vas deferens "freed up" the testes to direct energy to other mental and bodily functions, producing more youthful and healthy lives (Sengoopta 2003). The procedure retained some degree of popularity into the 1930s, at which point the discovery of the hormone testosterone proved the futility of the operation.

A far more serious misuse of sterilization was its employment in eugenic programs. Eugenics was a program of population control that began in the mid-19th century, largely through the efforts of English polymath Sir Francis Galton. Galton, acting on the discovery of the theory of evolution by his half-cousin Charles Darwin, argued that human evolution could be directed into a more promising direction by medical means. He proposed identifying those individuals who were of lesser mental or physical abilities and having them sterilized to prevent these undesirable traits from being passed on to future generations. Over the next century, eugenics became a very popular approach to population control in several limited, but significant, situations. It formed the basis, for example, of a program for "purifying" the human race by the Nazi Party in Germany in the 1930s (Carlson 2001; Drake, Mills, and Cranston 1999).

The sterilization procedures used in the applications described here were almost always involuntary. Boys and girls, women and men, did not usually want, ask for, choose, or agree to be sterilized. The act was performed because some individual or organization deemed the procedure necessary or desirable for their own purposes or for those of society at large.

A rise in an interest in voluntary sterilization as a form of birth control can be traced to the 1970s. A significant factor in this change was an increasing awareness among the general public of the need for and resources available for birth control. (The oral contraceptive pill was discovered in 1973.) Large-scale efforts were made to ensure that involuntary sterilization was no longer available in the United States, but that voluntary procedures would be both available and promoted (Tazkargy 2014). At one point, men who had had vasectomies were even encouraged to wear gold pins to indicate that they had undergone the procedure (and, thus, were "safe" sex partners) (Knowles 2012, 13–14). According to the most recent data available, the number of vasectomies performed in 2015 in the United States was estimated to be 527,476, with a decrease in vasectomy rates from 2007 to 2015 (Ostrowski et al. 2018).

Female sterilization is currently one of the three most popular forms of birth control in the United States, second only to the use of the oral contraceptive pill. According to the most recent data available, 21.8 percent of all women who use some form of contraceptive rely on some form of sterilization, compared to 25.3 percent who use the pill. These numbers have remained relatively constant since 2008, when corresponding rates were 26.6 percent and 27.5 percent, respectively (Kavanaugh and Jerman 2018, Table 1).

One of the most important reasons for the popularity of sterilization as a contraceptive technique is its very high rate of effectiveness. Studies have shown that it prevents pregnancy in more than 99 percent of all cases. One problem arises, however, with regard to that other 1 percent. On those rare cases, significant health, social, economic, and other problems may arise. A famous case involves a woman in Indiana who filed suit against her physician for *wrongful pregnancy*. (A similar, but not identical, legal term used for such instances is *wrongful birth*.) The woman had asked to be sterilized to ensure that she would no longer be able to become pregnant. The doctor performed the surgery, apparently with some errors in technique, such that the woman later became pregnant. She and her husband sued to recover financial costs and be compensated for emotional distress, as well as financial costs for the child's future upbringing. The court approved the initial expenses, but not the long-term costs of raising the child (*Chaffee v. Seslar*, 786 N.E.2d 705 [2003]). For a discussion of the differences among *wrongful pregnancy*, *wrongful birth*, and *wrongful life*, see What Are Prenatal Torts? Wrongful Pregnancy, Wrongful Birth, and Wrongful Life in Ohio 2018.

Developments in Birth Control Technology

Researchers are constantly searching for new methods of contraception and improvements on traditional methods. The rate of unplanned pregnancies in the United States is still very high, about 45 percent of all pregnancies in 2011, so new and better birth control measures are still needed (Finer and Zolna 2016). One of the most aggressive lines of research is the development of a male oral contraceptive pill. As of late 2019, two candidates had been developed for such a product: 11-beta-methyl-19-nortestosterone dodecylcarbonate (11-beta-MNTDC) and dimethandrolone undecanoate (DMAU). The first of these compounds mimics the action of natural testosterone in the body. It suppresses the action of hormones in the testes responsible for the production of sperm. It acts over a two- to three-month period so that discontinuing its use restores viability of sperm (New Study Reports Potential of DMAU as Male Birth Control Pill 2018; Phase I Trial of Male Birth Control Pill Reveals Positive Results 2019). Some researchers predict that a male oral contraceptive pill should be available in about 10 years (Nainggolan 2019).

A second development involved the approval of a mobile phone app by the FDA for tracking a woman's body temperature and menstrual cycle. The app is designed to alert a woman as to times at which she is most and least likely to become pregnant. In studies of the new device, a failure rate of 1.8 percent for "perfect use" was reported. "Perfect use" means the best possible outcome to be expected from the app. Critics of the FDA action pointed to unusually high failure rates in a study of Swedish women who used the app for their sole method of birth control (Andrews 2018).

Another line of research is focused on improvements of design and efficacy of some traditional birth control methods. One example is a product called Sayana Press, an injectable, a lower-dose formulation of Depo-Provera. It is a specially designed injection system that women can easily use themselves. It has become an especially popular contraceptive device in developing countries where traditional systems are more expensive and more difficult to find (Inject Sayana Press 2019).

The Efficacy of Birth Control

For many women and men, one question about birth control is predominant: what works? One can read about the history of birth control, techniques that have been developed, laws relating to birth control, current controversies over the use of contraceptives and abortion, and other issues relating to birth control. But the bottom line for many individuals is which practices among those available are most likely to protect a woman against pregnancy. Table 1.1 provides some basic

Table 1.1   Effectiveness of Various Contraceptive Methods

Method	Percentage of Women Experiencing an Unintended Pregnancy within the First Year of Use		Percentage of Women Continuing Use at One Year
	Typical Use	Perfect Use	
No method[1]	85.0	85.0	
Spermicides[2]	28.0	18.0	42.0
Fertility awareness–based methods	24.0		47.0
Standard days method		5.0	
Two-day method		4.0	
Ovulation method		3.0	
Symptothermal method		0.4	

Method	Percentage of Women Experiencing an Unintended Pregnancy within the First Year of Use		Percentage of Women Continuing Use at One Year
	Typical Use	Perfect Use	
Withdrawal	22.0	4.0	46.0
Sponge			36.0
Parous women[3]	24.0	20.0	
Nulliparous women[3]	12.0	9.0	
Condom[4]			
Female	21.0	5.0	41.0
Male	18.0	2.0	43.0
Diaphragm[5]	12.0	6.0	57.0
Combined pill and progestin-only pill	9.0	0.3	67.0
Evra patch	9.0	0.3	67.0
NuvaRing	9.0	0.3	67.0
Depo-Provera	6.0	0.2	56.0
Intrauterine contraceptives			
ParaGard (copper T)	0.8	0.6	78.0
Mirena (LNG)	0.2	0.2	80.0
Implanon	0.05	0.05	84.0
Female sterilization	0.5	0.5	100.0
Male sterilization	0.15	0.1	100.0
Abstinence[6]	0.0	0.0	100.0

For a complete description of all terms and methodology, see source below.

[1] No contraceptive use or discontinued contraceptive use.

[2] Foams, creams, gels, vaginal suppositories, and vaginal film.

[3] Parous: Having given birth to at least one child; Nulliparous: never having given birth to a child.

[4] Without spermicides.

[5] With spermicidal cream or jelly.

[6] Not included in this resource.

Source: "Appendix D: Contraceptive Effectiveness." Recommendations and Reports. Morbidity and Mortality Report. April 25, 2014. 63(RR04): 47-47. https://www.cdc.gov/mmWr/preview/mmwrhtml/rr6304a5.htm#Tab. Accessed on April 18, 2019.

information about that question. It shows the percentage (likelihood) of a woman's becoming pregnant if she relies on each of 17 commonly available birth control practices. Two sets of data are provided: typical use and perfect use. "Typical use" refers to data on an individual's actual and most likely practice, which may involve forgetting or otherwise missing the regimen recommended for each practice. "Perfect use" refers to evidence-based predictions of the best possible result obtained from a practice, assuming a person follows the regimen without fail. As Table 1.1 shows, the most effective methods of birth control, with more than 99 percent success, are abstinence, sterilization, an Implanon implantation, and IUDs. The least effective methods, with success rates of about 75 percent, are spermicides only, fertility-awareness approaches, withdrawal, and use of the sponge and female condom.

Population Control

Upon occasion, birth control becomes more than a matter of personal choice; it takes on the status of a national policy issue. It becomes the challenge of *population control*. Although that term has had a special significance in the United States and worldwide over the past half century, it has been a dominant theme going as far back as the earliest human civilizations. Both Greece and Rome struggled over the question of controlling their populations, although they took very different views as to what was best for the nations (Feen 1996).

Perhaps the best example of that situation in modern history is the so-called one-child policy adopted by the Chinese government in 1979. Concerned that the nation's mushrooming population would seriously damage its economic status, the government declared a family planning program in which a couple could have no more than one child. Individuals completely lost their control over birth decisions. That policy actually replaced an earlier "two-children" program that had not been effective enough. The one-child policy came to an end in 2015, at which point the Chinese government claimed that more than 400 million births had been prevented by the program (Hvistendahl 2017).

The modern history of population control efforts in the United States dates to the 1970s, largely as a result of concerns about the environmental effects of increasing population size. Among the many solutions suggested for population control in the country were a set of financial incentives designed to encourage families to have fewer children. For example, one population organization recommended changing the federal income tax policy to provide tax credits only to families with two children or less and to give a cash grant to low-income families for two children or less (Mann 1992). Using financial incentives such as these to control population size has a long history with only moderate measurable success in achieving that objective (Rabin 1972).

The United States also has adopted a birth control/population control policy for other nations. In 1984, the administration of President Ronald Reagan announced that it would no longer provide control funding for any foreign nongovernmental agency that provides any type of abortion services. That program, often known as the "Mexico City Policy," for the location in which it was first announced, has since been revoked by Democratic presidents and reinstated by Republican presidents (most recently by President Donald Trump) (The Mexico City Policy: An Explainer 2019).

Assisted Reproductive Technology

Thus far, the discussion of birth control in this book has focused exclusively on efforts to prevent or reduce the risk of pregnancy. But the term *birth control* has another meaning also, referring to efforts to *improve* or even *make possible* the likelihood of a pregnancy. Today, a number of technologies exist for such purposes, collectively known as *assisted reproductive technologies* or ARTs. Women and men who choose to make use of

ART are generally those who are infertile as a result of several possible medical conditions, including a diminished supply of eggs, inability to produce an adequate number and quality of sperm, endometriosis, a uterine disorder, pelvic inflammatory disease, or some combination of male and/or female conditions (Figures from the 2016 Assisted Reproductive Technology National Summary Report 2018, page 20).

The most common type of ART is in vitro fertilization (IVF), a process by which one or more eggs are removed from a woman's ovaries and a sample of sperm from a man. The two are then mixed outside the body in a petri dish and allowed to interact with each other. After fertilization of one or more eggs occurs, the young embryo is returned to a woman's uterus, where embryonic development may (or may not) continue. Other types of ART are also available, some more popular in the United States, and others more common in other countries. Two additional types of ART are intracervical and intrauterine insemination. In each case, a sample of semen (washed or unwashed) is injected directly into a woman's cervix or uterus, respectively, bringing sperm more directly in contact with an egg (Intrauterine Insemination [IUI]/Artificial Insemination 2018; Meher and Bag 2018).

ART procedures are not inexpensive. As of late 2019, the average cost of one "cycle" of treatment at one of the nation's 422 infertility clinics ranges from about $10,000 to about $15,000 (IVF Pricing Plans 2019). The success rate for most procedures is relatively low, depending on a woman's age:

- 31 percent in women younger than 35 years of age.
- 24 percent in women aged 35 to 37 years.
- 16 percent in women aged 38 to 40 years.
- 8 percent in women aged 41 to 42 years.
- 3 percent in women aged 43 to 44 years.
- 3 percent in women older than 44 years of age (Infertility FAQs 2019).

Conclusion

Women and men have been concerned about issues of birth control from the earliest stages of human history. Most methods for preventing pregnancy were based on trial-and-error techniques that were often as likely to fail as to succeed. Over the centuries, some of these methods were improved to the point where they could be used with some chance of success. Others fell by the wayside. Over the past century, newer and far more effective contraceptive methods have been developed so that a man and woman can have sexual intercourse with a very high expectation that pregnancy will not occur.

References

"Abortion." 2019. MediLexicon. https://www.medilexicon.com/dictionary/143. Accessed on April 26, 2019.

"Abortion and Religion." 2011. Education for Choice. https://www.brook.org.uk/attachments/Abortion_and_religion_leaflet_2011.pdf. Accessed on April 28, 2019.

Acevedo, Zoila. 1979. "Abortion in Early America." *Women & Health*. 4(2): 159-167.

Adelmann, Howard B. 1966. *Marcello Malpighi and the Evolution of Embryology*. Ithaca, NY: Cornell University Press.

Almukhtar, Naseer. 2018. "Define the Oogenesis?" Research Gate. https://www.researchgate.net/post/Define_the_oogenesis. Accessed on April 22, 2019.

Anderson, L. 2018a. "Types of Birth Control Pills (Oral Contraceptives)." Drugs.com. https://www.drugs.com/article/birth-control-pill.html. Accessed on April 22, 2019.

Anderson, L. 2018b. "What Are the Benefits and Risks of Taking Birth Control Pills?" Drugs.com. https://www.drugs.com/article/birthcontrolpill-risks-benefits.html. Accessed on April 24, 2019.

Andrews, Michelle. 2018. "FDA Stirs Contraception Debate with OK For 'Natural' Birth Control App." NPR. https://www.npr.org/sections/health-shots/2018/08/21/640274885/fda-stirs-contraception-debate-with-ok-for-natural-birth-control-app. Accessed on May 19, 2019.

Austin, Kathleen J. 2003. "Aristotle, Aquinas, and the History of Quickening." Thesis/dissertation. Montreal: McGill University Libraries. digitool.library.mcgill.ca/dtl_publish/5/79819.html. Accessed on April 29, 2019.

Bertram, Jerome, Fr. 2016. "The True History of Celibacy." Catholic Herald. https://catholicherald.co.uk/issues/august-19th-2016/the-true-history-of-celibacy/. Accessed on April 7, 2019.

Bigelow, Maurice Alpheus. 1916/2015. *Sex-education: A Series of Lectures Concerning Knowledge of Sex in Its Relation to Human Life*. n.p.: Forgotten Books.

"Birth Control Patch." 2019. Mayo Clinic. https://www.mayoclinic.org/tests-procedures/birth-control-patch/about/pac-20384553. Accessed on April 24, 2019.

Bosch, Mineke. 2017. "Aletta Jacobs and the Dutch Cap: The Transfer of Knowledge and the Making of a Reputation in the Changing Networks of Birth Control Activists." *GHI Bulletin*. https://www.ghi-dc.org/fileadmin/user-upload/GHI-Washington/Publications/Supplements/Supplement_13/167.pdf. Accessed on April 20, 2019.

Brundage, James A. 2009. *Law, Sex, and Christian Society in Medieval Europe*. Chicago: University of Chicago Press.

Bullough, Vern L., ed. 2002. *Encyclopedia of Birth Control*. Santa Barbara, CA: ABC-CLIO.

Capitan, Louise, and Henri Breuil. 1902. "Figures Préhistoriques De La Grotte Des Combarelles (Dordogne)." *Comptes Rendus Des Séances De L'académie*

Des Inscriptions et Belles-lettres Année. 46(1): 51–56. Available in French online at https://www.persee.fr/doc/ crai_0065-0536_1902_num_46_1_17072. Accessed on April 11, 2019.

Carlson, Elof Alex. 2001. *The Unfit: A History of a Bad Idea.* Cold Spring Harbor, NY: Cold Spring Harbor Laboratory Press.

Center for Young Women's Health. 2017. "Progestin-Only Oral Contraceptive Pill (POP) or Mini-pill." https:// youngwomenshealth.org/2014/07/08/progestin-only-oral-contraceptives/. Accessed on April 23, 2019.

"The Chemistry of Condom Materials—From Sheep Guts to Synthetic Rubber." 2018. Compound Interest. https:// www.compoundchem.com/2018/08/10/condoms/. Accessed on April 12, 2019.

"Choosing a Birth Control Pill." 2019. Mayo Clinic. https:// www.mayoclinic.org/healthy-lifestyle/birth-control/ in-depth/art-20044807. Accessed on April 23, 2019.

Clarke, Gary N. 2006. "A.R.T. and History, 1678-1978." *Human Reproduction.* 21(7): 1645–1650. https://academic .oup.com/humrep/article/21/7/1645/2938540. Accessed on April 6, 2019.

Cobb, Matthew. 2007. *The Egg & Sperm Race: The Seventeenth-century Scientists Who Unravelled the Secrets of Sex, Life and Growth.* London: Pocket Books.

Cobb, Matthew. 2012. "An Amazing 10 Years: The Discovery of Egg and Sperm in the 17th Century." *Reproduction in Domestic Animals.* 47(suppl. 4): 2–6. https://onlinelibrary .wiley.com/doi/pdf/10.1111/j.1439-0531.2012.02105.x. Accessed on April 6, 2019.

Cole, F. J. 1930. *Early Theories of Sexual Generation.* Oxford: Clarendon Press. https://archive.org/details/ EarlyTheoriesOfSexualGenerationByFrancisCole1930. Accessed on April 6, 2019.

Collier, Aine. 2007. *The Humble Little Condom: A History.* Amherst, NY: Prometheus Books.

"Contraception in Early Adolescence." 2011. Best Practice. https://bpac.org.nz/bpj/2011/april/docs/bpj_35_contraception_adolescence_pages_24-31.pdf. Accessed on April 23, 2019.

Creinin, Mitchell D. 2004. "Medical Termination of Early Pregnancy." Gynecology and Obstetrics. https://www.glowm.com/resources/glowm/cd/pages/v6/v6c126.html. Accessed on April 26, 2019.

Damian, Constantin-Iulian. 2010. "Abortion from the Perspective of Eastern Religions: Hinduism and Buddhism." *Romanian Journal of Bioethics.* 8(1): 124–136. https://web.archive.org/web/20120903233020/http://eng.bioetica.ro/atdoc/RRBv8n1_2010_Damian_EN.pdf. Accessed on April 27, 2019.

Dellapenna, Joseph W. 2006. *Dispelling the Myths of Abortion History.* Durham, NC: Carolina Academic Press.

Dembitsky, Valery M. 2008. "Natural Surfactants as Potential Contraceptive and Spermicidal Agents." *Inform.* 19(9): 641–643. http://aocs.files.cms-plus.com/inform/2008/9/641.pdf. Accessed on April 7, 2019.

"The Didache." 2011. http://www.thedidache.com/. Accessed on April 28, 2019.

"Dilation and Evacuation (D&E)." 2018. C. S. Mott Children's Hospital. University of Michigan. https://www.mottchildren.org/health-library/tw2462. Accessed on April 26, 2019.

Donaldson, I. M. L. 2009. "Ex Libris: William Harvey's Other Book." *Journal of the Royal College of Physicians of Edinburgh.* 39(2): 187–188. https://www.rcpe.ac.uk/sites/default/files/ex_libris_8.pdf. Accessed on April 21, 2019.

Drake, M. J., I. W. Mills, and D. Cranston. 1999. "On the Chequered History of Vasectomy." *BJU International.*

84(4): 475–481. https://onlinelibrary.wiley.com/doi/ pdf/10.1046/j.1464-410x.1999.00206.x. Accessed on April 30, 2019.

Dupont, Ellen M. 2008. "Regnier de Graaf (1641–1673)." The Embryo Project Encyclopedia. https://embryo.asu.edu/ pages/regnier-de-graaf-1641-1673. Accessed on April 21, 2019.

"The Early Church Fathers on Contraception." 2005. Stay Catholic. http://www.staycatholic.com/ecf_contraception .htm. Accessed on April 8, 2019.

Eig, Jonathan. 2014. *The Birth of the Pill: How Four Crusaders Reinvented Sex and Launched a Revolution.* New York: W. W. Norton & Company.

"Emergency Contraception: History and Access." 2013. Planned Parenthood. https://www.plannedparenthood.org/ uploads/filer_public/47/95/4795d527-cf88-4b7d-b4d6- e4a99b6767c0/emergency_contraception_history_and_ access.pdf. Accessed on April 24, 2019.

"Estrogen and Progestin Oral Contraceptives (Oral Route)." 2019. Mayo Clinic. https://www.mayoclinic.org/drugs- supplements/estrogen-and-progestin-oral-contraceptives-oral- route/side-effects/drg-20069422. Accessed on May 19, 2019.

"Eunuch." 2019. New World Encyclopedia. http://www .newworldencyclopedia.org/entry/Eunuch. Accessed on April 7, 2019.

Feen, Richard Harrow. 1996. "Keeping the Balance: Ancient Greek Philosophical Concerns with Population and Environment." *Population and Environment.* 17(6): 447–458.

Feldblum, Paul J., and Michael J. Rosenberg. 1989. "A Historical Perspective on Condoms." Prevention of Sexually Transmitted Diseases. Research Triangle Park, NC: American Social Health Association. https://pdf.usaid.gov/ pdf_docs/PNABG085.pdf. Accessed on April 11, 2019.

Feldman, David M. 1968. *Birth Control in Jewish Law; Marital Relations, Contraception, and Abortion as Set Forth in the Classic Texts of Jewish Law*. New York: New York University Press.

"Figures from the 2016 Assisted Reproductive Technology National Summary Report." 2018. Centers for Disease Control and Prevention. https://www.cdc.gov/art/pdf/2016-national-summary-slides/ART_2016_graphs_and_charts.pdf. Accessed on May 1, 2019.

Finer, Lawrence B., and Mia R. Zolna. 2016. "Declines in Unintended Pregnancy in the United States, 2008–2011." *New England Journal of Medicine*. 374: 843–852. https://www.nejm.org/doi/full/10.1056/NEJMsa1506575#t=article. Accessed on May 19, 2019.

"First Plastic Condom for Men Becomes Available Next Year." 1993. *Contraceptive Technology Update*. 14(10): 156–157. https://www.popline.org/node/329661. Accessed on April 13, 2019.

Foster, Angel M. 2005. "Medication Abortion: A Guide for Health Professionals." Ibis Reproductive Health. https://ibisreproductivehealth.org/publications/medication-abortion-guide-health-professionals. Accessed on April 26, 2019.

Fox, Pat. 2018. "Abortion in the Ancient and Premodern World." Thought Co. https://www.thoughtco.com/abortion-in-the-premodern-world-3528230. Accessed on April 27, 2019.

"Frequently Asked Questions Regarding Catholic Teaching on Contraception." n.d. Catholic Doors Ministry. https://www.catholicdoors.com/faq/1000/qu1342.htm. Accessed on April 8, 2019.

"From Penis Sheaths to Mandatory Condoms—A Journey Through Time." 2019. K-Portal. https://www.k-online.com/cgi-bin/md_k/lib/pub/tt.cgi/From_penis_

sheaths_to_mandatory_condoms_%E2%80%93_a_
journey_through_time.html. Accessed on April 12, 2019.

Fuller, Russell. 1994. "Exodus 21:22-23: The Miscarriage
Interpretation and the Personhood of the Fetus." *Journal of
the Evangelical Theological Society.* 37(2): 169–184. https://
pdfs.semanticscholar.org/50b2/064cf1d09be12389ecebc8c
235b1bd3ec628.pdf. Accessed on April 27, 2019.

Gelijns, Annetine. 1991. *Innovation in Clinical Practice: The
Dynamics of Medical Technology Development.* Washington,
DC: National Academy Press.

Gross, Alex. 1981. "Sex Through the Ages in China." *SIECUS
Report.* 10(2): 7–8.

Helig, Robert. 1905. "Birth Control in Ancient and Medieval
India." Medical Heritage Library. https://archive.org/
details/b28269366/page/1. Accessed on April 7, 2019.

Hester, J. David. 2005. "Queers on Account of the Kingdom
Of Heaven: Rhetorical Constructions of the Eunuch
Body." *Scriptura.* 90: 809–823. http://scriptura.journals.
ac.za/pub/article/view/1069/1024. Accessed on
April 7, 2019.

Hogan, Julie A. 2000. "The Life of the Abortion Pill in
the United States." LEDA at Harvard Law School.
https://dash.harvard.edu/bitstream/handle/1/8852153/
Hogan%2C_Julie.html. Accessed on April 26, 2019.

Hooper, Anne. 2008. *The Kama Sutra.* London: Dorling
Kindersley.

Horrocks, Alyssa. 2014. "The Soul and Abortion in
Ancient Greek Culture and Jewish Law." University of
North Carolina at Asheville. *Journal of Undergraduate
Research.* https://libres.uncg.edu/ir/unca/f/A_Horrocks_
Soul_JrnlUngRes_2014.pdf. Accessed on April 28,
2019.

"How Do I Use a NuvaRing?" 2019. Planned Parenthood.
https://www.plannedparenthood.org/learn/birth-control/

birth-control-vaginal-ring-nuvaring/how-do-i-use-nuvaring. Accessed on April 24, 2019.

Howards, Stuart S. 1997. "Antoine van Leeuwenhoek and the Discovery of Sperm." *Fertility and Sterility.* 67(1): 16–17. https://www.fertstert.org/article/S0015-0282(97)81848-1/pdf. Accessed on April 21, 2019.

Huber, Valerie J., and Michael W. Firmin. 2014. "A History of Sex Education in the United States Since 1900." *International Journal of Educational Reform.* 23(1): 25–51. https://www.loveandfidelity.org/wp-content/uploads/2014/10/Huber-Published-Sex-Ed-article.pdf. Accessed on May 2, 2019.

Hull, N. E. H., and Peter Charles Hoffer. 2010. *Roe v. Wade: The Abortion Rights Controversy in American History*, 2nd ed. Lawrence: University Press of Kansas.

Hvistendahl, Mara. 2017. "Analysis of China's One-child Policy Sparks Uproar." *Science.* 358(6361): 283–284. https://www.sciencemag.org/news/2017/10/analysis-china-s-one-child-policy-sparks-uproar. Accessed on May 1, 2019.

Imber, Michael. 1984. "The First World War, Sex Education, and the American Social Hygiene Association's Campaign Against Venereal Disease." *Journal of Educational Administration and History.* 16(1): 47–56.

"Induced Abortion in the United States." 2018. Guttmacher Institute. https://www.guttmacher.org/sites/default/files/factsheet/fb_induced_abortion.pdf. Accessed on April 26, 2019.

"Infertility FAQs." 2019. Centers for Disease Control and Prevention. https://www.cdc.gov/reproductivehealth/infertility/index.htm. Accessed on May 1, 2019.

"Inject Sayana Press." 2019. http://www.injectsayanapress.org/. Accessed on May 19, 2019.

"Intrauterine Insemination (IUI)/Artificial Insemination." 2018. Creating a Family. https://creatingafamily.org/

infertility/resources/intrauterine-insemination-iui/. Accessed on May 1, 2019.

"IUD." 2019. Planned Parenthood. https://www .plannedparenthood.org/learn/birth-control/iud. Accessed on April 25, 2019.

"IVF Pricing Plans." 2019. Your Fertility Friend. https:// yourfertilityfriend.com/ivf-pricing-plans/. Accessed on May 1, 2019.

Jastrow, Morris, Jr. 1921. "An Assyrian Law Code." *Journal of the American Oriental Society*. 41: 1–59. https://www.jstor .org/stable/593702. Accessed on April 27, 2019.

Jensen, Robin E. 2007. "Using Science to Argue for Sexual Education in U.S. Public Schools: Dr. Ella Flagg Young and the 1913 'Chicago Experiment'." *Science Communication*. 29(2): 217–241. https://www.academia .edu/2501883/Using_Science_to_Argue_for_Sexual_ Education_in_US_Public_Schools_Dr._Ella_Flagg_ Young_and_the_1913_Chicago_Experiment_. Accessed on May 2, 2019.

Jones, Richard E., and Kristin H. Lopez. 2014. *Human Reproductive Biology*, 4th ed. Amsterdam: Elsevier.

"The Kama Sutra of Vatsayayana." 2008. History of India. http://indohistory.com/kamasutra.html. Accessed on April 10, 2019.

Kavanaugh, Megan L., and Jenna Jerman. 2018. "Contraceptive Method Use in the United States: Trends and Characteristics Between 2008, 2012 and 2014." *Contraception*. 97(1): 14–21. https://www.ncbi.nlm.nih .gov/pmc/articles/PMC5959010/. Accessed on April 30, 2019.

Khan, Fahd, et al. 2013. "The Story of the Condom." *Indian Journal of Urology*. 29(1): 12–15. https://www.ncbi .nlm.nih.gov/pmc/articles/PMC3649591/. Accessed on April 11, 2019.

Khan, Javed A., M. A. Siddiqui, and Shagufta Nikhat. 2013. "Contraceptives in Greek Literature: A Review." *International Research Journal of Pharmacy.* 2(9): 22–24. https://irjponline.com/admin/php/uploads/1984_pdf.pdf. Accessed on April 11, 2019.

Knowles, Jon. 2012. "A History of Birth Control Methods." Planned Parenthood Federation of America. https://www.plannedparenthood.org/files/2613/9611/6275/History_of_BC_Methods.pdf. Accessed on April 6, 2019.

Kroon, Lisa A. 2007. "Drug Interactions with Smoking." *American Journal of Health System Pharmacy.* 64(18): 1917–1921. https://academic.oup.com/ajhp/article/64/18/1917/5135045. Accessed on May 19, 2019.

Lawrence, Cera R. 2010. "On the Generation of Animals, by Aristotle." The Embryo Project Encyclopedia. https://embryo.asu.edu/pages/generation-animals-aristotle. Accessed on April 21, 2019.

"Levonorgestrel—Drug Summary," 2019. Prescribers' Digital Reference. https://www.pdr.net/drug-summary/Plan-B-One-Step-levonorgestrel-573. Accessed on April 24, 2019.

"Loestrin® 21." 2013. Warner Chilcott. https://www.accessdata.fda.gov/drugsatfda_docs/label/2014/017354s045lbl.pdf. Accessed on May 19, 2019.

"Long-Acting Reversible Contraception: Intrauterine Device and Implant." 2018. American College of Obstetricians and Gynecologists. https://www.acog.org/Patients/FAQs/Long-Acting-Reversible-Contraception-Intrauterine-Device-and-Implant. Accessed on April 25, 2019.

Luo, Michael. 2005. "On Abortion, It's the Bible of Ambiguity." *The New York Times.* https://www.nytimes.com/2005/11/13/weekinreview/on-abortion-its-the-bible-of-ambiguity.html. Accessed on April 28, 2019.

Maguire, Daniel C. 2009. *Sacred Choices: The Right to Contraception and Abortion in Ten World Religions.* Minneapolis: Fortress Press.

Mann, Donald. 1992. "Why We Need a Smaller U.S. Population and How We Can Achieve It." Negative Population Growth, Inc. https://npg.org/wp-content/uploads/2015/03/WhyWeNeedASmallerU.S.Population.pdf. Accessed on May 1, 2019.

Marfatia, Y. S., Ipsa Pandya, and Kajal Mehta. 2015. "Condoms: Past, Present, and Future." *Indian Journal of Sexually Transmitted Diseases and AIDS*. 36(2): 133–139. https://www.ncbi.nlm.nih.gov/pmc/articles/PMC4660551/. Accessed on April 12, 2019.

Margulies, Lazar. 1975. "History of Intrauterine Devices." *Bulletin of the New York Academy of Medicine*. 51(5): 662–667. https://www.ncbi.nlm.nih.gov/pmc/articles/PMC1749527/pdf/bullnyacadmed00161-0098.pdf. Accessed on April 25, 2019.

McCarthy, Susan. 1999. "Don't Worry, Darling, I Have Giant Fennel." Salon. https://www.salon.com/1999/07/01/fennel/. Accessed on April 8, 2019.

"Medical Management of First-Trimester Abortion." 2016. Women's Health Care Physicians. https://www.acog.org/Clinical-Guidance-and-Publications/Practice-Bulletins/Committee-on-Practice-Bulletins-Gynecology/Medical-Management-of-First-Trimester-Abortion. Accessed on April 27, 2019.

Meher, Raju, and Sudeepta Bag. 2018. "Zoology Seminar." SlideShare. https://www.slideshare.net/rudramadhab1/assisted-reproductive-technology-90588655. Accessed on May 1, 2019.

"Methotrexate (MTX) for Early Abortion." 2014. Feminist Women's Health Center. http://www.fwhc.org/abortion/mtxinfo.htm. Accessed on April 27, 2019.

"The Mexico City Policy: An Explainer." 2019. Henry J Kaiser Family Foundation. https://www.kff.org/global-health-policy/fact-sheet/mexico-city-policy-explainer/. Accessed on May 1, 2019.

Mohr, James C. 1978. *Abortion in America: The Origins and Evolution of National Policy, 1800–1900.* New York: Oxford University Press.

Molnar, Charles, and Jane Gair. 2012. "Hormonal Control of Human Reproduction." Concepts of Biology, 1st Canadian Edition. https://opentextbc.ca/biology/chapter/24-4-hormonal-control-of-human-reproduction/. Accessed on April 22, 2019.

Moran, Jeffrey P. 1996. " 'Modernism Gone Mad': Sex Education Comes to Chicago, 1913." *Journal of American History.* 83(2): 481–513. http://www.academicroom.com/article/modernism-gone-mad-sex-education-comes-chicago-1913. Accessed on May 2, 2019.

Moran, Jeffrey P. 2000. *Teaching Sex: The Shaping of Adolescence in the 20th Century.* Cambridge, MA: Harvard University Press.

Mudaliar, Anuj. 2019. "The Process of Spermatogenesis Explained." Biology Wise. https://biologywise.com/the-process-of-spermatogenesis-explained. Accessed on April 21, 2019.

Nainggolan, Lisa. 2019. "10 Years to a Male Contraceptive?" Medscape. https://www.medscape.com/viewarticle/910887#vp_1. Accessed on May 19, 2019.

Nelson, Anita, and Natasha Massoudi. 2016. "New Developments in Intrauterine Device Use: Focus on the US." *Open Access Journal of Contraception.* 7: 127–141. https://www.dovepress.com/new-developments-in-intrauterine-device-use-focus-on-the-us-peer-reviewed-fulltext-article-OAJC. Accessed on April 25, 2019.

"New Developments in Vaginal Contraception." 1984. Population Reports. https://www.k4health.org/sites/default/files/021000.pdf. Accessed on April 20, 2019.

"New Study Reports Potential of DMAU as Male Birth Control Pill." 2018. Drug Development. https://www.drugdevelopment-technology.com/news/

new-study-reports-potential-dmau-male-birth-control-pill/. Accessed on May 19, 2019.

"Nexplanon." 2019. RxList. https://www.rxlist.com/ nexplanon-drug.htm#description. Accessed on April 24, 2019.

"Onanism." 2019. Jewish Virtual Library. https://www .jewishvirtuallibrary.org/onanism. Accessed on April 11, 2019.

"Oral Contraceptives and Cancer Risk." 2018. National Cancer Institute. https://www.cancer.gov/about-cancer/ causes-prevention/risk/hormones/oral-contraceptives-fact-sheet. Accessed on May 19, 2019.

Ostrowski, Kevin A., et al. 2018. "Evaluation of Vasectomy Trends in the United States." *Urology*. 118: 76–79.

"Outercourse." 2019. Urban Dictionary. https://www .urbandictionary.com/define.php?term=Outercourse. Accessed on April 10, 2019.

"Paragard." 2019. https://www.paragard.com/. Accessed on April 25, 2019.

Parmelee, Maurice. 1916. *Poverty and Social Progress*. New York: Macmillan. https://archive.org/details/ povertysocialpro00parmuoft/page/n5. Accessed on May 3, 2019.

Paul VI. 1968. Humanae Vitae. http://w2.vatican.va/content/ paul-vi/en/encyclicals/documents/hf_p-vi_enc_25071968_ humanae-vitae.html. Accessed on April 28, 2019.

Payne, Sarah Ruth. 2010. "Cleaning Up After Sex: An Environmental History of Contraceptives in the United States, 1873–2010." University of New Mexico. https:// digitalrepository.unm.edu/hist_etds/62/. Accessed on April 20, 2019.

"Phase I Trial of Male Birth Control Pill Reveals Positive Results." 2019. Drug Development. https://www .drugdevelopment-technology.com/news/trial-11-beta-mntdc/. Accessed on May 19, 2019.

"The Pill for Men." 2019. NHS Inform. https://www
.nhsinform.scot/healthy-living/contraception/the-pill/the-
pill-for-men. Accessed on April 22, 2019.

Piroreschi, Plinio. 1995. "Contraception and Abortion in
the Greco-Roman World." *Vesalius: Acta Internationales
Historiae Medicinae.* 1(2): 77–87. http://www.biusante
.parisdescartes.fr/ishm/vesalius/VESx1995x01x02x077
x087.pdf. Accessed on April 4, 2019.

Potts, D. M. 1972. "Limiting Human Reproductive
Potential." In C. R. Austin and R. V. Short, eds.
Reproduction in Mammals, vol. 5. "Artificial Control of
Reproduction," 32–66. New York: Cambridge University
Press.

Potts, Malcolm. 2019. "Birth Control." Encyclopedia
Britannica. https://www.britannica.com/science/birth-
control. Accessed on April 4, 2019.

Prescott, Heather Munro. 2011. *The Morning After: A History
of Emergency Contraception in the United States.* New
Brunswick, NJ: Rutgers University Press.

Rabin, Edward H. 1972. "Population Control through
Financial Incentives." *Hastings Law Journal.* 23(5): 1353–
1399. https://repository.uchastings.edu/hastings_law_
journal/vol23/iss5/2. Accessed on May 1.

Reagan, Leslie J. 2008. *When Abortion Was a Crime: Women,
Medicine, and Law in the United States, 1867–1973.*
Berkeley, CA: University of California Press.

"Reproduction and Development." 2019. Slide Player.
https://slideplayer.com/slide/4639066/. Accessed on
April 22, 2019.

Riddle, John M. 1992. *Contraception and Abortion from the
Ancient World to the Renaissance.* Cambridge, MA: Harvard
University Press.

"Risky Contraceptive Methods Some Women Are Forced to
Use—In Pictures." 2018. The Guardian. https://www

.theguardian.com/global-development/gallery/2018/jul/11/
risky-family-planning-methods-contraceptives-in-pictures.
Accessed on April 11, 2019.

Roberts, William C. 2015. "Facts and Ideas from Anywhere."
Baylor University Medical Center Proceedings. 28(3):
421–432. https://www.ncbi.nlm.nih.gov/pmc/articles/
PMC4462239/. Accessed on April 23, 2019.

Roffman, Deborah. 1991. "The Power of Language." *SIECUS
Reports*. 19(5): 1–6. https://siecus.org/wp-content/
uploads/2015/07/19-5.pdf. Accessed on April 10, 2019.

"The Samahita Blog." 2019. Samahita Retreat. https://
samahitaretreat.com/brahmacharya/. Accessed on April 8,
2019.

Samuel, Anand A. 2005. "FDA Regulation of Condoms:
Minimal Scientific Uncertainty Fuels the Moral
Conservative Plea to Rip a Large Hole in the Public's
Perception of Contraception." LEDA at Harvard
Law School. https://dash.harvard.edu/bitstream/
handle/1/8965574/Samuel05.html. Accessed on April 12,
2019.

Schwarcz, Joe. 2016. "The Right Chemistry: Condom
Technology." Montreal Gazette. https://montrealgazette
.com/opinion/columnists/the-right-chemistry-condom-
technology. Accessed on May 22, 2019.

Secura, Gina M. 2013. "Trends in Adolescent Contraceptive
Use from the Contraceptive CHOICE Project." The
Contraceptive Choice Project. https://www.hhs.gov/
ash/oah/sites/default/files/ash/oah/oah-initiatives/teen_
pregnancy/training/Assests/latest_contraceptiveuse.pdf.
Accessed on April 25, 2019.

Sengoopta, Chandak. 2003. " 'Dr Steinach Coming to Make
Old Young!': Sex Glands, Vasectomy and the Quest for
Rejuvenation in the Roaring Twenties." *Endeavour*. 27:
122–126.

"Sex Hygiene Is Discussed." 1913. Newspaper Archive. https://newspaperarchive.com/eau-claire-leader-nov-14-1913-p-4/. Accessed on May 2, 2019.

"Sex Using Tantra—II." 2000. Tantra Shashtra. http://indiansaga.com/tantra/tantra8.html. Accessed on April 19, 2019.

Sheldon, Tony. 2013. "Arie Haspels." *BMJ*. 346: f901. https://www.bmj.com/content/346/bmj.f901. Accessed on April 24, 2019.

Singer, Natasha. 2009. "Contraceptive Sponge Makes a Return to Pharmacy Shelves." *The New York Times*. https://www.nytimes.com/2009/05/23/business/23sponge.html. Accessed on April 20, 2019.

Sivananda, Sri Swami. 1997. "Practice of Brahmacharya." Divine Life Society. https://static1.squarespace.com/static/54482313e4b059dd18a323fa/t/57dea472414fb546195ce728/1474208889232/Brahmacharya+by+Swami+Sivananda.pdf. Accessed on April 8, 2019.

Smith, Lori. 2018. "10 Most Common Birth Control Pill Side Effects." Medical News Today. https://www.medicalnewstoday.com/articles/290196.php. Accessed on April 23, 2019.

"Sperm Release Pathway." 2019. Medline Plus. https://medlineplus.gov/ency/anatomyvideos/000121.htm. Accessed on April 21, 2019.

"Spermatogenesis." 2019. Repropedia. https://www.repropedia.org/spermatogenesis. Accessed on April 21, 2019.

Stacey, Dawn. 2019. "Must-Know Facts About Starting and Stopping Depo Provera." Verywell Health. https://www.verywellhealth.com/starting-and-stopping-depo-provera-906708. Accessed on April 24, 2019.

"Sterilization." 2019. HHS.gov. Office of Population Affairs. https://www.hhs.gov/opa/pregnancy-prevention/sterilization/index.html. Accessed on April 30, 2019.

Stern, Jacob. 2002. "The Female Condom at Antoninus Liberalis 41.5." In Jørgen Mejer and Bettina Amden, eds. *Noctes Atticae: 34 Articles on Graeco-Roman Antiquity and its Nachleben: Studies Presented to Jørgen Mejer on His Sixtieth Birthday March 18, 2002*. Copenhagen: Museum Tusculanum Press.

Strevens, Summer. 2017. "A Provision for Pleasure: Georgian London's Booming Sex Industry & STDs." Summer Strevens. http://www.summerstrevens.com/a-provision-for-pleasure-georgian-londons-booming-sex-industry-stds/. Accessed on April 12, 2019.

Tazkargy, Ariel S. 2014. "From Coercion to Coercion: Voluntary Sterilization Policies in the United States." *Law & Inequality: A Journal of Theory and Practice*. 32(1): 135–168. https://scholarship.law.umn.edu/lawineq/vol32/iss1/5/. Accessed on April 30, 2019.

Tissot, Samuel Auguste David. 1765. *Advice to the People in General with Regard to Their Health*. Dayboro, Queensland, Australia: Emereo Publishing. https://www.gutenberg.org/files/39044/39044-h/39044-h.htm. Accessed on April 20, 2019.

Tone, Andrea. 2002. *Devices and Desires: A History of Contraceptives in America*. New York: Hill & Wang.

Tsaraklis, Athanasios, et al. 2017. "Preventing Syphilis in the 16th Century: The Distinguished Italian Anatomist Gabriele Falloppio (1523–1562) and the Invention of the Condom." *The Infections in the History of Medicine*. 24(4): 395–398. https://www.infezmed.it/media/journal/Vol_25_4_2017_16.pdf. Accessed on April 12, 2019.

Tulandi, Togas, and Haya M. Al-Fozan. 2019. "Spontaneous Abortion: Risk Factors, Etiology, Clinical Manifestations." UpToDate. https://www.uptodate.com/contents/pregnancy-loss-miscarriage-risk-factors-etiology-clinical-manifestations-and-diagnostic-evaluation. Accessed on April 26, 2019.

"Vacuum Aspiration for Abortion." 2018. C. S. Mott Children's Hospital. University of Michigan. https://www.mottchildren.org/health-library/tw1078. Accessed on April 26, 2019.

Wallechinsky, David, and Irving Wallace. n.d. "History of Sex and Sexuality from 1866 to 1877." Trivia Library. https://www.trivia-library.com/b/history-of-sex-and-sexuality-from-1866-to-1877.htm. Accessed on April 11, 2019.

Wear, Sarah Klitenic. 2014. "The Ancients on Abortion." First Things. https://www.firstthings.com/article/2014/04/the-ancients-on-abortion. Accessed on April 28, 2019.

"What Are Prenatal Torts? Wrongful Pregnancy, Wrongful Birth, and Wrongful Life in Ohio." 2018. Dyer, Garofalo, Mann & Schultz. https://ohiotiger.com/wrongful-birth-claim/. Accessed on May 27, 2019.

"What Does the Bible Say about Abortion?" n.d. Freedom from Religion Foundation. https://ffrf.org/component/k2/item/18514-what-does-the-bible-say-about-abortion. Accessed on April 28, 2019.

Wood, Thomas D. 1922. *Health Service in the City Schools of the U.S.* Joint Committee on Health Problems in Education. https://books.google.com/books?id=YdIOAQAAMAAJ. Accessed on May 3, 2019.

Wortman, Judith. 1976. "The Diaphragm and Other Intravaginal Barriers: A Review." *Population Reports*. Series H, Number 4. Washington, DC: Department of Medical and Public Affairs, The George Washington University Medical Center. https://www.k4health.org/sites/default/files/760013.pdf. Accessed on April 19, 2019.

Zhuhong. 2009. "Ancient Chinese Contraceptive Choices." Women of China. http://www.womenofchina.cn/womenofchina/html1/culture/lifestyle/9/9194-1.htm. Accessed on April 7, 2019.

2 Problems, Controversies, and Solutions

Birth control is a topic of considerable interest to young adults, to their parents, to governmental agencies, to religious organizations, and to many other groups of individuals in the United States and every other part of the world. It is a topic involving many complex and controversial issues. One cannot talk about the subject or develop views about birth control without first of all having an understanding of the biological processes that occur during fertilization, gestation, and birth, as well as the problems that may arise during these events. But developing a store of knowledge is only a first step in thinking about birth control. Reproduction is not some neutral, remote, unimportant topic that one can choose to think about or not. It is a critical part of almost everyone's life at some time or another. Decisions about contraception, abortion, sterilization, assisted reproductive technology, and other issues are very much influenced by a host of factors other than scientific knowledge. What does one's religious beliefs, if any, for example, have to say on the subject? Does a person's economic status or place in society have anything to do with the positions one takes on these issues? How about one's emotional feelings about intimate relations with other boys and girls, men and women? Do

Cecile Richards, cofounder of political action group Supermajority, addresses the Ann Arbor Stop the Bans protest organized by Planned Parenthood on May 21, 2019. (Smontgom65/Dreamstime.com)

these—or should these—feelings have any influence on the viewpoints one eventually develops about birth control? This chapter presents some of the personal, moral, economic, social, political, and other issues relating to birth control, along with arguments on all sides of each issue.

Sex Education

Should you be reading this book? Some people might respond without hesitation, "Of course" or "Why not?" Most young adults are eager to learn more about the process of reproduction and the implications it has for the way they live their lives. Why would it *not* be a good idea to gather as much as unbiased information as possible on this topic?

Others may take a somewhat different view. Yes, they say, information about birth control is probably a good thing. The more young adults know about human reproduction, the better the decisions they will eventually make. *But (!)* reading books on the topic or going to a class on sex education is not the best way to deal with this controversial topic: much better to let parents, religious leaders, or other qualified adults take on the education of children and young adults about such a personal question.

This debate has gone on since the late 19th century. Prior to that time, teaching children and young adults about human sexuality was, if not ignored and/or frowned upon, treated as a topic handled exclusively by parents, older siblings, priests, nuns, and other religious leaders. Prior to 1900, only a handful of sex education programs in more formal settings, such as schools, existed (Huber and Firmin 2014). The focus of these programs was largely on moral issues and sexual disease. That is, courses were designed to teach girls and boys about sexual standards of the time—the things a "good" boy or girl could be expected to do—and the problems of avoiding syphilis, gonorrhea, or other types of sexual infections. Some versions of sex education were motivated by strong, negative attitudes about human sexuality in general. An example is the position taken by some members of the late 19th-century group called the Social Purity Movement. These individuals argued, perhaps surprisingly, that sex education in the schools was essential. The reason, they said, was that such courses could reveal to young women and men the evils of all types of sexual behaviors and repress any sexual desires and behaviors they might have adopted (Strong 1972). None of the courses of the time were designed to provide instruction on the actual mechanics of human sexuality, such as contraception, abortion, sterilization, and related topics. (The strongly negative attitudes about just about all aspects of human sexuality were reflected in some of the comments by the individual for whom the period was named, Queen Victoria. At one point, after the birth of her first child, she commented that childbearing was "a complete violence to all one's feelings of propriety (which God knows receive a shock enough in marriage alone)" [Greenspun 2017].)

That situation began to change in the United States only in the early 20th century. One factor in revising the goals of sex education to some modest extent was the experience of young men in World War I. Sexually transmitted infections (STIs) were rampant among the military during the time, and some observers suggested that such a problem could be avoided in the future by providing young men (and, possibly, young women) with the "facts of life" as to how STIs are contracted and spread (Imber 1984).

The first concrete realization of that view of sex education (and, some say, the beginning of modern sex education in the United States) dates to 1912, when the National Education Association adopted a resolution affirming the need for the training of teachers to implement sex education programs in the nation's schools. (It followed with an even stronger resolution on the topic in 1914 [Carrer 1971].) Only a year after that resolution was adopted, an important, large-scale experiment on its realization took place in the Chicago Public School system. There, Ella Flagg Young, the first female administrator of a major school system in the country, outlined a program consisting of three lectures on human biology and STIs. At one point, Young pointed to the absurdity of the city's failure to teach some version of sex education in its schools. It appeared to reflect the view, she said, that "people have no sex organs" (Moran 1996; for her exact quote, see Sex Hygiene Is Discussed 1913). Reaction to the program was so strong, however, that it was canceled after only one semester, and Young resigned from her post in protest (Jensen 2007).

In the half century following the so-called Chicago experiment, Americans became more amenable to the idea of formal sex education classes in high schools and, sometimes, junior high schools and even elementary schools. Reflecting that growing acceptance of sex education in secondary schools was the finding of a 1922 research study that about a quarter of schools contacted provided some type of sex education program within their curriculum (Wood 1922, 25). Compare that number to similar data from 1914, when only 1 percent of schools were teaching a sex education class (Moran 2000, 61). During this period, the federal government was also becoming involved in the support of sex educational programs. The U.S. Office of Education, the Public Health Service (PHS), and other agencies began to publish pamphlets about sex education in schools. As an example, the PHS released a manual of more than 100 pages: "High Schools and Sex Education," offering "suggestions on education related to sex." The manual was many decades ahead of most other material widely available on sex education in the United States (Gruenberg 1922).

The emphasis of sex education programs from the 1920s to the 1960s was constantly changing, reflecting the views of the general population and educators on human sexuality and the recommended focus in sex education classes on that topic. Throughout that period, however, two themes predominated (as they had for virtually all of previous history): (1) a better understanding of sexuality is critical to and will contribute to a decrease in sexually transmitted infections and unwanted pregnancies, and (2) abiding by traditional social values by not engaging in premarital sex is the best policy for both individuals and society as a whole. The idea that sex might have a recreational component in addition to its procreative function was sometimes, but only very rarely, mentioned (Carter 2001).

That situation began to change in the late 1960s as a result of three factors: (1) a more open and accepting view of human sexuality, mostly among younger adults living in the so-called sexual revolution of the time; (2) the availability (for the first time) of an oral contraceptive pill that made worry-free sex a much more likely option; and (3) research on male and female sexuality by researcher Alfred Kinsey and his colleagues at the Institute for Sex Research at Indiana University, research showing a far greater diversity of sexual activity than most Americans had ever imagined (Escoffier 2015; Huber and Firmin 2014).

These three events contributed to a shift in sex education priorities. Newer programs in sex education began to modify their exclusive emphasis on morality and disease prevention, probably presented in a handful of boys-only and girls-only lectures, often by the school physical education instructor, to full-blown classes covering a range of topics related to human sexuality. This new curriculum, often referred to as *comprehensive sex education*, involves at least a semester's worth of work not only on traditional topics such as abstinence and sexually transmitted infections but also on subjects such as contraception, reproduction, puberty, menstruation, body image, media literacy, decision-making, gender roles, healthy relationships, communication, dating, and relationships (Lindberg, Maddow-Zimet, and Boonstra 2016; Sexuality Education. Frequently Asked Questions 2019; a good review of the current status of sex education in the United States is Hall et al. 2016).

This shift in emphasis within many school systems and other educational programs constitutes the basis on which vigorous debates about the nature of sex education continue today. That debate consists of two major questions. First, should young adults be required to participate in school-based sex education at all? Or should any instruction of that type be limited to the family and religious organizations? Second, if there are to be school programs, what topics are or are not appropriate for those programs?

Existing data suggest that the first of these questions may already have been answered. Although very few (if any) public opinion surveys exist prior to the late 20th century, recent studies suggest that large majorities of the general public tend to support the teaching of human sexuality in schools. One recent study, for example, reported that, in general, "more than 93 percent of parents place high importance on sex education in both middle and high school" (Kantor and Levitz 2017). Earlier research cited in this report suggests that these numbers reflect a trend that has existed in the United States for at least the past few decades (see, for example, Parents and Teens Talk about Sexuality: A National Poll 2012; Sex Education in America 2004). The caveat implied for these data, however, is that the devil may be in the details; that is, respondents may not understand or report as to what they precisely mean by their answers, which can range from a vague "teaching about sex is a good idea" to "the whole range of sexual issues should be discussed in a school program."

The more interesting question, then, is what it is that parents, students, and other interested individuals and groups would like to see as a program of sex education in the schools. Do they want a more classical "birds and bees" and sexual disease program, or do they prefer a more extensive comprehensive sex education approach? (For a review of the topics actually covered in sex education classes in the United States in 2014, see Results from the School Health Policies and Practices Study 2014 2015.) Probably the single most contentious issue in this debate was the rise of the Abstinence-Only-Until-Marriage (AOUM) movement in the early 1980s. Proponents of this movement argue that the only effective method of sex education is to encourage young adults to abstain from any sexual contact until they marry.

Abstinence-Only-Until-Marriage

The early 1980s saw the confluence of two factors that were to influence the direction of sex education over at least the next three decades. In the first place, public opinion had reached a point at which there no longer remained much controversy as to the need for sex education in the schools. Approval ratings for such programs were close to or well into the 90 percent range, and opponents of the practice began to recognize that there was not much point in objecting to sex education overall. Also, the advance of the HIV/AIDS epidemic in the United States shone a spotlight on the need for more and better education about avoiding sexual infections. Largely in response to these factors, some individuals and organizations began to speak out about the need for a single-issue form of sex education, one in which abstinence was essentially the only option for the content of such courses (History of Sex Education n.d.).

The federal government first weighed in on this issue in 1981 when the U.S. Congress passed the Adolescent Family Life Act, Title XX of the Public Health Service Act. The act was designed to encourage and support sex education conducted by parents, religious and charitable organizations, voluntary groups, and other interested associations. Its goal was to teach young adults "self-discipline" as a way of avoiding pregnancy, as well as providing ways of caring for the children of unwed mothers. The act provided funding in the amount of $30 million annually from 1981 through 1985 (Public Health Service Act 2018, Title XX, page 1314). Since 1981, two additional sources of funding for abstinence-only programs have been created, Title V of the Temporary Assistance for Needy Family Act of 1996 and the Special Projects of Regional and National Significance—Community-Based Abstinence Education (SPRANS—CBAE) Act of 2000. These three avenues of funding have resulted in an ever-increasing flow of money to abstinence-only programs, rising from about $60 million in 1998 to $100 million in 2003 to $180 million in 2008 (Donovan 2017; A History of Federal Funding for Abstinence-Only-Until-Marriage Programs 2018).

One feature of the 1996 act was of special significance: its clearly stated definition as to what the term *abstinence* means, at least as far as the federal government is concerned. That definition is sometimes referred to as the *A-H definition* because of the eight (A through H) conditions essential to the meaning of abstinence education. Programs that can be funded under the act must

A. have as its exclusive purpose teaching the social, psychological, and health gains to be realized by abstaining from sexual activity,

B. teach abstinence from sexual activity outside marriage as the expected standard for all school-age children,

C. teach that abstinence from sexual activity is the only certain way to avoid out-of-wedlock pregnancy, sexually transmitted diseases, and other associated health problems,

D. teach that a mutually faithful, monogamous relationship in the context of marriage is the expected standard of sexual activity,

E. teach that sexual activity outside the context of marriage is likely to have harmful psychological and physical effects,

F. teach that bearing children out-of-wedlock is likely to have harmful consequences for the child, the child's parents, and society,

G. teach young people how to reject sexual advances and how alcohol and drug use increases vulnerability to sexual advances,

H. teach the importance of attaining self-sufficiency before engaging in sexual activity (110 Stat. 2354 Public Law 104–193, Sec. 912, Title V, available at https://www.con gress.gov/104/plaws/publ193/PLAW-104publ193.pdf. Accessed on May 9, 2019).

It would be helpful to a discussion of federal support for AOUM sex education programs if comparable data about federal funding for comprehensive sex education courses were also available. The problem is that there are few such programs; Congress has never approved a dedicated mechanism for funding comprehensive sex education in the country (State Profiles Fiscal Year 2017 2017). The closest approach to federal support for comprehensive sex education was a pair of programs implemented by the administration of President Barack Obama in 2010, the Personal Responsibility Education Program and the Teen Pregnancy Prevention Program, both enacted as part of the president's Affordable Care Act (ACA) of that year. The former program has been funded at the rate of about $75 million per year and the latter program at about $100 million annually (State Profiles Fiscal Year 2017 2017). As of 2019, the administration of President Donald Trump indicated a reduction in funding for these two programs, with any remaining grants set aside for abstinence-only-type programs (Abstinence Education Programs: Definition, Funding, and Impact on Teen Sexual Behavior 2018).

One question that was seldom asked in the early years of interest in AOUM programs was simply, "Do they work?" That is, are young men and women who enroll in these programs more likely not to indulge in premarital sex, to remain in monogamous relationships longer, to have lower rates of sexually transmitted infections, and, in general, to become the kind of men and women proponents of AOUM sex education hope and promise that they will be? The first definitive answer to that question came in 2004 when U.S. representative Henry A. Waxman released a report prepared at his request on the 13 most popular AOUM programs funded by SPRANS at the time. Authors of the report said that "over 80% of the abstinence-only curricula, used by over two-thirds of SPRANS grantees in 2003, contain false, misleading, or distorted information about reproductive health." The specific problems they noted were that such programs contain false information about the effectiveness of contraceptives and the risks of abortion, blur the boundaries between religion and science, treat stereotypes about boys and girls as scientific fact, and contain scientific errors (The Content of Federally Funded Abstinence–Only Education Programs 2004). Probably not surprisingly, some supporters of AOUM found flaws in the Waxman report itself and rejected its findings as unreliable (Waxman Report Is Riddled with Errors and Inaccuracies 2004).

Over the next two decades, the effectiveness of AOUM programs was the subject of several additional research studies. Almost without exception, those studies reported the same findings as did the Waxman study. In one such study, authors found that "at present, there does not exist any strong evidence that any abstinence program delays the initiation of sex, hastens the return to abstinence, or reduces the number of sexual partners. In addition, there is strong evidence from multiple randomized trials demonstrating that some abstinence programs chosen for evaluation because they were believed to be promising actually had no impact on teen sexual behavior. That is, they did not delay the initiation of sex, increase the return to abstinence or decrease the number of sexual partners" (Kirby 2007). A second study noted that no program (of abstinence-only sex education) helped teens abstain from sex any longer than other teens, helped raise the age of first intercourse, helped reduce the number of teens' sex partners, helped teens use less marijuana and alcohol, and led to believe that condoms reduce the risk of infection (Trenholm, 2007). A recent review of many studies on AOUM programs concluded that "U.S. abstinence-only-until marriage policies and programs are not effective, violate adolescent rights, stigmatize or exclude many youth, and reinforce harmful gender stereotypes" (Santelli et al. 2017). In spite of this research, interest in abstinence-only sex education programs, downplayed by the Obama administration, has once again become a popular theme in the subsequent administration of President Donald Trump (Hellmann 2018).

Sources of Information on Birth Control

Some individuals may decide at some point in their lives that they would like to have more information about birth control than whatever they may (or may not) have gained in a formal school setting. For example, a woman and/or her partner may decide that they would prefer not to have any more children. She/they may then search out a source of birth control information to find out how best to deal with that decision.

One source of birth control information is one's own physician, physician assistant, or other medical specialist. Such an individual can provide private, helpful instruction about the types of contraception currently available and, if necessary, provide the appropriate medical services. Another common source of birth control information is a publicly funded family planning clinic, of which there are about 8,000 nationwide. In 2014, some 5.3 million women received services from such a facility. This number represented more than a quarter (27 percent) of all women who received contraceptive services at the time and nearly a half (44 percent) of all poor women receiving such services. Funding for family planning clinics may come from federal, state, regional, local, or nongovernmental agencies (Publicly Funded Family Planning Services in the United States 2016; Zolna and Frost 2016).

In 1970, the U.S. Congress passed the Family Planning Services and Public Research Act of 1970, often called the Title X Family Planning Program. The law was adopted as an amendment to the Public Health Service Act of 1944 (Public Law 91-572). The act is the only federal dedicated source of funding for family planning services in the United States (Title X 2019). It provided for federal funding grants, training, and research programs on virtually all aspects of birth control and family planning activities.

During debates over the act in Congress, and ever since that time, one issue has reoccurred: coverage for abortion activities. Many legislators, other public officials, and members of the general public have argued that federal funds should not be used for any program in which any aspect of abortion was also included. This restriction was meant to apply not only to actual abortion surgeries themselves but to any discussion of abortion as a possible birth control method as well as to agencies that provide a whole range of contraceptive services in which abortion was included in any form whatsoever (Nash et al. 2018; Vamos et al. 2011).

As of mid-2019, 18 states have passed some form of legislation that prohibits the use of public funds for any agency that includes some aspect of abortion information or service in its activities. Half of those states restrict the use of Title X funds for such services, 15 prohibit the use of state funds, three restrict the use of certain types of Medicare funding, and 12 states limit other forms of birth control funding, such as sexually transmitted infection and/or sex education if abortion is also included in such programs (State Family Planning Funding Restrictions 2019).

Funding restrictions are only one way in which the federal government and some states have attempted to restrict abortion services, as well as unrelated family planning activities, at publicly funded facilities. The whole range of such efforts have sometimes been called "targeted regulation of abortion providers" (TRAP) provisions. Other TRAP restrictions that have been imposed by various states include requirements that physicians working at family planning clinics have hospital-admitting privileges, that physical structures of such facilities be equivalent to full-service surgical centers, that they be located at distances of no more than some given number of miles from a full-service hospital, or that room sizes in the clinic meet certain minimum standards. Most of these limitations have little to do with abortion procedures and essentially nothing to do with other family planning activities (Targeted Regulation of Abortion Providers 2019). As with many other issues related to human sexuality, actions by governmental agencies, as well as public opinion on a topic, are much impacted by dominant political trends at a time (see, for example, Kodjak 2016, and President Trump Signs Measure Reversing Obama Era Rule Protecting Women's Access to Basic Health Care 2017).

The Future of Abortion

There may never have been a time in U.S. history when the right to abortion was not a matter of controversy. There may never be such a time in the future. Some optimists may have thought that the U.S. Supreme Court ruling in the case of *Roe v. Wade* in 1973 settled the matter. That decision might be viewed, one might argue, as a reasonable compromise with which each side of the abortion debate could live. But such was not the case. Almost from the moment that decision was announced, individuals and organizations opposed to abortion began to ask how that decision could be avoided, modified, or overturned.

The first highly visible expression of this campaign against abortion came exactly one year after the *Roe v. Wade* decision in a national March for Life, held in Washington, D.C. The purpose of that event was to "end abortion by uniting, educating, and mobilizing pro-life people in the public square." Originally designed as a one-time event, the march has been held annually on or about the anniversary of the *Roe v. Wade* ruling (About the March for Life 2019).

Over the next half century, many opponents of abortion rights hoped and planned for an orderly transition in the makeup of the U.S. Supreme Court that would eventually result in a majority willing to overturn *Roe v. Wade*. With the confirmation of each new justice (and chief justice), many observers have hoped that the Court had taken a more conservative turn, increasing the likelihood of an antiabortion majority. But, as of 2018, that hope had been dashed. The addition of Clarence Thomas (1991), John Roberts (2005), Samuel Alito (2006), and Neil Gorsuch (2017) had not yet produced a guaranteed 5–4 majority to reverse *Roe v. Wade*. The addition of the potential vote in that debate, Brett Kavanaugh, in 2018, has been seen yet once again as the turning point on which an antiabortion vote might finally be obtained. As of late 2019, those hopes had not yet come true as a recent vote on a restrictive abortion law passed in Louisiana had been blocked by a 5–4 Court vote, with the deciding vote being that of Chief Justice Roberts (Ollstein 2019). (For an abbreviated history of federal legislation on abortion from 1973 to recent periods, see Abortion History Timeline n.d.; Martin 2014.)

As an alternative strategy to waiting, working, and hoping for a majority on the Supreme Court, some antiabortion groups have focused on a state-by-state approach to overturning *Roe v. Wade*. The premise behind that strategy is a "death-by-a-thousand-cuts" approach in which several types of restrictive abortion laws are created for, introduced into, and adopted by individual states (An Overview of Abortion Laws 2019; one of the most complete reviews of legal restrictions on reproductive rights is the annual "State of the States" report of the Center for Reproductive Rights; see, for example, A Pivotal Time for Reproductive Rights 2016).

One of the most common legal methods of making life difficult for abortion providers is the TRAP laws, described earlier. Two other approaches that have been tried are the so-called personhood laws and amendments and fetal heartbeat legislation. In this context, the term *personhood* means that human beings from the very moment of conception are legally "persons." As such, they are entitled to all of the rights and privileges to which all "persons" of any age or other characteristics are entitled. Killing an embryo or fetus, then, is as much a crime as it is for any other living human (Rights of Personhood 2019).

The first personhood law was proposed in the U.S. Congress by Representative Lawrence Hogan (R-MD) under the title "Human Life Amendment to the U.S. Constitution." Hogan submitted the bill the week following the Supreme

Court's decision in 1973. The first section of the proposed amendment read:

> Neither the United States nor any State shall deprive any human being, from the moment of conception, of life without due process of law; nor deny to any human being, from the moment of conception, within its jurisdiction, the equal protection of the laws. (Human Life Amendments: Major Texts 2004)

The act never received serious attention in the Congress, but it soon became a model for similar legislation at the state level. Indeed, over the next 40 years, more than 330 versions of the act were introduced in state legislatures (Martin 2014). Many variations of the act became known as fetal homicide bills. These forms of legislation established that human life begins at conception and that a person responsible for the death of an embryo or fetus is guilty of homicide. Minnesota passed the first of such acts in 1986, and, as of 2018, 29 states overall had some form of that type of legislation on their books (State Laws on Fetal Homicide and Penalty-enhancement for Crimes Against Pregnant Women 2018).

Opposition to personhood laws ultimately involves the murky depths of the most basic of all birth control issues: When does life begin? For individuals who believe that human life begins at conception, these laws make at least some degree of sense, since the fertilized egg is by its very nature defined as being "human." A very different view is the argument that science (and other fields of human scholarship) cannot definitively say when human life begins. The existing legal standard in the United States in 2019 is the position taken by the Supreme Court in *Roe v. Wade*, namely that there is no rational basis for saying life begins at conception. In his majority opinion, Justice Harry Blackmun wrote:

We need not resolve the difficult question of when life begins. When those trained in the respective disciplines of medicine, philosophy, and theology are unable to arrive at any consensus, the judiciary, in this point in the development of man's knowledge, is not in a position to speculate as to the answer. (*Roe v. Wade.* 410 U.S. at 159)

As an example of the way this view is presented in recent years is an editorial in the *Aurora* (Colorado) *Sentinel,* in stating its opposition to the state's 2014 initiative petition in favor of personhood:

Plain and simple, Amendment 67 would bestow constitutional rights on fertilized human eggs, creating a labyrinth of medical and legal nightmares for women, hospitals and doctors. It's a dangerous idea that even the most ardent critics of legalized abortion have worked previously to defeat. (Colorado Definition of "Personhood" Initiative, Amendment 67 [2014] 2014)

Personhood laws are still a popular line of resistance to *Roe v. Wade* in the United States today. Legislators and citizens in many states across the country continue to propose such acts or amendments to state constitutions of this kind (Shea 2019).

In recent years, one of the most common types of antiabortion legislation has been the so-called fetal heartbeat bill. Bills of this kind are based on the belief that the presence of a fetal heartbeat is an indication that human life has begun, and performing an abortion at any time after that moment constitutes murder of a human being. Fetal heartbeats can sometimes be detected as early as the sixth week of pregnancy, significantly before a woman may know that she is pregnant.

The first bill of this type was submitted to the Ohio legislature in 2011 by a group known as Faith2Action. The bill failed, but it became the model for similar bills in several other states. The first state in which such a bill passed was North

Dakota in 2013. The federal appeals court later ruled this bill unconstitutional but, interestingly, strongly recommended to the U.S. Supreme Court that it reverse the ruling in *Roe v. Wade* (Lithwick 2015; the current status of fetal heartbeat bills in the United States is available at Heartbeat Bans 2019; the text of all such bills can be found at Sabetai 2019).

Campaigns to increase restrictions on abortion heated up in 2019. During the year, eight states adopted revised abortion laws: Alabama, Arkansas, Georgia, Kentucky, Mississippi, Missouri, Ohio, and Utah. Arkansas and Utah passed the least restrictive of the new laws, limiting abortions to the middle of the second trimester. (*Roe v. Wade* allows states to set standards such as this one.) Georgia, Kentucky, Missouri, Mississippi, and Ohio all adopted some version of the fetal heartbeat bill, banning abortions at the point at which a heartbeat can be detected. This point varies from individual to individual but usually occurs at six to eight weeks of pregnancy. Alabama took the most extreme position, banning essentially all abortions at any time of pregnancy. The only exceptions to the law are for cases in which the fetus will be unable to survive and those in which a woman's life is at risk. No exceptions are provided for rape or incest. Although pregnant women themselves are not subject to prosecution, doctors who perform an abortion can be sentenced to a prison term of up to 99 years (Lai 2019; text of the Alabama bill is available at Gore 2019).

The Georgia law is somewhat different from the Alabama statute. It adopts the principle of personhood and declares that life begins at conception. In this scenario, any women who had an abortion, either from an abortion provider or by taking an abortifacient drug, might be guilty of murdering her unborn child. Legal experts are currently unsure about the interpretation of this provision of the law, although some think that a murder prosecution is possible (Rankin 2019).

Proabortion groups are by no means unaware of state (and federal) efforts to limit or restrict abortion in the United States. Much of their efforts go into countering antiabortion initiatives, such as personhood and fetal heartbeat bills. Debates over these bills are often of the "he said, she said" type, in which the two sides cannot agree on the most basic of issues, such as when life begins. As an example, the organization National Advocates for Pregnant Women has prepared a long and detailed response to personhood legislation. In that document, the author argues that the basic science on which personhood bills are based is flawed; the legislation has, in any case, been designed to overturn *Roe v. Wade* rather than serve a legitimate health issue for women; and, most important, such laws will actually cause harm to pregnant women (Paltrow n.d.).

But proabortion groups also focus their attention on ways in which safe and inexpensive (or free) abortions can still be available to women who want them. Some of the proactive measures that have been proposed or adopted in 2019 include the following:

1. The Rhode Island House of Representatives passed a bill repealing all pre-*Roe* antiabortion bills still listed in state law and repealing all state and local laws banning Medicaid and private insurance plans coverage for abortion.

2. The Hawaii Senate approved a bill that would allow registered nurses to conduct abortions.

3. Legislation specifically confirming a woman's right to an abortion was proposed and/or enacted in 24 states. The one state in which such a bill actually became law was New York.

4. The most popular type of bill removed pre-*Roe* prohibitions on abortion and/or introduced new protections against personhood, fetal heartbeat, and similar antiabortion bills being proposed and/or enacted.

5. At least 17 states are considering or have adopted legislation specifically requiring the state to provide free FDA-approved birth control measures.

6. Tennessee and some other states are considering bills designed to increase access to long-acting reversible contraceptives (LARCs).

7. Legislation allowing pharmacists to dispense contraceptives has been introduced into more than ten states, including Connecticut, Delaware, Indiana, Kentucky, Mississippi, New Hampshire, and Rhode Island (items 1–4 from State Policy Updates 2019; items 5–7 from State of the States 2018; both sites are updated annually).

8. The state of Vermont approved legislation that added a guaranteed right to abortion for women to the state constitution (Rathke 2019).

The Contraceptive Mandate

A basic theme throughout this book has been that many women and men want, and have always wanted, access to some type of birth control. Over the centuries, individuals have developed a broad array of methods for avoiding pregnancy, from pessaries and crocodile dung to an oral contraceptive pill and IUD (intrauterine device). The benefits of effective birth control are clear. On the personal level, they allow women and their partners to make reliable decisions about the size of their family. When individuals cannot afford to have more children, are unable to do so, and simply want to limit their family size, they should have access to contraception. On a broader level, birth control methods provide a simple and inexpensive way to place a rein on population growth, an issue often blamed for many of the social, economic, environmental, political, and other problems the world currently faces.

Over the past half century, this scenario has begun to have a larger governmental component than at almost any time in the past. That is, many experts have been arguing that birth control technology should be a right for women and men, just as a living wage is now considered to be a right for all Americans.

That principle has formed the basis of actions taken at both federal and state levels to ensure that women and men have access to the birth control technologies that they want and need. Among the states, these actions date to the late 20th century, with the passage of laws requiring contraceptive coverage by employers and insurance companies. Maryland passed the first such law in 1998, followed a year later by California, Connecticut, Georgia, Hawaii, Maine, Nevada, New Hampshire, North Carolina, and Vermont. By 2019, 29 states had passed such laws covering one or more forms of contraception, such as over-the-counter methods, prescription methods, extended supplies of a contraceptive, and male and female sterilization procedures. Fourteen states required that coverage come at no cost to participants, and eight states specifically prohibited delays in individuals receiving service and/or treatment (Dailard 2004; Insurance Coverage of Contraceptives 2019).

Action by the federal government followed closely on that of the states. In 2000, the Equal Employment Opportunity Commission (EEOC) was asked to rule on a case in which a woman complained that her employer declined to provide coverage for oral contraceptive pills even though it paid for many other prescription and contraceptive devices. The EEOC ruled that the company was in violation of Title VII of the Civil Rights Act of 1964. It said that any company that covered any type of prescription drugs in its insurance plan must also cover all types of prescription contraceptives (Decision 2000).

The most recent iteration of the contraceptive mandate was included in the 2010 Affordable Care Act, also known as Obamacare. The act required that all new health insurance plans adopted after August 1, 2012, include free coverage for all contraceptive devices and methods approved by the Food and Drug Administration (Group Health Plans and Health Insurance Issuers Relating to Coverage of Preventive Services Under the Patient Protection and Affordable Care Act 2012, 8725–8729). That list included 18 contraceptive methods and two forms of emergency contraception (Birth Control Guide n.d.).

A fundamental problem with which the act had to deal was that many organizations and groups affected by the law were certain to have religious and/or moral objections to the use (and, therefore, the provision) of contraceptives. The law specifically exempted churches and other houses of worship from complying with the law. But the status of other related organizations, such as hospitals maintained by religious groups, was unclear. Many groups involved in health-care issues argued that a religious exemption, if provided at all, should be as narrowly drawn as possible. The broader the exemption, they pointed out, the larger the number of women who would be excluded from provisions of the act (Sonfield 2012).

Forces opposed to the contraceptive mandate continued, however, to lobby vigorously for more generous exemption policies in implementation of the ACA. Multiple law suits were brought by religious organizations, for-profit corporations, and individuals to invalidate or at least cut back on requirements for contraceptive coverage. In response to these actions, the federal government offered a series of compromise proposals, the most significant of which allowed religious organizations not to follow provisions of the law, as long as the companies with which they had insurance plans did so (Flicker 2013).

These compromise proposals proved not to be satisfactory to opponents of the ACA provisions, and legal and legislative efforts continued. Probably the most significant of all these cases was decided by the U.S. Supreme Court in 2014, *Burwell v. Hobby Lobby Stores, Inc.* The owners of the Hobby Lobby arts and crafts stores claimed that the contraceptive mandate of ACA posed an unreasonable burden on their operations because the family that owned the company had always held very strong Christian values. The Court agreed with the company and ruled, by a 5–4 margin, that it and other "closely held" companies must be exempted from the contraceptive mandate. Although the term *closely held* typically refers to companies with a small number of stockholders, such as family-owned businesses, it was not clear precisely to whom the

Court's ruling applied. The U.S. Department of Health and Human Services (HHS) proposed changes in exemptions from ACA regulations that would comply with the Court's position on the matter. It said that exemptions *would* be granted to any company whose shares were not publicly traded. The compromise proved satisfactory to some companies but clearly not to many individuals who opposed the entire concept of the government's providing contraceptive devices to individuals (Denniston 2014).

Refusal of Birth Control Services

For opponents of the contraceptive mandate, the battle continues. Some physicians, nurses, pharmacists, and other health-care providers continue to assert their own right *not* to take part in a government program about which they have serious religious and/or moral objections. Consider the following scenario.

Some birth control devices are available on an over-the-counter (nonprescription) basis. These include male and female condoms, the birth control sponge, and spermicides. These devices tend to be generally and easily available, usually at low cost. The problem is that these devices are also among the least effective of contraceptive methods. The more reliable methods, such as the birth control pill, birth control patch, vaginal ring, IUD, diaphragm, and cervical cap, all require a doctor's prescription.

But what if your physician is a member of the Roman Catholic Church working at a health facility operated by that church? Church doctrine prohibits the use of any type of contraceptive except some form of natural family planning, so your doctor is not allowed to write you a prescription for a contraceptive device. That issue became a national problem in 2010 with passage of the Affordable Care Act, otherwise known as Obamacare. The act required all federal and state health plans to offer access to all FDA-approved contraceptive methods and devices free of charge. If your doctor's hospital is a member of one of the facilities covered by the ACA, it might be subject to this regulation.

Except that it probably isn't. The ACA has, as do most other health-care laws, an exception that allows physicians and other medical personnel to refuse to provide contraceptive services if doing so violates their religious or moral beliefs. According to the most recent data, nine states, in addition to the federal government, have specific provisions allowing health-care providers to refuse contraceptive services on religious or moral grounds. Some laws require physicians to refer a patient to colleagues who will provide those services, but some do not have that requirement (Refusing to Provide Health Services 2019; for the position of the American College of Obstetricians and Gynecologists on this issue, see Committee Opinion 2015; for a specific example of this issue, see Morris and Arora 2018).

Refusal policies for abortion services are even more extensive than those for contraceptive services. The federal government includes these exemptions in a variety of acts, laws, administrative rulings, and other directives. In addition, 46 states have adopted specific legislation allowing individual health-care providers to abstain from performing abortions. Only slightly fewer (44) states also allowed hospitals and other health-care institutions to refuse to perform abortions. Thirteen of these states allow exemptions to private institutions only and one to religious institutions only (Refusing to Provide Health Services 2019).

Probably a more common and more relevant aspect of this issue involves not the position of physicians in prescribing contraceptives but that of pharmacists who may be asked to fill those prescriptions. No regulations at the federal level similar to those in place for abortion exist for contraception. And many fewer states allow exemptions for individual providers (nine states), health-care institutions (eight states), and pharmacists themselves (six states). As a consequence of this patchwork system of regulations and exemptions, it is likely to be much more difficult for a person to get a prescription for contraceptives than it is to have that prescription filled (Refusing to Provide Health Services 2019).

Given some of these hindrances in obtaining contraceptives, some groups are working to find ways of expanding a person's access to such products. One approach has been to make it possible for a person to obtain a contraceptive medication or device directly from a pharmacy. Ten states (California, Colorado, Hawaii, Maryland, New Hampshire, New Mexico, Oregon, Tennessee, Washington, and Utah) and the District of Columbia have passed laws making this procedure legal within their borders. The first step in that procedure is to locate a pharmacy participating in the program. Online websites are available for conducting this kind of search. Once a participating pharmacy has been located, the individual must fill out a short questionnaire and have his or her blood pressure taken. If he or she has no medical problem, the pharmacist will provide the contraceptive onsite, with all costs normally covered by the person's health insurance (Joslin and Greenhut 2018; Sarna, Vinson, and Fink III 2018).

Another new procedure for gaining access to abortion and contraceptive information is through telemedicine (also known as telehealth). Telemedicine is a system by which an individual is connected via the Internet to a health-care provider who may be located at some significant distance away from the user. The two participants, then, can discuss the issue in which the user is interested, such as the appropriate contraceptive device to use or access to emergency contraceptive medication. The expert can then provide answers to the user's questions and recommend additional actions that he or she can take (Brown 2017).

The technology of telemedicine appears to be moving ahead more rapidly than are state efforts to monitor and regulate the system. Thus far, states have taken two general approaches to the use of telemedicine for contraceptive purposes. In some states, the use of telemedicine for contraceptive counseling has been banned, although some of those bans have later been invalidated by courts as being unconstitutional. In 2019, for example, District Judge Franklin Theis of the Third Judicial District of Kansas ruled that the state's recently passed telemedicine bill banning its use for contraceptive purposes was unenforceable (Wicklund 2019).

Other states have taken a quite different approach, approving of and encouraging individuals to use telemedicine to learn more about contraceptive and family planning issues. The state of California, for example, has a policy of allowing individuals to obtain information and expert opinion on a host of medical issues, among which is reproductive health. The state's health insurance plan, Medi-Cal, is required to include this coverage in all of its plans, as are private insurers in the state. These plans also require payment parity, meaning that no additional charges can be made for telemedicine services over those for standard in-person sessions (California Knox-Keene Health Care Service Plan Act and Regulations 2019; for a complete list and discussion of state telemedicine laws, see State Telehealth Laws and Medicaid Program Policies 2018).

One might hope and expect that decisions about contraception be made on the basis of the best interests of a woman's needs and desires and that those decisions be made in consultation with her partner and health-care provider. But, as the earlier discussion has illustrated, such has not been the case in the United States for some time. The federal and state governments are now deeply involved in decisions as to whether women should have access to contraceptive devices, under what circumstances, and at what costs. These decisions have often become political decisions as much as decisions based on what is best for women (and, often, men). Each political party has had its own views about the distribution of contraceptive information and devices and the role that government should have, if any, in those activities. Thus, policies adopted during the administration of President Barack Obama (2008–2016) inevitably reflected the philosophy of one political party, the Democrats, about this issue. That philosophy was one based on the belief that contraceptive methods should be more widely available to as many women as possible, at as little cost as possible. It also held that an individual or organization's own personal beliefs should not interfere with the right of women to have access to those products.

The election of Donald Trump to the office of president in 2016 and the accession of the Republican Party to power in both executive and legislative branches of the government introduced an alternative view of the contraceptive mandate to American politics. The new view has held, in the first place, that the ACA should be eliminated entirely and a new health-care policy should be developed for the nation. Lacking in that effort, there has been an effort to reverse individual parts of the health-care act, the contraceptive mandate being one of them.

In 2017 and 2018, the new administration issued revised rules regarding exemptions from the contraceptive mandate. These rules were generally more generous in determining which individuals and groups would be eligible for exemption from the mandate. For example, any employer with an objection to the contraceptive mandate based on religious or moral arguments would be allowed to drop contraceptive coverage from health insurance plans under which it operates (Moral Exemptions and Accommodations for Coverage of Certain Preventive Services Under the Affordable Care Act 2018; Religious Exemptions and Accommodations for Coverage of Certain Preventive Services Under the Affordable Care Act 2018). In addition to these changes, the Trump administration announced the creation of a new office, the Conscience and Religious Freedom Division of the Department of Health and Human Services, for the arbitration of cases in which individuals feel their religious and/or moral conscience has been violated by enforcement of the contraceptive mandate or comparable federal rulings (Huetteman 2018). How the contraceptive mandate would be interpreted and implemented under a different political party at some time in the future is a question that no one can answer at this point in history.

The preceding discussion illustrates the fact that individuals, political parties, governmental agencies, advocacy groups, and other organizations tend to have very different philosophies about the role of birth control in American society. One side believes that birth control information and methods should be readily available to everyone at little or no cost. Employers and insurance providers must then develop and institute plans that will make that philosophy a reality. The Affordable Care Act of 2010 was written largely from that position. Another side argues that birth control is not an issue with which the government or private businesses should be directly involved. Birth control may be a worthy program, but individuals who need and use contraception should be responsible for seeking out and paying for their needs in this regard. The policy statements from the U.S. Department of Health and Human Services of 2018 reflect this view. The debate between these two sides is hardly a new one, and one might expect that it will continue with some fervor into the future.

Free Condom Distribution

In the early 1980s, the HIV/AIDS epidemic had just begun to appear in the United States. The suddenly growing number of deaths from this terrible disease created panic among at least some portion of the nation's population. People began to ask what could be done to offer protection from the virus (which had not yet been identified). One of the earliest efforts in that direction took place at the 1983 Gay Pride Parade in San Francisco when staff members of the San Francisco AIDS Foundation handed out free condoms, along with information about the disease and condom use (A Brief History of Free Condoms 2017).

Several school systems also began to ask what they could do to raise students' awareness of the threat posed by HIV/AIDS and, more concretely, what they could actually do to increase their level of protection. In 1990, the New York Public

School System devised a plan for providing free condom distribution in all public high schools. A special room was set aside and staffed for instructions on the use of condoms, along with handouts of condoms to any student who requested them. Parents were allowed to "opt out" of the program. That is, they were permitted to prohibit their children from taking any part of the program. At around the same time, similar programs were being developed in several other school systems across the country (Waters 1997, 797, 810).

Not surprisingly, many parents were opposed to the availability of free condoms in their children's schools. They offered several arguments for their position, namely that all forms of sex education should be the purview of parents, not the schools; that condoms did not offer protection against HIV/AIDS or other sexually transmitted infections; that the use of condoms would have no effect on out-of-wedlock births; and that the availability of condoms would make students feel safer about engaging in sexual relations and would tend to increase the rate of promiscuity among the school population (Berger 1990; Dean 2007; Eisenberg, et al. 2004). All or some of these arguments can still be found in the literature today, although they tend to be less common than they were at the end of the 20th century.

In spite of the view of naysayers about condom distribution programs, they rapidly gained approval and popularity among both school personnel and parents. A 1992 public opinion poll conducted by Gallup and the *Phi Delta Kappa* journal found that 68 percent of parents surveyed approved the use of condom distribution in schools. More than half that number (43 percent) said that condoms should be provided for any student who requested one, while another 25 percent approved the practice only for students whose parents had given permission for them to do so. Authors of the report commented on the relatively high level of approval of condom distribution, pointing out that such a result "undoubtedly would have been lacking a few years ago" (Elam, Rose, and Gallup 1992, 42, 44).

At about the same time, the Guttmacher Institute was studying the characteristics of condom distribution programs in 431 schools in 50 school districts nationwide. This sample led to the conclusion that such programs were available in 2.2 percent of the nation's schools and 0.3 percent of all school districts. The most common method of supplying condoms in these programs was through school nurses (54 percent of all programs), followed by teachers (52 percent) and counselors (47 percent). Some type of parental consent was required in 81 percent of all programs, and counseling for students was required in 49 percent of schools. The average number of condoms per student ranged from less than 0.5 to more than 12, with about six condoms per student as the national average (Kirby and Brown 1996; recent data on condom distribution programs in the United States do not appear to be available).

Most of the concern about the ineffectiveness and/or possible harm of using condoms expressed in the late 20th century has now largely been dismissed. Any number of studies have shown that proper condom use can significantly reduce the risk of pregnancy and sexually transmitted infections and does not tend to increase the timing or frequency of an individual's earliest sexual experimentation. That is, scientific arguments in opposition to the use of condoms are largely absent, although moral and other objections remain (School-Based Condom Availability Programs 2019; The Truth about Condoms 2011). Based on that reality, several professional societies have adopted resolutions in support of condom use, in general, and condom distribution programs, in particular. The American Academy of Pediatrics, for example, has adopted a policy statement regarding the use of condoms by adolescents. Its specific recommendations about distribution programs are as follows:

• Restrictions and barriers to condom availability should be removed, given the research that demonstrates that increased availability of condoms facilitates use. Beyond retail distribution of condoms, sexually active adolescents should have ready access to condoms at free or low cost where possible. Pediatricians and other clinicians are encouraged to provide condoms within their offices and to support availability within their communities.

- Condom availability programs should be developed through a collaborative community process and accompanied by comprehensive sequential sexuality education to be most effective. This is ideally part of a K–12 health education program, with parental involvement, counseling, and positive peer support.

- Schools should be considered appropriate sites for the availability of condoms because they contain large adolescent populations and may potentially provide a comprehensive array of related educational and health-care resources. Training of youth to improve communication skills around condom negotiation with partners can occur in school-based settings (Committee on Adolescence 2013).

Over-the-Counter Pill

After more than a half century of availability, oral contraceptive pills have become widely used. In the vast majority of cases, they are highly effective at preventing pregnancy and generally safe to use. One recognition of that fact is that more than 100 countries worldwide now permit distribution of the pill without a prescription. That is, a woman in Mexico, Egypt, India, or China can walk into a pharmacy, ask for, and receive an oral contraceptive pill (Moving Oral Contraceptives Over-the-Counter 2019). Such is not the case in the United States, where the only type of oral contraceptive available without a prescription is the emergency contraceptive pill. (A partial exception to this situation is in the 10 states and District of Columbia that have adopted some form of "prescriptive authority for pharmacists" law, described earlier.)

Many American women support the idea of making oral contraceptive pills available over the counter. In a 2018 study, 39 percent of all adult women and 29 percent of teenage girls said that they favored the implementation of nonprescriptive oral contraceptive drugs. Those numbers were even higher (46 percent and 40 percent, respectively) if provisions were available for having the cost of those drugs covered by their insurance plans. In addition, about a quarter of women and girls who are currently not using oral contraceptive pills would begin to do so if they were available over the counter (Grindlay and Grossman 2018).

Several professional organizations also support making oral contraceptive (OC) pills available over the country. Among conclusions and recommendations in a 2018 position paper from the American College of Obstetricians and Gynecologists, for example, were the following suggestions:

- Weighing the risks versus the benefits based on currently available data, OCs should be available over the counter.
- Women should self-screen for most contraindications to OCs using checklists.
- Screening for cervical cancer or STIs is not medically required to provide hormonal contraception.
- Continuation rates of OCs are higher in women who are provided with multiple pill packs at one time (Over-the-Counter Access to Oral Contraceptives 2012/2018).

Objections to the delisting of oral contraceptive pills as prescription drugs exist. One objection is that, although contraceptive pills are generally safe, some adverse side effects may occur with their use, and some of those side effects can be serious and even life threatening. Women should see a health-care provider to be certain that they are not at risk for using the pill. The health-care provider can also offer an important general introduction to the way the pill works, how it should be used, and warning signs about possible side effects. Some research also suggests that women and girls who obtain prescriptions from a doctor are more likely to follow a recommended regimen and continue to see their physician to monitor drug use and general health.

There is some reason to believe that the most serious objections to a pharmacy access to oral contraceptives may be overblown. In the study cited earlier, girls and women were asked if they would continue to see their health-care providers if they could get their contraceptive pills at a pharmacy. About 85 percent of subjects interviewed said that they would continue to see their health-care provider on a regular basis to obtain gynecological services, such as pap smears. And a majority of those subjects who currently use a condom said that they would continue that practice even if they obtained their contraceptives on an over-the-counter basis.

Confidentiality and Access to Birth Control

Emmy Lou is a 13-year-old student at Middleview Middle School. She has just started having sex with a boy in her class. She has learned in her health class that using a contraceptive will prevent her from becoming pregnant. She can't decide if she should talk to her parents about obtaining a contraceptive. And she doesn't know if she is required to do by some state or federal law.

Let's take the easier question first. No, she is not required by any law to tell her parents that she wants, needs, or intends to start using a contraceptive. She is protected by the principle of *confidentiality*, namely that she is not required to share information about personal aspects of her life with anyone. There has been a long debate in the United States about this principle. As recently as the early 1980s, the federal government ruled that clinics were required to notify parents within 10 days of a child's requesting and/or receiving some form of birth control.

The courts have consistently taken a different view. In 1977, for example, the U.S. District Court for the Western District of Michigan ruled that a person of any age was allowed to withhold information about her or his contraceptive experiences from parents. The court said that "there is no magic age at which a person reaches maturity[;] some persons unfortunately never do" (*Doe v. Irwin*, 441 F. Supp. 1247 (W.D. Mich. 1977) 1977). The final word on this matter was written by the U.S. Supreme Court in the case of *Planned Parenthood Association of Utah v. Mattheson* in 1983. The court ruled that laws and administrative rulings denying a person, no matter her or his age, confidentiality in dealing with contraceptives were unconstitutional. In its decision, the court said that it was

> persuaded that the statements in *Akron* and *H.L.* [two earlier cases on the same issue] concerning the constitutionality of parental notification laws in the abortion context support the conclusion that the state may not impose a blanket parental notification requirement on minors seeking to exercise their constitutionally protected right to decide whether to bear or to beget a child by using contraceptives. (*Planned Parenthood Ass'n of Utah v. Matheson*, 582 F. Supp. 1001 (D. Utah 1983) 1983; for a good general review of this history, see Maradieguen 2003)

In theory, then, the issue of confidentiality with regard to contraceptive use by minors is legally a settled issue. But the matter is not quite so simple. Many individuals and organizations have strong feelings about the question and are constantly searching for ways to get around the court rulings on the issue. For some, the issue is one of ethics and morality. Parents are responsible for the raising, instruction, and well-being of their children until they reach their majority (usually about 18 years of age). It doesn't make any sense for them to be deprived of decision-making or decision-sharing in one of the most intimate and consequential areas of their children's lives: their sexual life.

The moral aspects of this issue are expressed by a statement from the United States Conference of Catholic Bishops. Laws and policies that deprive parents of the right of knowing about their children's contraceptive practice, it said,

> are affronts to parents' rightful role as the primary educators of their children. Government agencies or counselors cannot replace and should not interfere with the rights and responsibilities of loving parents, particularly in sensitive matters dealing with human sexuality and the transmission of human life. (Parental Notification Needed in Title X Program 2019)

Individuals often express some version of this argument in their statements opposing confidentiality for contraceptive topics. In one pro and con discussion online about the subject, for example, one participant wrote: "You shouldn't even be having sex as simple as that. If your not ready for sex then just wait until your married that way you don't have to worry about getting pregnant" [as in the original throughout] (Should Teens Be Allowed to Obtain Birth Control Without Parental Consent? 2013).

These views tend to be a minority opinion about the role of confidentiality in contraceptive topics. Several surveys have been conducted about the attitudes of health-care providers, parents, and children and adolescents about the need for confidentiality in obtaining contraceptive information and devices. For example, one study asked 1,800 obstetricians and gynecologists if they would provide contraceptive services for an imaginary 17-year-old girl who did not want her parents to know about her request. Ninety-four percent of respondents said that, yes, they would provide those services without notifying a parent. Half would also advise the girl to notify her parents anyway, and half would recommend that she remain abstinent until marriage (Lawrence, et al. 2011).

Surveys of parental attitudes about notification practices are somewhat more complex. In one study, for example, about half (49.1 percent) of respondents said that they thought that a child's receiving information about and methods for contraception is generally a good thing. But about three-quarters identified at least one negative result of such a practice, and 10 percent more mentioned three or four negative results. The most common negative effects mentioned were that children and adolescents would turn to nonclinic methods of birth control or that they would be more likely to have unprotected sex. Possible positive consequences of a parental notification law were that children would think more about sex (42.2 percent of respondents) and talk more to their parents about sex (33.1 percent). Neither of these possible results is confirmed by research into the issue (Eisenberg, et al. 2005).

Children and adolescents' views about parental notification laws are generally not very positive. This trend is reflected in a 2002 survey of more than 1,000 girls and young women using clinic-based contraceptive services in Wisconsin. When asked what they would do if parental notification laws were in place, 59 percent of respondents said that they would "stop using all sexual health care services, delay testing or treatment for HIV or other STDs, or discontinue use of specific (but not all) sexual health care services." The authors concluded from their research that "mandatory parental notification for prescribed contraceptives would impede girls' use of sexual health care services, potentially increasing teen pregnancies and the spread of STDs" (Reddy Fleming, and Swain 2002).

Attitudes of children and adolescents about contraceptive information are a bit more complex than those indicated by this study. Somewhat later research found that an important factor in a girl's or woman's attitudes about confidentiality was whether her parents already knew about her situation. Nearly 80 percent of respondents whose parents knew about the use of clinics for contraception would continue to do so if parental notification laws were in place. By contrast, just less than 30 percent of those whose parents did *not* know would continue to use clinic services. Parental notification would, therefore, have a profound effect on the types of contraceptive services girls and women might receive on pregnancy, sexually transmitted infections, and other sex-related topics (Jones, et al. 2005). In general, available research suggests that parental notification laws would, in general, have significantly more negative impacts, most unintended, on the sexual health of girls and young women than it would positive impacts (Jones and Boonstra 2005).

(The debate over parental notification for abortions for girls and women is very different from the one presented here for contraception and is not discussed in this chapter.)

Reproductive Justice

Reproductive justice is a term that was first used in 1994 by a group of African American women in preparation for the International Conference on Population and Development, held in Cairo, Egypt. The term is a combination of two other concepts, reproductive rights and environmental justice. The former concept was developed in 1984 at the first International Women and Health Meeting, held in Amsterdam, Netherlands. It was an expression of the idea that women everywhere had a fundamental right to make their own decisions about their sexuality: whether or not to have children and, if so, when, as well as having access to information about and methods for contraceptive of all types (Ross 2006). The second term dates to the early 1980s when communities of race, color, low income, national origin, or some other minority status began to acknowledge and act upon the reality that they were the victims of environmental harm far out of proportion of their numbers in the general population (Newton 2009).

Founders of the Reproductive Justice movement were convinced that leaders of the reproductive movement in the 1980s and 1990s were largely middle- and upper-class, white individuals who did not understand or represent the special needs and hopes of women of color. They felt that they needed a new organization whose members lived lives fundamentally different from those of mainstream sexual rights activists. In 1997, the concept of Reproductive Justice was expanded significantly when 16 autonomous groups joined together to create Sister-Song Women of Color Reproductive Health Collective. The collective consists of Indigenous, African American, Arab and Middle Eastern, Asian and Pacific Islander, and Latina women and LGBTQ people. Membership also includes white, male, and pro-life allies "who support women's human right to lead fully self-determined lives" (Reproductive Justice 2019).

SisterSong and Reproductive Justice have ambitious programs designed to promote interest in and action on programs designed to support the reproductive needs of otherwise poorly served women. These include actions such as lobbying of the U.S. Congress, the United Nations, and other governmental agencies; conducting research on Reproductive Justice issues and publishing the results of that research; sponsoring conferences; promoting the role of Reproductive Justice in mainstream civil rights and women's rights movements; training individuals to recognize and incorporate Reproductive Justice issues into their own lives and workplaces; and organizing a range of events to promote the solution of Reproductive Justice issues (Reproductive Justice 2019; Ross and Solinger 2017).

Birth Control and Population Control

Loss of fresh water, species extinction, lower life expectancy, depletion of natural resources, increased numbers of epidemics and pandemics, less individual freedom and more government regulations, increased loss of habitat, increased climate change, more intensive farming practices, and elevated crime rates are an impressive list of social, environmental, and political problems facing the world today. Some writers say that all of these problems are caused, in one way or another, by overpopulation (Effects of Overpopulation 2014).

Concerns about the rapid increase in the world's population and its possible effects on humans and the environment date to the mid-20th century. After more than 10,000 years of relatively slow growth, the planet's human population began to increase exponentially in about 1950. It took 697 years for the population to double from 0.25 billion to 0.5 billion in 1543, but only 37 years for it to double from 2.5 billion to 5 billion in 1987 (Effects of Overpopulation 2014). Over the past seven decades, then, there has been a constant, if sometimes subdued, drumbeat for efforts to slow human population growth.

One obvious way to achieve that objective has been through birth control. Thus, governmental and nongovernmental agencies and other organizations of all kinds have analyzed the problem of population growth and the role that birth control can play in solving the problem. Their work has been driven by a number of motivations and produced a variety of birth control options. The rise of the eugenics movement and the Chinese one-child policy, discussed in Chapter 1, are two examples of these efforts.

But many other examples are available. One of the most popular approaches has been the involuntary sterilization of women. The most common subjects of these programs have been poor, mentally ill, racial minority, or otherwise disadvantaged women. Such individuals have been blamed for many of the social problems that exist and have been treated with incorrect information, or no information at all, as to the reason for their sterilization. A 1976 government report, for example, found that more than 3,400 Native American women had been sterilized without adequate information about the procedure. Several states have also passed legislation authorizing women of illegitimate children who also receive benefits from the federal Aid to Families with Dependent Children. (An exhaustive review about this history is available at DePaul College of Law 1979.)

Many rationales have existed for the use of birth control for population control programs over time. As an example, both federal governmental and business interests have felt the need to control population, not so much in the United States as in other parts of the world (especially developing nations) for either economic or political reasons or both. One illustration of that view was the so-called Kissinger Report (National Security Study Memorandum, NSSM-200). The report was motivated by concerns that rapid population growth in developing nations might interfere with America's access to critical raw materials from nations such as India, Bangladesh, Pakistan, Nigeria, Brazil, and Ethiopia. It recommended that assistance for birth control programs be implemented in these countries to counteract the threats posed by increased populations in the countries. Some of the actions specifically recommended were the legalization of abortion, financial assistance to nations for birth control programs, indoctrination of children in the need for birth control, and the withholding of U.S. aid to countries that did not make adequate progress in the development of birth control programs (Clowes 2017; also see Connelly 2008).

Another more recent manifestation of the "birth control for population control" philosophy has been the concern about environmental degradation and climate change. Several observers have argued that both phenomena are fundamentally an effect of overpopulation. The most effective way of dealing with these changes, therefore, is to develop and institute birth control programs to reduce population growth. That approach has some relatively simple elements: just provide women with more and more accurate birth control information and the devices needed for birth control (Potts and Campbell 2011). Also, provide girls and women with greater educational opportunities. The more education they have, the more empowered they become; the longer they delay marriage, the better they are able to care for their children. All these factors tend to reduce birth rates. According to one estimate, simply providing girls and women with more educational opportunities can reduce population growth by a billion less than current projections by 2050 (Furst 2015; Heikkinen, Niina. 2014).

The use of birth control for population control has its opponents. A number of objections can be raised to such a plan. For example, they may be motivated less by a concern for the health of the planet than by an ensured flow of resources from less developed to more developed nations. In that respect, they may be nothing other than a revival and continuation of imperialistic policies by stronger over weaker countries. Also, some birth control policies could conceivably be implemented more frequently among disadvantaged women, an echo of eugenics policies that were so popular during the mid-20th century. Such programs may, furthermore, inevitably involve an element of coercion, in which individual humans rights are disregarded or violated. As one writer has suggested,

> Casting family planning in developing countries as a solution to resource stress, migration, or rising carbon emissions not only unfairly pins blame for these crises on poor women, it also misdiagnoses the problem. It's not population numbers, but global inequalities—in resource consumption, health care access, political power, etc.—that determine which countries are flush, and which lack enough to go around. (Galavotti and Williams 2017)

Assisted Reproductive Technologies

Infertility is a common problem among women and men during their childbearing years. In the United States about 12 percent of either women or men (or both) within that age range are infertile. That amounts to about 7.3 million women and men who are unable to become pregnant. Some of these couples explore assisted reproductive technologies (ART) as avenues to achieving pregnancy. By far the most common of these technologies is in vitro fertilization (IVF), although other methods are also available. ART is also available to same-sex couples (who, by their very nature, are unable to become pregnant), single women who would like to have a child, and other specialized nontraditional heterosexual couples (Asch and Marmor n.d.).

Two general schemes are available for ART. The more common involves two members of a couple who provide their own egg and sperm, which are then fertilized artificially, with the hope of achieving pregnancy. The success rates of such procedures depend strongly on the age of the woman involved. In a summary of one clinic's experiences in the field, 48.6 percent of women under the age of 35 achieved a live birth, of which 12 percent were twins or triplets. The success rate for women in the 35–37 age group was 41.2 percent; for those 38–40, 23.5 percent; for women 41–42, 11.6 percent; and those over 42, 3.8 percent (Clinic Summary Report 2016).

A second ART methodology makes use of a donor egg, sperm, or uterus (or some combination of these three) to achieve pregnancy. That is, a couple may obtain an egg from a fertile woman to be fertilized by the sperm of the couple, sperm from a donor male with which to fertilize a fertile woman, or a surrogate mother who brings to term an embryo conceived by one or a combination of these methods.

Any method of ART carries with it a host of personal, social, economic, political, and moral issues. One such issue involves the question as to what should be done with embryos produced by an ART procedure. Many couples choose to use multiple eggs for the fertilization problem, based on the expectation that that process will increase the likelihood of at least one embryo. That decision also, however, increases the likelihood of more than one egg being fertilized, leading to multiple births (twins, triplets, etc.). Any fertilized eggs or embryos produced by this process, but not brought to term, must be treated by some other means. Often, they are frozen with the expectation that they might be used later for future pregnancies. (According to current data, about 620,000 embryos are being stored in a frozen state [cryopreserved]; Embryo Adoption 2019.) That expectation is often not realized, and large numbers of eggs and/or embryos remain frozen for extended periods of time. What option is available, then, for the eventual fate of these products?

In some cases, individuals or couples eventually decide that they do not want any more children, and they just stop paying the storage fees for frozen embryos. In other cases, mechanical failures at a clinic may result in the loss of thousands of frozen embryos. Some facilities also may have conscious, active programs for destroying embryos after some period of time has passed (Almendrala 2018; Tens of Thousands of Embryos Are Stuck in Limbo in Fertility Clinics 2019). These outcomes are often problematic because of differences of opinion as to when life begins. As noted previously, many individuals and groups believe that life begins at conception. Therefore, frozen embryos are not just clumps of cells but actual, living human beings. "Disposing of them," then, is tantamount to murder and cannot be condoned by society (Baden and Moss 2014).

For the most part, federal and state governments have not yet developed consistent laws dealing with these issues. Some states have passed legislation on one or another aspect of ART, such as the harvesting of eggs for IVF or the use of surrogates for a procedure (see, for example, Sreenivas and Campo-Engelstein 2010; Think Again for a Human Future 2019). But most aspects of ART remain in a legal state of limbo (Basic Law of In Vitro Fertilization 2018).

The one possible exception to this generalization is in the area of insurance. IVF and other forms of ART can be expensive procedures, with an average cost of more than $12,000 for each attempt. At these prices, such procedures tend to be unavailable to poor women and men. To help deal with this problem, several states have adopted legislation mandating some form of insurance coverage for diagnostic studies of infertility and/or one or more forms of ART. As of late 2019, 15 states—Arkansas, California, Connecticut, Hawaii, Illinois, Louisiana, Maryland, Massachusetts, Montana, New Jersey, New York, Ohio, Rhode Island, Texas, and West Virginia—had such laws. In most cases, those laws required insurance companies to provide coverage for either diagnosis or therapeutic treatment (or both) for infertility, including ART procedures. In a few states, laws had the opposite intent, preventing companies from offering coverage for one or another aspect of ART procedures (State Laws Related to Insurance Coverage for Infertility Treatment 2018).

References

"Abortion History Timeline." n.d. National Right to Life. https://nrlc.org/archive/abortion/facts/abortiontimeline .html. Accessed on May 14, 2019.

"About the March for Life." 2019. March for Life Education & Defense Fund. https://marchforlife.org/ about-us/. Accessed on May 14, 2019.

"Abstinence Education Programs: Definition, Funding, and Impact on Teen Sexual Behavior." 2018. Henry J. Kaiser Family Foundation. https://www.kff.org/womens-health-policy/fact-sheet/abstinence-education-programs-definition-funding-and-impact-on-teen-sexual-behavior/. Accessed on May 9, 2019.

Almendrala, Anna. 2018. "No One Knows How Many Frozen Embryos Are Lost or Destroyed Each Year." Huffpost. https://www.huffpost.com/entry/the-destruction-of-thousands-of-embryos-reveals-just-how-under-regulated-fertility-clinics-are_n_5aab04bfe4b0c33361af1b45. Accessed on May 22, 2019.

Asch, Adrienne, and Rebecca Marmor. n.d. The Hastings Center. https://www.thehastingscenter.org/briefingbook/ assisted-reproduction/. Accessed on May 22, 2019.

Baden, Joel, and Candida Moss. 2014. "Praying for a Child." Slate. https://slate.com/human-interest/2014/09/ the-catholic-church-and-infertility-emily-herxs-lawsuit-describes-the-problem.html. Accessed on May 22, 2019.

"Basic Law of In Vitro Fertilization." 2018. Law Offices of Stimmel, Stimmel, & Smith. https://www.stimmel-law

.com/en/articles/basic-law-vitro-fertilization. Accessed on May 22, 2019.

Berger, Joseph. 1990. "Condoms in Schools." *The New York Times*. https://www.nytimes.com/1990/12/22/nyregion/condoms-in-schools.html. Accessed on May 17, 2019.

"Birth Control Guide." n.d. U.S. Food and Drug Administration. https://www.fda.gov/media/99605/download. Accessed on May 16, 2019.

"A Brief History of Free Condoms." 2017. The Jaded Project. https://www.thejadedproject.org/home/2017/11/10/a-brief-history-of-free-condoms. Accessed on May 17, 2019.

Brown, Brittany S. 2017. "Increasing Access to Oral Contraceptives, State by State: There's an App for That." *Asia Pacific Journal of Health Law & Ethics*. 10(3): 107–144. http://eible-journal.org/index.php/APHLE/article/view/75/28. Accessed on May 15, 2019.

"California Knox-Keene Health Care Service Plan Act and Regulations." 2019. Department of Managed Healthcare. https://www.dmhc.ca.gov/Portals/0/Docs/OLS/KKA_2019.pdf. Accessed on May 15, 2019.

Carrera, Michael A. 1971. "Preparation of a Sex Educator: A Historical Overview." *The Family Coordinator*. 20(2): 99–108.

Carter, Julian B. 2001. "Birds, Bees, and Venereal Disease: Toward an Intellectual History of Sex Education." *Journal of the History of Sexuality*. 10(2): 213–249.

"Clinic Summary Report." 2016. Penn Fertility Care. University of Pennsylvania. https://www.sartcorsonline.com/rptCSR_PublicMultYear.aspx?ClinicPKID=2297. Accessed on May 22, 2019. (More recent data may be available.)

Clowes, Brian. 2017. "Exposing the Global Population Control Agenda." Human Life International. https://www.hli.org/resources/exposing-the-global-population-control/. Accessed on May 18, 2019.

"Colorado Definition of "Personhood" Initiative, Amendment 67 (2014)." 2014. Ballotpedia. https://ballotpedia.org/ Colorado_Definition_of_%22Personhood%22_Initiative,_ Amendment_67_(2014)#Opposition_2. Accessed on May 14, 2019.

Committee on Adolescence. 2013. "Condom Use by Adolescents." American Academy of Pediatrics. *Pediatrics*. 132(5): 973-981. https://pediatrics.aappublications.org/ content/132/5/973. Accessed on May 17, 2019.

"Committee Opinion." 2015. The American College of Obstetricians and Gynecologists. https://www.acog.org/-/ media/Committee-Opinions/Committee-on-Health-Care-for-Underserved-Women/co615.pdf. Accessed on May 15, 2019.

Connelly, Matthew. 2008. *Fatal Misconception: The Struggle to Control World Population*. Cambridge, MA: Harvard University Press.

"The Content of Federally Funded Abstinence-Only Education Programs." 2004. United States House of Representatives. Committee on Government Reform— Minority Staff. Special Investigations Division. https:// spot.colorado.edu/~tooley/HenryWaxman.pdf. Accessed on May 9, 2019.

Dailard, Cynthia. 2004. "Contraceptive Coverage: A 10-Year Perspective." Guttmacher Institute. https://www .guttmacher.org/gpr/2004/06/contraceptive-coverage-10-year-retrospective. Accessed on May 16, 2019.

Dean, Tony, and Pamela. 2007. "Making Sex Safe: Condoms, Agendas, and the Truth." Moriah Ministries. http://users .adam.com.au/moriah/textarchive/mss.htm. Accessed on May 17, 2019.

"Decision." 2000. U.S. Equal Employment Opportunity Commission. https://www.eeoc.gov/policy/docs/decision-contraception.html. Accessed on May 16, 2019.

Denniston, Lyle. 2014. Rules for Birth-Control Mandate after Hobby Lobby (UPDATED)." SCOTUSblog. https://www

.scotusblog.com/2014/08/rules-for-birth-control-mandate-after-hobby-lobby/. Accessed on May 16, 2019.

DePaul College of Law. 1979. "Sterilization Abuse: A Proposed Regulatory Scheme." *DePaul Law Review.* 731–768. https://pdfs.semanticscholar.org/cb71/ce09c9ec0d81fedf1c4f51d73c5500d7790f.pdf. Accessed on May 19, 2019.

"Doe v. Irwin, 441 F. Supp. 1247 (W.D. Mich. 1977)." 1977. Justia US Law. https://law.justia.com/cases/federal/district-courts/FSupp/441/1247/1427533/. Accessed on May 20, 2019.

Donovan, Megan K. 2017. "The Looming Threat to Sex Education: A Resurgence of Federal Funding for Abstinence-Only Programs?" Guttmacher Institute. https://www.guttmacher.org/gpr/2017/03/looming-threat–sex-education-resurgence-federal-funding-abstinence-only-programs. Accessed on May 8, 2019.

"Effects of Overpopulation." 2014. Everything Connects. http://www.everythingconnects.org/overpopulation-effects.html. Accessed on May 18, 2019.

Eisenberg, Marla E., et al. 2004. "Parents' Beliefs About Condoms and Oral Contraceptives: Are They Medically Accurate?" *Perspectives on Sexual and Reproductive Health.* 36(2): 50-57.

Eisenberg, Marla E., et al. 2005. "Parental Notification Laws for Minors' Access to Contraception: What Do Parents Say?" *Archives of Pediatric Adolescent Medicine.* 159(2): 120–125. https://jamanetwork.com/journals/jamapediatrics/fullarticle/485929. Accessed on May 21, 2019.

Elam, Stanley M., Lowell C. Rose, and Alec M. Gallup. 1992. "The 24th Annual Gallup/Phi Delta Kappa Poll of the Public's Attitudes Toward the Public Schools." http://www.pdkmembers.org/members_online/publications/

GallupPoll/kpoll_pdfs/pdkpoll24_1992.pdf. Accessed on May 17, 2019.

"Embryo Adoption." 2019. Office of Population Affairs. HHS.gov. https://www.hhs.gov/opa/about-opa/embryo-adoption/index.html. Accessed on May 22, 2019.

Escoffier, Jeffrey. 2015. "The Sexual Revolution, 1960–1980." glbtq. http://www.glbtqarchive.com/ssh/sexual_revolution_S.pdf. Accessed on May 5, 2019.

Flicker, Lauren Sydney. 2013. "Religious Employers and Exceptions to Mandated Coverage of Contraceptives." *Virtual Mentor.* 15(3): 220–225. https://journalofethics.ama-assn.org/article/religious-employers-and-exceptions-mandated-coverage-contraceptives/2013-03. Accessed on May 16, 2019.

Furst, Niki. 2015. "To Save the Environment, Let's Put Humans on Birth Control." Quartz. https://qz.com/452614/to-save-the-environment-lets-put-humans-on-birth-control. Accessed on May 18, 2019.

Galavotti, Christine, and Casey Williams. 2017. "Contraception Is a Human Right, Not a Tool for Population Control." *New Statesman America.* https://www.newstatesman.com/politics/feminism/2017/07/contraception-human-right-not-tool-population-control. Accessed on May 18, 2019.

Gore, Leada. 2019. "Alabama Abortion Bill Passes: Read the Bill." AL.com. https://www.al.com/news/2019/05/alabama-abortion-ban-passes-read-the-bill.html. Accessed on May 19, 2019.

Greenspun, Philip. 2017. "Queen Victoria in the Domestic Sphere." https://philip.greenspun.com/blog/2017/01/13/queen-victoria-in-the-domestic-sphere/. Accessed on May 7, 2019.

Grindlay, Kate, and Daniel Grossman. 2018. "Interest in Over-the-Counter Access to a Progestin-Only Pill among

Women in the United States." *Women's Health Issues*. 28(2): 144–151.

"Group Health Plans and Health Insurance Issuers Relating to Coverage of Preventive Services Under the Patient Protection and Affordable Care Act." 2012. Federal Register. https://www.govinfo.gov/content/pkg/FR-2012-02-15/pdf/FR-2012-02-15.pdf. Accessed on May 16, 2019.

Gruenberg, Benjamin C. 1922. "High Schools and Sex Education." Washington, DC: United States Public Health Service. https://iiif.lib.harvard.edu/manifests/view/drs:2574361$1i. Accessed on May 4, 2019.

Hall, Kelli Stedham, et al. 2016. "The State of Sex Education in the United States." *The Journal of Adolescent Health*. 58(6): 595–597. https://www.ncbi.nlm.nih.gov/pmc/articles/PMC5426905/#R16. Accessed on May 8, 2019.

"Heartbeat Bans." 2019. Rewire.news. https://rewire.news/legislative-tracker/law-topic/heartbeat-bans/. Accessed on May 15, 2019.

Heikkinen, Niina. 2014. "Birth Control Could Help the Environment, but Not Quickly." *Scientific American*. https://www.scientificamerican.com/article/birth-control-could-help-the-environment-but-not-quickly. Accessed on May 18, 2019.

Hellmann, Jessie. 2018. "Abstinence-Only Education Making a Comeback Under Trump." The Hill. https://thehill.com/policy/healthcare/377304-abstinence-only-education-making-a-comeback-under-trump. Accessed on May 9, 2019.

"A History of Federal Funding for Abstinence-Only-Until-Marriage Programs." 2018. SIECUS. https://siecus.org/wp-content/uploads/2018/08/A-History-of-AOUM-Funding-Final-Draft.pdf. Accessed on May 8, 2019.

"History of Sex Education." n.d. Future of Sex Education. http://www.futureofsexed.org/background.html. Accessed on May 8, 2019.

Huber, Valerie J., and Michael W. Firmin. 2014. "A History of Sex Education in the United States Since 1900." *International Journal of Educational Reform.* 23(1): 25–51. https://www.loveandfidelity.org/wp-content/uploads/2014/10/Huber-Published-Sex-Ed-article.pdf. Accessed on May 2, 2019.

Huetteman, Emmarie. 2018. "At New Health Office, 'Civil Rights' Means Doctors' Right to Say No to Patients." Kaiser Health News. https://khn.org/news/at-new-health-office-civil-rights-means-doctors-right-to-say-no-to-patients/. Accessed on May 16, 2019.

"Human Life Amendments: Major Texts." 2004. Human Life Action. https://www.humanlifeaction.org/downloads/sites/default/files/HLAmajortexts.pdf. Accessed on May 15, 2019.

Imber, Michael. 1984. "The First World War, Sex Education, and the American Social Hygiene Association's Campaign Against Venereal Disease." *Journal of Educational Administration and History.* 16(1): 47–56.

"Insurance Coverage of Contraceptives." 2019. Guttmacher Institute. https://www.guttmacher.org/state-policy/explore/insurance-coverage-contraceptives. Accessed on May 16, 2019.

Jensen, Robin. 2007. "Using Science to Argue for Sexual Education in U.S. Public Schools." *Science Communication.* 29(2): 217–241.

Jones, Rachel K., and Heather D. Boonstra. 2004. "Confidential Reproductive Health Services for Minors: The Potential Impact of Mandated Parental Involvement for Contraception." *Perspectives on Sexual and Reproductive Health.* 36(5): 182–191. https://www.guttmacher.org/journals/psrh/2004/confidential-reproductive-health-services-minors-potential-impact-mandated. Accessed on May 21, 2019.

Jones, Rachel K., et al. 2005. "Adolescents' Reports of Parental Knowledge of Adolescents' Use of Sexual Health

Services and Their Reactions to Mandated Parental Notification for Prescription Contraception." *JAMA*. 293(3): 340–348. https://jamanetwork.com/journals/jama/fullarticle/200191. Accessed on May 21, 2019.

Joslin, Courtney M., and Steven Greenhut. 2018. "Birth Control in the States: A Review of Efforts to Expand Access." R Street. https://2o9ub0417chl2lg6m43em6psi2i-wpengine.netdna-ssl.com/wp-content/uploads/2018/11/Final-159.pdf. Accessed on May 15, 2019.

Kantor, Leslie, and Nicole Levitz. 2017. "Parents' Views on Sex Education in Schools: How Much Do Democrats and Republicans Agree?" *PLoS One*. 12(7): e0180250. https://www.ncbi.nlm.nih.gov/pmc/articles/PMC5495344. Accessed on May 6, 2019.

Kirby, Douglas. 2007. "Emerging Answers." The National Campaign to Prevent Teen and Unplanned Pregnancy. https://powertodecide.org/sites/default/files/resources/primary-download/emerging-answers.pdf. Accessed on May 9, 2019.

Kirby, Douglas B., and Nancy L. Brown. 1996. "Condom Availability Programs in U.S. Schools." *Family Planning Perspectives*. 28(5): 196–202. https://www.guttmacher.org/journals/psrh/1996/09/condom-availability-programs-us-schools. Accessed on May 17, 2019.

Kodjak, Alison. 2016. "Obama Administration Moves to Protect Planned Parenthood's Federal Funding." NPR. https://www.npr.org/sections/health-shots/2016/12/14/505595090/obama-administration-moves-to-protect-planned-parenthoods-federal-funding. Accessed on May 11, 2019.

Lai, K. K. Rebecca. 2019. "Abortion Bans: 8 States Have Passed Bills to Limit the Procedure This Year." *The New York Times*. https://www.nytimes.com/interactive/2019/us/abortion-laws-states.html. Accessed on May 19, 2019.

Lawrence, Ryan E., et al. 2011. "Adolescents, Contraception, and Confidentiality: A National Survey of Obstetrician–Gynecologists." *Contraception*. 84(3): 259–265. https://www.ncbi.nlm.nih.gov/pmc/articles/PMC3156985/. Accessed on May 21, 2019.

Lindberg, Laura Duberstein, Isaac Maddow-Zimet, and Heather Boonstra. 2016. "Changes in Adolescents' Receipt of Sex Education, 2006–2013," *Journal of Adolescent Health*. 58(6): 621–627. https://www.ncbi.nlm.nih.gov/pmc/articles/PMC5426905. Accessed on May 8, 2019.

Lithwick, Dahlia. 2015. "A Regrettable Decision." Slate.com. https://slate.com/human-interest/2015/07/north-dakota-fetal-heartbeat-bill-court-opinion-an-anti-science-states-rights-call-to-ban-abortion.html. Accessed on May 15, 2019.

Maradiegue, Ann. 2003. "Minor's Rights Versus Parental Rights: Review of Legal Issues in Adolescent Health Care." *Journal of Midwifery and Womens Health*. 48(3): 170–177. https://www.medscape.com/viewarticle/456472_6. Accessed on May 20, 2019.

Martin, Nina. 2014. "The Personhood Movement." ProPublica. The Personhood Movement. Accessed on May 14, 2019.

"Moral Exemptions and Accommodations for Coverage of Certain Preventive Services Under the Affordable Care Act." 2018. Federal Register. https://www.federalregister.gov/documents/2018/11/15/2018-24514/moral-exemptions-and-accommodations-for-coverage-of-certain-preventive-services-under-the-affordable. Accessed on May 16, 2019.

Moran, Jeffrey P. 1996. "'Modernism Gone Mad': Sex Education Comes to Chicago, 1913." *Journal of American History*. 83(2): 481–513.

Morris, Jane, and Kavita Shah Arora. 2018. "Should Clinicians Challenge Faith-Based Institutional Values

Conflicting with Their Own?" *AMA Journal of Ethics*. 20(7): E630–E636. https://journalofethics.ama-assn.org/sites/journalofethics.ama-assn.org/files/2018-06/cscm3-1807.pdf. Accessed on May 15, 2019.

"Moving Oral Contraceptives Over-the-Counter." 2019. Ibis Reproductive Health. http://ocsotc.org/faqs/. Accessed on May 20, 2019.

Nash, Elizabeth, et al. 2018 *Laws Affecting Reproductive Health and Rights: State Policy Trends at Midyear, 2018*. New York: Guttmacher Institute. https://www.guttmacher .org/article/2018/07/laws-affecting-reproductive-health-and-rights-state-policy-trends-midyear-2018. Accessed on May 11, 2019.

Newton, David E. 2009. *Environmental Justice: A Reference Handbook*. Santa Barbara, CA: ABC-CLIO.

Ollstein, Alice Miranda. 2019. "Supreme Court Blocks Restrictive Louisiana Abortion Law." Politico. https://www .politico.com/story/2019/02/07/supreme-court-abortion-louisiana-1152680. Accessed on May 14, 2019.

"Over-the-Counter Access to Oral Contraceptives." 2012. Reaffirmed 2018. The American College of Obstetricians and Gynecologists. https://www.acog.org/Clinical-Guidance-and-Publications/Committee-Opinions/Committee-on-Gynecologic-Practice/Over-the-Counter-Access-to-Oral-Contraceptives. Accessed on May 20, 2019.

"An Overview of Abortion Laws." 2019. Guttmacher Institute. https://www.guttmacher.org/state-policy/explore/overview-abortion-laws. Accessed on May 14, 2019.

Paltrow, Lynn M. n.d. "American Life League: Anti-Abortion 'Personhood' Measures Really Will Hurt All Pregnant Women." National Advocates for Pregnant Women. http://advocatesforpregnantwomen.org/ALL_PersonhoodMeasuresReallyDoHurt.pdf. Accessed on May 15, 2019.

"Parental Notification Needed in Title X Program." 2019.
United States Conference of Catholic Bishops. http://
www.usccb.org/issues-and-action/human-life-and-dignity/
contraception/fact-sheets/parental-notification-needed-in-
title-x-program.cfm. Accessed on May 20, 2019.

"Parents and Teens Talk about Sexuality: A National
Poll." 2012. Planned Parenthood. https://www
.plannedparenthood.org/files/8313/9610/5916/LT_2012_
Poll_Fact_Sheet_final_2.pdf. Accessed on May 6, 2019.

"A Pivotal Time for Reproductive Rights." 2016. Center for
Reproductive Rights. https://www.reproductiverights
.org/sites/crr.civicactions.net/files/documents/USPA_
StateofStates_11.16_Web_Final.pdf. Accessed on May 14,
2019.

"Planned Parenthood Ass'n of Utah v. Matheson, 582 F.
Supp. 1001 (D. Utah 1983)." 1983. Justia US Law.
https://law.justia.com/cases/federal/district-courts/
FSupp/582/1001/1761144/. Accessed on May 20, 2019.

Potts, Malcolm, and Martha Campbell. 2011. "Foreign Policy:
Without Birth Control, Planet Doomed." NPR. https://www
.npr.org/2011/05/11/136201025/foreign-policy-without-
birth-control-planet-doomed. Accessed on May 18, 2019.

"President Trump Signs Measure Reversing Obama Era
Rule Protecting Women's Access to Basic Health Care."
2017. Center for Reproductive Rights. https://www
.reproductiverights.org/press-room/president-trump-signs-
measure-reversing-obama-rule-protecting-women-access-
to-health-care. Accessed on May 11, 2019.

"Public Health Service Act." 2018. https://legcounsel.house.
gov/Comps/PHSA-merged.pdf. Accessed on May 8, 2019.

"Publicly Funded Family Planning Services in the United
States." 2016. New York: Guttmacher Institute. https://
www.guttmacher.org/sites/default/files/factsheet/fb_
contraceptive_serv_0.pdf. Accessed on May 11, 2019.

Rankin, Bill. 2019. "New: Who Could Be Prosecuted Under Georgia's 'Heartbeat' Law?" News 95.5 https://www .wsbradio.com/news/local/who-could-prosecuted-under-georgia-heartbeat-law/sjmrBSuG3ZT4eM9kkAKPuL/. Accessed on May 20, 2019.

Rathke, Lisa. 2019. "Republican Governor Signs Bill Protecting Abortion Rights." US News. https://www .usnews.com/news/best-states/vermont/ articles/2019-06-11/vermont-governor-signs-bill-protecting-abortion-rights. Accessed on August 11, 2019.

Reddy, Diane M., Raymond Fleming, and Carolyne Swain. 2002. "Effect of Mandatory Parental Notification on Adolescent Girls' Use of Sexual Health Care Services." *JAMA*. 288(6): 710–714. https://jamanetwork.com/ journals/jama/fullarticle/195185. Accessed on May 21, 2019.

"Refusing to Provide Health Services." 2019. Guttmacher Institute. https://www.guttmacher.org/state-policy/explore/ refusing-provide-health-services. Accessed on May 15, 2019.

"Religious Exemptions and Accommodations for Coverage of Certain Preventive Services Under the Affordable Care Act." 2018. Federal Register. https://www.federalregister .gov/documents/2018/11/15/2018-24512/religious-exemptions-and-accommodations-for-coverage-of-certain-preventive-services-under-the. Accessed on May 16, 2019.

"Reproductive Justice." 2019. SisterSong. https://www .sistersong.net/reproductive-justice. Accessed on May 21, 2019.

"Results from the School Health Policies and Practices Study 2014." 2015. U.S. Department of Health and Human Services. Centers for Disease Control and Prevention. https://www.cdc.gov/healthyyouth/data/shpps/pdf/shpps-508-final_101315.pdf. Accessed on May 8, 2019.

"Rights of Personhood." 2019. Abort73.com. https://abort 73.com/abortion/personhood/. Accessed on May 14, 2019.

Ross, Loretta J. 2006. "Understanding Reproductive Justice." Sister Song. https://d3n8a8pro7vhmx.cloudfront .net/rrfp/pages/33/attachments/original/1456425809/ Understanding_RJ_Sistersong.pdf. Accessed on May 21, 2019.

Ross, Loretta J., and Rickie Solinger. 2017. *Reproductive Justice.* Berkeley: University of California Press.

Sabetai, Isaac. 2019. "A Look at Abortion Bills around the U.S. in 2019." AJC. https://www.ajc.com/news/ state--regional-govt-politics/look-abortion-bills-around- the-2019/rjgjwPxL6ZKBOOPBJ1SqmK/. Accessed on May 15, 2019.

Santelli, John S., et al. 2017. "Abstinence-Only-Until- Marriage: An Updated Review of U.S. Policies and Programs and Their Impact." *Journal of Adolescent Health.* 61(3): 273–280.

Sarna, Kelly A., Mayce N. Vinson, and Joseph L. Fink III. 2018. "Prescriptive Authority for Pharmacists: Oral Contraceptives." Pharmacy Times. https:// www.pharmacytimes.com/publications/issue/2018/ november2018/prescriptive-authority-for-pharmacists-oral- contraceptives. Accessed on May 20, 2019.

"School-Based Condom Availability Programs." 2019. American Civil Liberties Union. https://www.aclu .org/other/school-based-condom-availability-programs. Accessed on May 17, 2019.

"Sex Education in America." 2004. National Public Radio/Kaiser Family Foundation/Kennedy School of Government. https://www.npr.org/programs/morning/ features/2004/jan/kaiserpoll/publicfinal.pdf. Accessed on May 6, 2019.

"Sex Hygiene Is Discussed." 1913. The Eau Claire Leader. https://newspaperarchive.com/eau-claire-leader-nov-14-1913-p-4/. Accessed on May 4, 2019.

"Sexuality Education. Frequently Asked Questions." 2019. Oregon Department of Education. https://www.oregon.gov/ode/students-and-family/healthsafety/Documents/sexedfaq.pdf. Accessed on May 5, 2019.

Shea, Brie. 2019. "Legislative Lowlights: Lawmakers in Four States Want to Bring Fetal 'Personhood' to the Ballot Box." Rewire.News. https://rewire.news/article/2019/01/28/legislative-lowlights-fetal-personhood-ballot-box/. Accessed on May 14, 2019.

"Should Teens Be Allowed to Obtain Birth Control Without Parental Consent?" 2013. Debate.org. https://www.debate.org/opinions/should-teens-be-allowed-to-obtain-birth-control-without-parental-consent. Accessed on May 20, 2019.

Sonfield, Adam. 2012. "The Religious Exemption to Mandated Insurance Coverage of Contraception." *Virtual Mentor*. 14(2): 137–145. https://journalofethics.ama-assn.org/article/religious-exemption-mandated-insurance-coverage-contraception/2012-02. Accessed on May 16, 2019.

Sreenivas, Kiran, and Lisa Campo-Engelstein. 2010. "Domestic and International Surrogacy Laws: Implications for Cancer Survivors." *Cancer Treatment Research*. 156: 135–152. https://www.ncbi.nlm.nih.gov/pmc/articles/PMC3086466/. Accessed on May 22, 2019.

"State Family Planning Funding Restrictions." 2019. New York: Guttmacher Institute. https://www.guttmacher.org/state-policy/explore/state-family-planning-funding-restrictions. Accessed on May 11, 2019.

"State Laws on Fetal Homicide and Penalty-Enhancement for Crimes Against Pregnant Women." 2018. National

Conference of State Legislatures. http://www.ncsl.org/ research/health/fetal-homicide-state-laws.aspx. Accessed on May 14, 2019.

"State Laws Related to Insurance Coverage for Infertility Treatment." 2018. National Conference of State Legislatures. http://www.ncsl.org/research/health/ insurance-coverage-for-infertility-laws.aspx. Accessed on May 22, 2019.

"State of the States." 2018. Center for Reproductive Rights. https://www.reproductiverights.org/sites/crr.civicactions .net/files/documents/SotS_2018.pdf. Accessed on May 15, 2019.

"State Policy Updates." 2019 [or current year]. Guttmacher Institute. https://www.guttmacher.org/state-policy. Accessed on May 15, 2019.

"State Profiles Fiscal Year 2017." 2017. SIECUS. https:// siecus.org/wp-content/uploads/2018/07/SIECUS-SP-FY17-Federal-Funding-Overview.pdf. Accessed on May 9, 2019.

"State Telehealth Laws and Medicaid Program Policies." 2018. Center for Connected Health Policy. https://www.cchpca .org/sites/default/files/2018-10/CCHP_50_State_Report_ Fall_2018.pdf. Accessed on May 15, 2019.

Strong, Bryan. 1972. "Ideas of the Early Sex Education Movement in America, 1890–1920." *History of Education Quarterly.* 12(2): 129–161.

"Targeted Regulation of Abortion Providers." 2019. New York: Guttmacher Institute. https://www.guttmacher.org/ state-policy/explore/targeted-regulation-abortion-providers. Accessed on May 11, 2019.

"Tens of Thousands of Embryos Are Stuck in Limbo in Fertility Clinics." 2019. CBS News. https://www.cbsnews .com/news/embryos-are-stuck-in-limbo-in-fertility-clinics/. Accessed on May 22, 2019.

"Think Again for a Human Future." 2019. The Center for Bioethics and Culture Network. http://www.cbc-network .org/wp-content/uploads/2019/01/CBC_ThinkAgainTPR_ Study_Guide_1-13-19.pdf. Accessed on May 22, 2019.

"Title X." 2019. National Family Planning & Reproductive Health Association. https://www.nationalfamilyplanning .org/title_x. Accessed on May 11, 2019.

Trenholm, Christopher. 2007. "Impacts of Four Title V, Section 510 Abstinence Education Programs. Final Report." U.S. Department of Health and Human Services. https://aspe.hhs.gov/system/files/pdf/74961/report.pdf. Accessed on May 9, 2019.

"The Truth about Condoms." 2011. Planned Parenthood. https://www.plannedparenthood.org/files/9313/9611 /6384/truth_about_condoms.pdf. Accessed on May 17, 2019.

Vamos, Cheryl A., et al. 2011. "Approaching 4 Decades of Legislation in the National Family Planning Program: An Analysis of Title X's History From 1970 to 2008." *American Journal of Public Health*. 101(11): 2027– 2037. https://www.ncbi.nlm.nih.gov/pmc/articles/ PMC3222394/. Accessed on May 11, 2019.

Waters, Camille. 1997. "A, B, C's and Condoms for Free: A Legislative Solution to Parents' Rights and Condom Distribution in Public Schools." *Valparaiso University Law Review*. 31(2): 787–832. https://scholar.valpo.edu/vulr/ vol31/iss2/26. Accessed on May 17, 2019.

"Waxman Report Is Riddled with Errors and Inaccuracies." 2004. The Heritage Foundation. https://www.heritage .org/education/report/waxman-report-riddled-errors-and- inaccuracies. Accessed on May 9, 2019.

Wicklund, Eric. 2019. "Kansas Judge Rules against New Law Banning Telemedicine Abortions." mHealth Intelligence. https://mhealthintelligence.com/news/

kansas–judge–rules-against-new-law-banning-telemedicine-abortions. Accessed on May 15, 2019.

Wood, Thomas Denison. 1922. *Health Service in the City Schools of the U.S: Report of the Joint Committee of the N.E.A. and the American Medical Association, 1922.* n.p. n.pub. https://books.google.com/books?id=YdIOAQAAMAAJ. Accessed on May 4, 2019.

Zolna, Mia R., and Jennifer J. Frost. 2016. *Publicly Funded Family Planning Clinics in 2015: Patterns and Trends in Service Delivery Practices and Protocols.* New York: Guttmacher Institute. https://www.guttmacher.org/sites/default/files/report_pdf/publicly-funded-family-planning-clinic-survey-2015_1.pdf. Accessed on May 11, 2019.

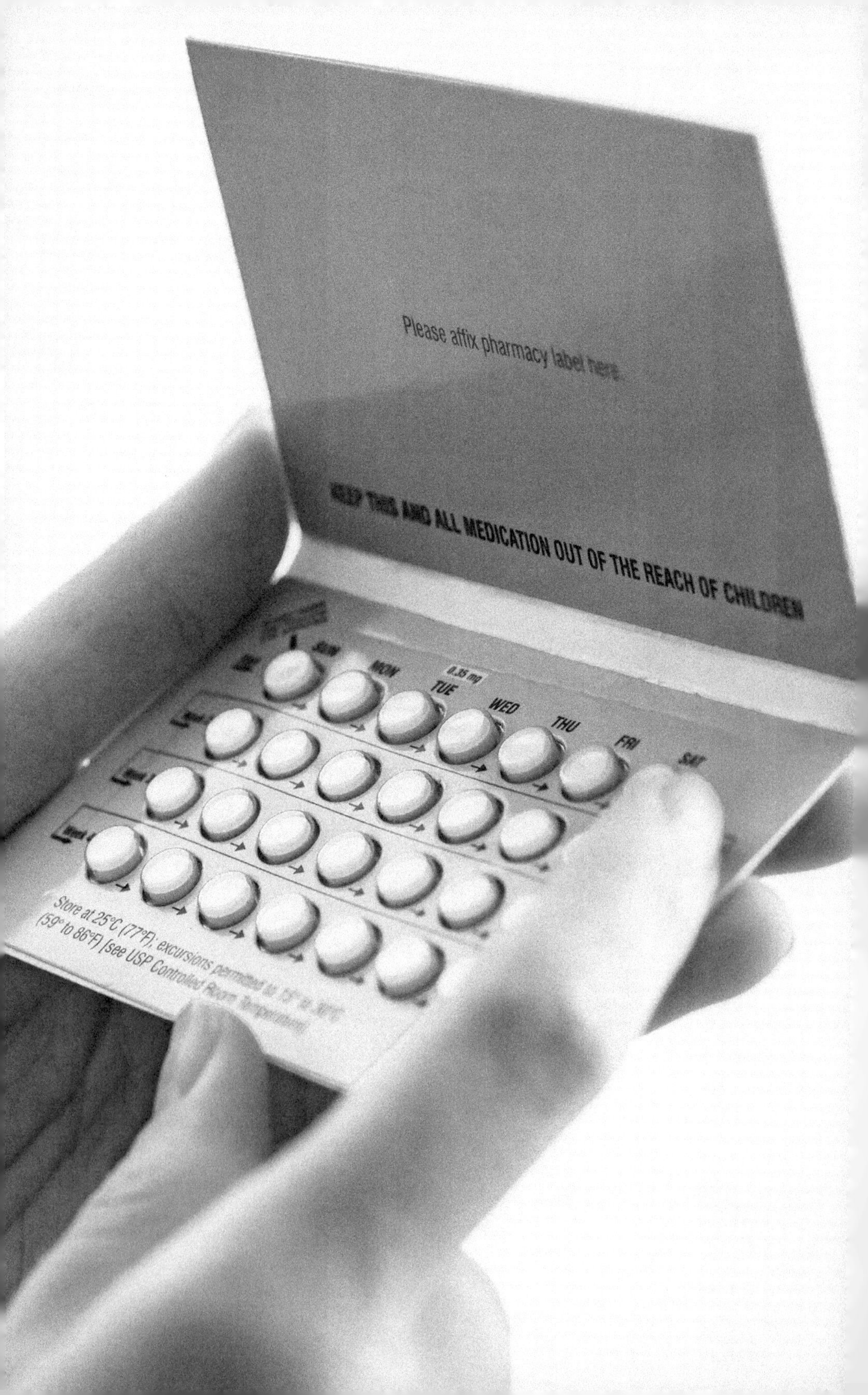
Please affix pharmacy label here.
KEEP THIS AND ALL MEDICATION OUT OF THE REACH OF CHILDREN
SUN
MON
0.35 mg
TUE
WED
THU
FRI
SAT
Store at 25°C (77°F); excursions
(59° to 86°F) [see USP Controlled

Birth control is of interest to many people because of the technical issues involved. Which contraceptive method is easiest to use? Least expensive? Most effective? These questions are all of paramount interest for women and men who want to practice responsible family planning. But birth control also has profound effects on people's lives. It determines how many children a couple can have and what that decision means to their lives. The essays in this chapter present personal viewpoints on both aspects of birth control. They are designed to encourage readers to think about a wide range of issues relating to contraception.

Family Planning Affects More Than Just Families
Sandy Becker

At present there are about 7.6 billion people on Planet Earth (Current World Population 2019). Fifty years ago, within my lifetime, there were half that many. Just think how much better the traffic in New York or Los Angeles might be if there were only half as many people trying to drive in and out! Or how much less polluted the air in Beijing or Kolkata might be if only

A woman holds regular monthly birth control pills, a combination of female hormones and the mineral iron used as contraception to prevent pregnancy. (Yaroslav Sabitov/Dreamstime.com)

127

half as many people lived there! Or how much less carbon dioxide would be spewed into the air if only half as many people were driving, cooking, heating, and lighting their houses! We are currently facing climate changes that will probably make it even harder to feed and house and transport our population, and our efforts to do so only accelerate these changes.

For example, we cut down forests in Indonesia to grow palm trees for palm oil. We cut down rain forests in Brazil to make room for livestock pasture. We drill for oil in offshore locations that disturb ocean life and risk catastrophic oil spills. And as millions more people are lifted out of poverty, the pressure on our ecosystem will only grow.

If there were fewer people, the goal of "sustainable development" would likely be achievable. With seven-and-a-half billion people (and counting), it's probably not.

A misanthropic curmudgeon like me might harbor sci-fi-esque fantasies of alien invasions or apocalyptic pandemics, to quickly cut the human population back to a more manageable size. (Well, at the rate pathogens are becoming resistant to antibiotics, maybe an apocalyptic pandemic isn't completely science fiction.) But let's face it, the much more humane—though somewhat slower—way to do this is to make sure all the babies we bear are born on purpose. That is, safe and reliable birth control must be made available to everyone who wants it, always and everywhere.

Scientists have been doing their part to bring this about. When I was in college in the early 1960s, avoiding pregnancy was rather a fuss and bother. Relying on a condom or diaphragm likely meant you had to interrupt yourself to put it on or put it in, at a moment when you really, really didn't want to be interrupted. (Oh yes, and sometimes they didn't work.) Or you could just abstain from having sex. Birth control pills were invented in my junior year in college, and many of us co-eds breathed a sigh of relief. You do need a prescription, and you do need to take them responsibly, but they work pretty well.

Planned Parenthood's website (www.plannedparenthood.org/learn/birth-control) now lists 18 different methods of birth control, including their cost, effectiveness, permanence, and convenience of use. Most of them are designed to be used by women. In the developed world most women do have access to birth control, at least middle-class women. In less-affluent communities and in less-developed parts of the world, many of them don't. And with access to abortions becoming more and more restricted in some parts of this country, it is crucial that contraceptives become more accessible. After all, the best way to prevent abortions is to prevent unplanned pregnancies.

The evidence suggests that most women in developed countries are choosing to have only one or two children, or even none. In Europe and North America, the fertility rate is below replacement level—that is, our population is falling (or would if not for immigration). In Asia and South America, it is slightly above replacement level. In Africa, however, the average family has five children (Current World Population 2019). Partly this is because they want to have several children, realizing that some of them will probably die, which brings up the seemingly counterintuitive point that improving health care in the poorest parts of the world would likely reduce the birth rate; if families had more confidence that their children would survive, they would likely choose to have fewer.

But partly this difference is because many women in Africa and some other developing areas don't have access to reliable, affordable birth control. A recent study conducted by US-AID found that "more than 225 million women in developing countries want to choose the number, timing, and spacing of their pregnancies but are not using a modern method of family planning" (Annual Progress Report to Congress: Global Health Programs FY 2014 2015, 24). The report goes on to point out that if women don't become mothers when they are too young or too old, if their children are spaced far enough apart so each baby can be better cared for, and if the total number is not too overwhelming, both mothers and children will be healthier.

At this point you may be thinking, "What about male contraceptives?" Shouldn't we be working harder to invent a pill or shot or treatment that would reversibly render a man infertile? Well, let's face it: the ones who gestate and lactate are going to be the ones most impacted by the unplanned babies. And a woman may not be able to convince her partner to take his pills reliably or get his shots or his vasectomy. Therefore, we women need to have reliable birth control methods easily available and affordable period.

We hear a lot nowadays about the high cost of childcare and the need for paid family leave. Maybe we should focus more on enabling families not to need childcare or family leave unless they really want to have children.

Access to birth control is not just a family matter of preventing teenagers from becoming accidental mothers or enabling couples to easily choose how many children to have. It's part of an effort to improve maternal and child health in poorer parts of the world. And it's also a global matter of gradually returning to a human population that is truly sustainable.

References

"Annual Progress Report to Congress: Global Health Programs FY 2014." 2015. USAID. https://www.usaid.gov/open/global-health-programs-annual-progress-report-congress/fy-2014. Accessed on June 2, 2019.

Current World Population. 2019. Worldometers. https://www.worldometers.info/world-population/#region. Accessed on June 2, 2019.

Sandy Becker was a cell biologist for several decades and is now retired. She moonlights as a science writer, covering biology in the broadest sense, environmental issues, and economics (which in her view are all connected).

That's It!?
Kirk Brennan

"Are we going to have more children?" I looked up from my paperwork and blinked at my partner. "I don't think so," I replied. "I am good with just the one." "Then we need to come up with a permanent form of birth control. I no longer want to be on the pill. It's not compatible with my other medication." "OK," I said, and that is what started the path to my eventual vasectomy. Investigating the different types of permanent birth control in 2005, I discovered there weren't many options. Men could wear condoms or have vasectomies. I had ruled out condoms as a permanent form of contraception the last time I used them regularly. I was coming of the age where stopping the stimulation of foreplay to put on a condom was causing my erection to start to go down. Having to keep condoms on hand for spontaneity sex wasn't ideal either. Having a three-year-old child in our lives, spontaneity was just about the only way we were able to squeeze in sex, usually in the afternoons. By bed time we were both too wiped to think about sex. With the pill and condoms out, that left IUD (intrauterine device), tubal ligation, and vasectomy.

Investigating IUDs, I found that they were not 100 percent effective, and they could move around, sometimes puncturing the uterus. The woman's body could reject it or have some other allergic reaction to it. Tubal ligation was definitely permanent. It was also invasive, and the woman would need to be admitted to the hospital for a few days and undergo surgery. Vasectomies were outpatient procedures; the man didn't have to be admitted to the hospital, and he would go home that same day. Vasectomies came in three main styles in 2005. Two of them could be easily reversed if I changed my mind and wanted to have more children. The third option could also be reversed, but the reversal would require surgery since the vas deferens would need to be connected back together. This procedure would cut the vas deferens from each testicle and cauterize the ends so they couldn't grow back together, nor would the ends leak sperm causing hard spots in the scrotum. I wasn't planning on having any more children, and this third option was 99.999999 percent effective. Only in one in a million cases did the vas deferens reattach itself enough to make a man fertile again. After my investigations were complete, the cauterization vasectomy was the best option for us and me.

I found the best urologist in San Francisco who used the cauterization technique. I didn't want to be worked on by someone who was willing to accept Blue Cross's low payments, so it was okay that he was out of network for my insurance. The meeting with the urologist was completed in less than an hour. He checked my overall health and asked me a handful of questions. I found it particularly interesting that he refused to give vasectomies to anyone under the age of 30 if they didn't have children yet. Even though the cauterization procedure could technically be reversed, it wasn't recommended. Since he chose to not accept patients outside of his parameters, that made me feel better as it seemed he was not a meat market type of doctor. Being in my 40s and having one child, I was within his parameters and he took me on as a patient. His office was willing to let me pay his fee in three installments, and the outpatient surgery room he used was in network. All appeared well, and I made an appointment for the procedure.

Three weeks after my initial consultation, I woke up at 6:00 a.m. and took a taxi to the surgery center and checked myself in for my vasectomy procedure. After 45 minutes of pre-op questions and checking my vitals, I was wheeled into the procedure room. The doctor came in and confirmed that I was ready to proceed and still wanted to have a vasectomy; I said "yes." He and his assistant put a sheet barrier between my upper body and lower body, and I was given local anesthesia in the scrotum. He checked my numbness level by thumping my scrotum, and when I couldn't feel it anymore it was time to start. He talked me through the whole procedure and answered all my questions as we went through the procedure. When he got to the part of cauterizing the ends, I could see smoke floating up over the sheet barrier, and it smelled like someone was cooking steak nearby; it took me a second to realize, that's me. I must admit it was a weird feeling to smell myself being cauterized and not be able to feel anything. The whole procedure took about 15 minutes. The doctor looked up and said I was finished and wheeled me into the post-op waiting room. My first thought was, that's it? It should take longer than 15 minutes to sterilize someone. It should be a major ordeal. After 45 minutes in the post-op waiting room, I was cleared to go, and they walked me to the door. As I walked down the hallway, the nurses were chuckling and told me I had the after-vasectomy walk. My after-procedure instructions were simple: When I arrived home, I was to stay in bed with ice on my scrotum for the day. Do not have sex for a week. If there was still discomfort after two weeks, follow up with the doctor. After the week wait, have as much sex as possible to flush out any sperm past the place of the procedure. After 60 days, bring a sample in for testing.

Not all went according to plan. When I arrived home, I discovered there was a work crew there installing fire sprinklers throughout the building. I was trying to ice my scrotum and had to keep moving around to stay out of their way. I received a lot of funny looks that day. I didn't make it a whole week before having sex. My partner was very much in the mood about three days later, and I ended up having sex. The next morning I had a little discomfort on the right side of my scrotum. I called the doctor and asked him about it. He said to me, "You had your vasectomy only four days ago and you have a little discomfort on one side? You should consider yourself lucky. You are fine."

I was fine. The discomfort went away after a week, and at 60 days I took my sample in and was declared at zero sperm count. I had achieved permanent contraception. Fourteen years later, and I still believe it was the best decision. The vasectomy hasn't caused any erectile dysfunction issues at all. The strength of my erections is normal or better than that of the average 50-plus-year-old male. My sex life is very satisfying mainly because we can let spontaneity rule. No prescriptions to remember, no condoms to buy, no worries. For men who are finished having children, the vasectomy is a very good choice.

Kirk Brennan is a retired software developer running a dog-walking and pet-sitting business with his wife. He lives in the San Francisco Bay Area with his wife and daughter.

Praying to the God of Birth Control
Linda Heiden

These days, I take birth control only in order to get pregnant. It is the height of irony that my reproductive endocrinologist hands me a pack of hormonal birth control pills before each IVF cycle or embryo transfer, all in an effort to achieve the thing The Pill was created to avoid: pregnancy.

I started out like every other girl—utterly terrified of unwanted pregnancy. The pill was a talisman against that, taken at *exactly* the same time each day, the alarm on my phone ringing out like the adhan, and I popped the pill like a religion, a prayer to the God of Birth Control, a plea against the terror of two pink lines showing up on a home pregnancy test. Finally, one day, it happened: a late period and two pink lines. I was 30, in a stable and loving relationship moving in an unhurried pace toward marriage, and after the initial nuclear shockwave blew up my psyche, we were happy. "Wow! We must be so fertile," I thought more than once, just a teeny bit smug that we hadn't even been trying to get pregnant and here we were. Sadly, a few weeks later the bleeding began, there was no heartbeat on an ultrasound, and a little fetal body that should have been 11 weeks measured only as 6 weeks, a grain of rice instead of a fig. This was a different kind of nuclear shockwave that tore me down instead of blowing me up, flattening me into the earth instead of throwing me into the sky. My brain had been rearranged, the fire had been lit, the marriage vows said, our life path was set: we wanted a baby, and I wanted it right now. So we had sex, so much sex, fun sex, boring sex, sex when we were sore, raw, sick, healthy, excited, aroused, or just wanting to cuddle and watch TV; it did not matter; we had so much sex without birth control. And yet, those two pink lines just would not show up; my period became an unstoppable metronome, pounding out the month after month of failure.

One in eight heterosexual couples will meet the diagnostic criteria for infertility, which means they've had unprotected and frequent sex for 12 months and haven't "achieved pregnancy" (and oh does it feel like an underachievement!). Nearly every gay couple is infertile within their relationship. After blood tests and intravaginal ultrasounds for me, and a date with a cup and a supply closet for my husband, we were declared, as I suspected after I got pregnant easily, so fertile. We looked perfect on paper. Husband had tons of great sperm; my hormones were balanced and on track; I ovulated each month. And yet, we couldn't get pregnant and were diagnosed with unexplained infertility. In total, I saw five reproductive endocrinologists, doing treatment with three of them at various times. We started with Clomid, the gateway drug of infertility and quickly moved on from there. Common reasons among heterosexual couples include low sperm count, endometriosis, or polycystic ovary syndrome. Approximately a third of infertility cases can be attributed to problems with the woman, one-third is problems with the man, and one-third is unexplained or a combination of both partners. Gay couples simply don't have all of the gametes necessary. Treatment consists of medications to address problems such as not ovulating. In *intrauterine insemination*, sperm is placed into the uterus at the correct time in the woman's cycle; in *in vitro fertilization* (IVF), a woman is stimulated to produce as many eggs as she can; they are harvested in a surgery, fertilized in a petri dish, grown for five days, and either frozen or placed back into the woman's uterus at the optimal time.

Infertility ate up years of my life. It dominated my marriage and even changed my routes in grocery stores so I could avoid even seeing the baby food aisle. There were times the pain was so great I could barely breathe, an aching longing draped over simmering rage that this was so hard for me when it was so easy for everyone else. My body became a battlefield in which I fought for the life I wanted, and the enemy was an unnamed and undiagnosed problem within my ovaries.

That brings me back to the birth control pills handed to me before starting my first round of IVF and my complicated feelings involving those four rows of tiny pills. I had spent so long in my youth trying to avoid pregnancy by taking these and spent so much money buying them and time researching various options, and now I am taking them to help me get pregnant. These pills that once helped me avoid those two pink lines now suppress my natural hormones so the doctor can build eggs using synthetic hormones instead, one tiny dot in the pointillistic portrait of infertility. Other dots include the online community of women who educated me and lifted me up (I still talk to them today), the many couples who do fertility treatments but do not walk away with a baby, my parents' retirement account that is $50,000 lighter than it was before four full rounds of IVF, and my lost chance for a daughter when my only XX embryo didn't create those two elusive pink lines. I pull back from these dots; I see all of them when I look at my beautiful, perfect son. And I think of all of this when I think about how we are transferring another embryo this summer, hoping for the amazing bounty of two children. Tiny pills, tiny dots, part of making up the larger and more beautiful painting of how my son came to be. Each time I pop one of those tiny pills, I pray a very different prayer than before to the God of Birth Control.

Linda Heiden is a lover of dogs, music, food, and cursing. She lives in the Midwest with her baby, a dog, her garden of herbs, and a wonderful husband, Zack.

Birth Control Pills Should Be Over the Counter
Emily Hirsch

While facilitating sex education and family planning workshops as a Peace Corps Volunteer in Zambia, I became really focused on access to information and access to various forms of birth control. I learned a lot from the people in the village about both barriers and possibilities for the future. Community members were far more receptive than I had anticipated to having open conversations about birth control. We did condom demonstrations and had workshops about birth control pills. Most of the biggest advocates, in fact, were also highly involved in the church. They were able to reconcile their religious beliefs with the urgency of women's reproductive rights and health. One time, a village headman helped me translate a session on family planning for a group of 30 women.

Because of this support in Zambia, a place where I did not necessarily expect to get it, I started to question why access surrounding birth control was so tenuous in the United States. Why, given that the country has far more access to wealth, education, and technology than Zambia and is presumably a secular government, is there not a better solution to getting birth control to people who need it? Why is it so difficult and expensive to obtain, especially for those without insurance?

One way that I argue this could improve is if birth control pills were over the counter in the United States, that is, available at any drugstore without a prescription or visit to the doctor. This idea has recently come to the forefront of Congress, in large part due to members of Congress voicing their opinions on Twitter. In June 2019, the freshman congresswoman from New York, Alexandria Ocasio-Cortez, tweeted, "Psst! Birth control should be over-the-counter, pass it on" (North 2019). Her sentiment has resonated with Democrats and some Republicans, as well as her widespread public following and reproductive justice activists.

When I initially heard about the over-the-counter proposition, it seemed straightforward. Birth control pills are said to be just as safe as a lot of other over-the-counter medications, and this policy has already been implemented in 12 states. Why shouldn't the rest of the country do the same? It is complicated because as the Affordable Care Act stands now, if the FDA were to approve over-the-counter birth control pills, insurance companies nor employers would be required to cover it, and thus it could drive up the price, making the contraceptive method just as inaccessible. This is likely why some Republicans are supporting the idea (North 2019).

Thankfully, freshmen members of Congress, including Alexandria Ocasio-Cortez and Ayanna Pressley of Massachusetts, are seeking to change that stipulation and pass a bill that makes birth control both over the counter and covered by the Affordable Care Act. Pressley stressed in a statement, "Bodily autonomy is a basic human right. Reproductive justice is not only a healthcare issue, it is an economic issue and a civil rights issue" (Tso 2019). If they are able to pull this bill off, it could be a game changer particularly for people facing interlocking forms of oppression as a result of race, gender, sexuality, class, religion, and more.

In a moment when getting an abortion, another aspect of basic health care, is becoming even more challenging for people with marginalized identities and inadequate resources in the United States, I think that it is important to make preventative birth control measures, like oral contraception, as accessible as we can (Williams and Blinder 2019). Exploring the potential of over-the-counter birth control is only one strategy. This is also not to say that if birth control was available over the counter, people could not still go to a doctor and weigh different options depending on their medical history. However, they would not have to do that.

Lawmakers and private citizens could do more to make birth control accessible in the United States in a multitude of ways. The point is that despite any political backlash or hesitation (or outright refusal) based on religion, people should have a choice how and when the they want to reproduce. They should have an equal degree of choice if they never want to reproduce, in terms of both preventative birth control and abortion. Right now, those choices, those fundamental rights given the context and history of the United States, are under attack.

After my years as a Peace Corps Volunteer in Zambia, I have found it perplexing and hypocritical how the United States often props itself up as the best place for women, as a country that is so advanced regarding women's rights compared to poorer countries in the Global South. Within its context, I thought Zambia was remarkable in how it embraced changes that would improve the health of its citizens. Even if birth control is not fully accessible there yet, I was impressed with the nuanced conversations and the level of community support. Since the United States, unlike Zambia, has practically unlimited resources and access to education, it needs to do much better in its commitment to reproductive health and rights and, in particular, with access to affordable birth control. Making birth control pills over the counter would be a promising start.

References

North, Anna. 2019. "The Strange Politics of Over-The-Counter Birth Control, Explained." https://www.vox .com/identities/2019/6/13/18677710/ted-cruz-birth-control-aoc-otc-counter. Accessed on June 14, 2019.

Tso, Tiffany. 2019. "The Beyoncés of Birth Control: Freshman Reps Introduce OTC Bill." https:// www.refinery29.com/en-us/2019/06/235328/

alexandria-ocasio-cortez-ted-cruz-birth-control-bill. Accessed on June 14, 2019.

Williams, Timothy and Blinder, Alan. 2019. "Lawmakers Vote to Effectively Ban Abortion in Alabama." https:// www.nytimes.com/2019/05/14/us/abortion-law-alabama .html. Accessed on June 14, 2019.

Emily Hirsch earned her MA in sustainable international development at The Heller School for Social Policy and Management at Brandeis University in 2019 and wrote her graduate thesis on feminist philanthropy. She now works in the nonprofit and philanthropy sector in New York City. She served in Peace Corps Zambia from 2015 to 2017, through which she facilitated gender equality and sex education programs, participated in the Let Girls Learn Madagascar Summit in 2016, and cofounded Peace Corps Zambia's first Gender Committee.

When Is Safe Sex Not Safe?
Joyce Krensky

For the record, I wish you lives with heart-pounding orgasmic sex, if that's what you want. I wish you warm, face-to-face close connections with another, if that's what you want. I wish you pleasure from your body and with another's, if that's what you want.

But when we think we've checked off the boxes for using birth control, and think that we are prepared to have safe sex, you may not be anything close to it. Because what I'm suggesting is that what is known as "safe sex" is often only about staying physically safe.

But for it really to be safe sex, for your whole vulnerable self, it needs to be emotionally, physically, and spiritually safe for both you and your partner. This kind of safe sex won't happen in a context where you're doing someone else a favor, when you feel unworthy to be seen for who you are, when you're not in a situation to get your own needs met, or when you are unable or not ready to know what you really want. You need to be able to self-reflect on whether you're in the right situation for you.

Let's think about what permission looks like.

For starters, emotionally safe sex requires your permission. How can you know in a specific time and place what is vital, true, and nonnegotiable for you? Once we know that, and have communicated our needs to a potential intimate partner, have you got that same information back from your partner? In other words, what does clarity for safe sex look and feel like to you and then, of course, to the other?

Often people have very different interpretations of what permission looks like. Some think it's implicit even if your words say "no"—that if you go anywhere secluded, such as to a dorm room, or apartment, or car—that they've got your permission for sex. A miscommunication I've heard often looks like this—you think that you are going to the beach to just talk and walk under the moonlight together. And the person you're with thinks that the act of going to the beach together at night implies that you are giving permission to have sex.

Pay Attention to Your Desires

You can train yourself to access the clarity and wisdom that is in you, which you have available for your use in all areas of your life. You can use it to look at your desires and if they're coming from a place in you that you recognize as your true self. You can recognize the times when the thought of sex may be scary but feels right and is exciting scary. Or when it's blissful intimacy and the connection you hope for. Or if you're looking for a time to have terrifically awesome fun. And you can also recognize the times you need to access your self-control.

What is self-control in sexual relationships about? Have you heard that it might be more romantic to lose control? Please remember that alcohol and other drugs allow people to engage in activities that would otherwise be unappealing, uncomfortable, or not in their value system.

Sometimes teens want to get their virginity over with. Does that make sense for you? Take time to think about all the desires you have and what you really want for yourself. Can you pay attention to them, and set intentions for yourself, even when you might be feeling the peer pressure from the culture or perhaps from an individual person? Mindfulness is an antidote to impulsivity. We can take a few deep breaths and respond then by making choices for ourselves.

Honoring Our Truths

Let's just acknowledge how challenging all of this communicating can be. This is not because you are in adolescence or are a young adult but because it's hard for most anyone at any age. Often a great deal of miscommunication and hurt comes from assumptions that have never been agreed to.

Once you're in a sexual relationship with someone, it doesn't mean you've given permission for the next sexual encounter with that person. If you'd like to continue, permission needs to be ongoing, including conversations about the frequency you have sex with this partner, or the particular activities you feel comfortable and not comfortable doing, even if you've done them before. It might mean that you are exclusive if that's important to you, or it might be about the role of social media. Remember this can include even something that does not look "too private or personal," like being in public together somewhere and then having that appear on social media. Furthermore, certainly you need to be confident that you and your partner will honor the privacy of anything more detailed, more personal, and potentially even more invasive or violating than just taking a walk somewhere together.

Remember that everything about your privacy needs to be clearly articulated for you to be ultimately protected and respected, and that is according to your definition and your needs. Make sure you trust in the person's integrity; be sure that the person is telling you the truth and not what the person thinks you want to hear.

Ultimately, Treat Yourself Like You Matter

Please be compassionate with yourself as you grow and learn more about you. Expect frustrations, disappointments, and that feeling of "what was I thinking?" Be respectful and tender with your vulnerability. Your confusions and mistakes are normal. It takes courage to know yourself and also to communicate to another. Remember to dream big and not think that you have to lower your expectations. And know that you'll learn the balance of these complexities only after a lot of life experience.

Finally, remember that your life is sacred, and then fill yourself with respect and dignity. You're worth it.

Joyce Krensky was health educator for 20 years at the Cambridge School of Weston in Weston, Massachusetts. Currently, she has a private practice for people of all ages; her work on well-being and self-care allows her to continue the joy of working with adolescents and their families. You may find her at joycekrenskyconsulting.com.

Jewish Law and Birth Control
David L. Levine

Most of us have heard the words "Be fruitful and multiply." It comes from the Bible and constituted God's instructions to Adam and Eve about how to lead their lives. "And you, be ye fruitful, and multiply; bring forth abundantly in the earth, and multiply therein" (Genesis 1:28).

The Bible is taken literally by Orthodox Jews, the most religious Jews. According to a Pew Report survey, Orthodox Jews are much younger and tend to have much higher fertility than the overall Jewish population—an average of 4.1 children among Orthodox Jews in the survey ages 40–59 compared with 1.9 children per Jewish adult overall. The Orthodox share of the Jewish population is growing, compared to Conservative or Reformed Jews (Cooperman and Smith 2003).

Traditional Jewish law has strict rules on birth control. Since Orthodox Jews follow these rules, I asked several Orthodox rabbis what Jewish law says about birth control.

In Jewish law, birth control applies only to females, not males. That is because wasting seed (sperm) is forbidden. This law has its origins in the story of Onan. When Onan's brother died, their father Judah ordered him to have sex with his brother's widow Tamar to give her offspring (Onan 2019). However, when Onan had sex with Tamar, he withdrew before his orgasm, spilling his semen on the ground. He was slain by God for this evil (Genesis 38:9).

"This idea, called Onanism, of avoiding getting your wife pregnant through wasting seed, is one of the cornerstones of the laws about birth control," according to Rabbi Mendel Adelman, an Atlanta-based rabbi who answers questions sent to Chabad (Chabad-Lubavitch is a major movement within mainstream Jewish tradition with its roots in the Chassidic movement of the 18th century).

"The Talmud speaks quite harshly about the prohibition against wasting seed, writing that it delays redemption and the like," Rabbi Adelman said. "Another source is the prohibition against causing impotency to men. This pretty much takes surgeries to remove potency, even reversible ones, out of the question." (Halacha is the collective body of Jewish religious laws consisting of the Torah and the Talmud. The Torah was given to Moses at Mount Sinai. The Talmud began as commentary on the Torah.)

"However, there are many cases where birth control is allowed and encouraged," Rabbi Adelman said.

The Talmud writes an argument about the use of a female condom for women for whom there are serious side effects, such as lack of milk for another baby, and danger to health, and the like. Some hold that a condom may be used in such cases, while the majority forbids it. Based on this (after much debate over the centuries), the accepted rule is that anything that affects the sperm during intercourse, such as condoms or spermicides, are forbidden. In cases of danger to health, they may be used, but still only as a last resort, as there are other options.

Marriage, in Jewish law, is referred to as "kiddushin," which comes from the Hebrew word for "holy." That is why Jewish authorities disapprove of premarital sex because it does not take place within the context of kiddushin.

It is common for Orthodox women to take birth control pills before they get married so they won't have their period on the wedding night (Bob 2019). That is because the Torah prohibits sex between a man and a woman who is menstruating (known as a niddah). This prohibition is in place until the woman's period is complete and she immerses in a mikveh, or ritual bath. Rabbi Strauss notes that this restriction applies to both married and unmarried couples, though it is considered inappropriate for a nonmarried woman (except for a soon-to-be bride) to immerse in a mikveh.

For the Orthodox, the use of birth control can be done only when it comes from a competent halachic authority, or a rav. Each person must speak to his or her own rabbi about his or her individual case. There is no "one-size-fits-all" answer, as each case is to be handled individually (Adelman 2019).

The preferred method of birth control for Orthodox women is the pill. That is because unlike condoms or spermicides, which are forbidden, it does not interfere with sperm.

According to the Talmud, the methods of acceptable birth control are listed in descending order of severity. The first ones should be used. Only if those are not available should others be tried:

- Pills or medicines that prevent the sperm from reaching the cervix (progesterone, for example)
- Pills that cause temporary infertility
- Tying tubes temporarily

- Cleaning out the area after intercourse
- Permanent implantations that prevent sperm from reaching the cervix
- Spermicides
- Female condom use during intercourse
- Birth control that affects the egg after it has been fertilized
- Male condom (Chabad.org)

There is some debate about the exact order. The general goal is to avoid affecting the sperm, as the Torah prohibition was about wasting seed.

Among the factors that play in the decision of whether to allow birth control include the following:

- Danger to physical health
- Danger to mental health
- Ability to care for the child
- Financial burdens
- Has the couple already fulfilled the biblical obligation of being fruitful and multiplying by having one boy and one girl? (Chabad.org)

Many rabbis allow birth control to space between children, to ease the burden of childcare. But again, each case is handled individually.

Can unmarried women use birth control? If for health reasons, the answer is "yes." For example, many female teenagers have menstrual migraines. For these reasons, taking the pill is sanctioned because it is for medical reasons and does not have anything to do with sex. When I asked a Chabad rabbi, who did not wish to be identified, about teenagers who have sex and are not married. He said, "We know that this exists, of course. And they don't usually come to a rabbi to discuss this. I would personally rather see unmarried couples use birth control to avoid the consequences of being a single mother. It is not sanctioned by Jewish law, but I feel it is for the best. Others might disagree."

References

Adelman, Mendel. 2019. "The Difference Between a Rabbi and a Rav." Chabad.org. https://www .chabad.org/library/article_cdo/aid/3753331/jewish/ The-Difference-Between-a-Rabbi-and-a-Rav.htm. Accessed on May 30, 2019.

Bob, Channa. 2019. "A Detailed Explanation of Niddah, or "Family Purity" Laws." Jewish Learning. https://www .myjewishlearning.com/article/the-laws-of-niddah/. Accessed on May 30, 2019.

Cooperman, Alan, and Gregory A. Smith. 2013. "Eight Facts about Orthodox Jews from the Pew Research Survey." Pew Research Center. https://www.pewresearch.org/ fact-tank/2013/10/17/eight-facts-about-orthodox-jews-from-the-pew-research-survey/. Accessed on May 30, 2019.

"Onan." 2019. Encylopedia.com. https://www.encyclopedia .com/people/philosophy-and-religion/biblical-proper-nam es-biographies/onan. Accessed on May 30, 2019.

David L. Levine is cochairman of Science Writers in New York (SWINY) and a member the National Association of Science Writers (NASW) and the Association of Healthcare Journalists. He has written for The New York Times, Reuters Health, Scientific American Mind, Nature Medicine, *the* Los Angeles Times, Nautilus, *and the* Smithsonian.

Coercive Contraception: When Choice Is Taken Away
Liesl Nydegger

Using birth control is a woman's choice in whether she wants to have a child. There are numerous forms of birth control a woman can choose to use: an implant, intrauterine device, a shot, vaginal ring, a patch, pills, diaphragm, sponge, cervical cap, spermicide, and sterilization (tubal ligation). While there are always side effects when it comes to medication, it is often the case where a woman hears about someone having a very negative experience with one form of birth control and assumes it is more common of an occurrence than it really is. This is extremely problematic as this form of contagious panic can spread rapidly through communities, particularly with the use of social media, and prevent women from using birth control who otherwise may choose to. There are also common myths believed by many women that prevent them from taking birth control, such as that birth control increases chances of infertility or cancer. There are no studies that show any association between taking birth control and infertility or cancer. Once a woman stops taking birth control, she can conceive unless she has other medical conditions preventing her from doing so. Similarly, women who do not take birth control are just as likely to have cancer as those who do take birth control. It is similar to the association that almost all serial killers ate white bread when they were children; so did most everyone else. It is essential to dispel myths surrounding birth control because women who want to take birth control should. Unfortunately, there are other factors that affect women's choice to take birth control or of getting pregnant, and those include doctors, significant others, and others with significant influence in their life.

Reproductive coercion occurs when a woman's significant other tries to impregnate her to establish control by interfering with contraception or pressuring her to get pregnant (Centers for Disease Control and Prevention 2019). Based on my research, I have had numerous women who stated that they thought their partners had unsuccessfully tried to get them pregnant, or their pregnancies were a result of tampering with contraception. One participant stated that her partner said the condom was on when it was not, another stated that her partner told her that he was infertile, and another said her partner told her he "pulled out" when he did not.

Conversely, other women experienced reproductive coercion where people pushed birth control or sterilization on them in order for them not to get pregnant. After one woman had her twins who were already from reproductive coercion from her partner, her doctor had her sign a form while she was under heavy medication after a cesarean section stating she would have a tubal ligation. She had no idea what she was signing and had no intention of having a tubal ligation as she wanted more children later on. When I interviewed her, she was extremely upset by the fact that she could not have any more children and had looked into having the procedure reversed, which would cost approximately $13,000. Another woman, who had a learning disability, had a child with her husband. His parents did not approve of their marriage or their having a child, and so her mother-in-law convinced the doctor that my participant was not in the right state of mind to make decisions since she has a severe learning disability, which she does not. He not only sterilized her but also removed her tubes altogether so she could never have the surgery reversed. My participant woke up from the surgery without any idea of what happened and was distraught that she could never have any more children. Another example is a participant who had a baby and, without even receiving a request for pills, her doctor sent her home with birth control pills. What is the one thing that all of these women have in common? They are all African American.

The United States has a long history of sterilizing African American women against their will or coercing them into using birth control. Throughout the 1990s, numerous states proposed coercive policies targeting women on welfare, which disproportionately affected African American women. The policies required women on welfare to take birth control, would pay women on welfare to obtain long-lasting birth control, and required the women to pay for early removal of devices. No policies were passed, but private citizens took it upon themselves to implement programs to pay women who used drugs to have tubal ligations or obtain long-lasting birth control. Rather than coerce African American women's reproductive rights, states have turned to criminalizing them. Although white women use illegal drugs while pregnant at higher rates than African American women, African American women are significantly more likely to be tested, arrested, convicted, and incarcerated, leading to decreased likelihood of receiving prenatal care and thus poorer health outcomes for mother and baby.

Birth control is the one method that women have control over to choose whether or not they want to have a child, and that choice should be theirs and theirs alone. Education is essential to dispel the current myths surrounding birth control and to increase awareness of different reproductive coercion methods that men use to impregnate women. In addition, reproductive coercion within relationships often occurs when there is intimate partner violence (IPV). Women and healthcare providers should be educated about the signs of different forms of IPV in order to provide resources and help to women so they do not remain in violent situations. Finally, hospitals/clinics should be screened for how many sterilizations are performed by race/ethnicity, and doctors who tend to perform more sterilizations among minority women should be supervised carefully to ensure their patients are actually consenting to surgeries. Birth control is a woman's right and should not be something she has to fight for or second-guess due to outside influences. It is our job as a society to ensure women take back control of their bodies and their choice to have children.

Reference

Centers for Disease Control and Prevention. 2019. "Understanding Pregnancy Resulting from Rape in the United States." https://www.cdc.gov/violenceprevention/datasources/nisvs/understanding-RRP-inUS.html. Accessed on May 6, 2019.

Liesl Nydegger, PhD, MPH, is assistant professor in health behavior and health education and director of the Gender Health Equity Lab in the Department of Kinesiology and Health Education at The University of Texas at Austin. Dr. Nydegger earned her PhD in health promotion sciences with a concentration in global health and her master's in public health in health promotion, education, and evaluation from Claremont Graduate University, School of Community and Global Health. In 2015, Dr. Nydegger was awarded a two-year Ruth L. Kirschstein Institutional National Research Service Award Postdoctoral Research Fellowship at the Center for AIDS Intervention Research at the Medical College of Wisconsin. Dr. Nydegger was awarded a Fulbright-Fogarty Fellowship in 2012–2013 that took place in Durban, South Africa. Dr. Nydegger's research interests focus on sexual health equity among vulnerable and underserved populations such as illicit drug users and racial/ethnic minorities who experience health disparities. Specifically, she is interested in HIV and sexually transmitted infection (STI) risk and prevention by considering substance abuse, violence (e.g., structural violence, community violence, intimate partner violence, and childhood sexual abuse), and structural factors (e.g., housing and poverty). Dr. Nydegger's current research combines intra-, inter-, and community-level theories to prevent HIV and STIs among high-risk women.

Queering Birth Control
Marissa Quenqua

"Are you sexually active?" It's a question I've been asked since my first gynecological visit in 1998, at age 13.

"Yes," I answered, my face burning hot, despite being out to my family and my open attitude toward sex.

I remember staring at the wall above the doctor's head, at a framed photograph of blooming flowers. I glanced at the numerous pamphlets on safe-sex practices, anything to avoid looking her in the eye. My mother's advice "Never lie to your doctor" rang in my ears. My mouth turned dry.

"Do you use condoms?" the doctor asked me, her lipstick-covered mouth turning up into an easy smile.

"No."

Her back stiffened, eyes slightly wide.

"Do you use birth control?"

"No."

She nearly gasped then, but was able to stifle it, her face turning serious. We were about to have a very difficult conversation.

"I'm having sex with a woman," I blurted out. "I have a girlfriend."

"Oh!" she laughed, face falling toward my medical chart. "I guess you don't have to worry about that then!" she said awkwardly, face flushed, and nearly slammed my chart shut.

The doctor didn't tell me what, if anything, I did have to worry about as a young gay teen. The doctor asked me to lie back and put my feet in the stirrups for my pelvic examination, and the topic of sex never came up again. I wasn't used to this kind of silence. Usually doctors and teachers went on and on about safe-sex practices, statistics, sex acts themselves, and the risks associated with each. There was nothing.

According to a 2008 study comprising nearly 8,000 queer women, it's estimated that "1.3% to 1.9% of US women aged 15 to 44 years were lesbians and that 3.1% to 4.8% were bisexual. Viral STD rates were significantly higher among bisexual women (15.0% to 17.2%) than among lesbians (2.3% to 6.7%)" (Tao 2008). These extremely low numbers as well as the lack of studies done on women who have sex with women, period, may account for my experience.

I've lived in New York my entire life. That first exam took place on Long Island, and I've lived in New York City since 2006. You'd think my experience at the doctor would change over time, living in such a liberal mecca, but that's not the case. I've been out of the closet for over 20 years, and I've had this uncomfortable conversation with gynecologists more times than I can count. My wife actually lists "sex with women" as her preferred method of birth control on medical intake forms.

It usually garners a hearty laugh but no advice from doctors on how to protect herself. Now in my mid-30s, I'll drag the interaction out a bit.

"Are you sexually active?"

"Yes."

"Do you use condoms?"

"No."

"Spermicide?"

"No."

"Birth control?"

"No."

"Do you want a baby?"

"Nope."

At this point, the medical professional is looking at me like I either have three heads or am exceedingly stupid. Thick silence hangs in the air. I am femme in my presentation, I wear makeup every day, and at this point I am forced to come out of the closet. There are no visual clues that will help fill in the blanks here.

"I'm married to a woman."

"Oh, my God! OK, of course! I'm so sorry."

They are always very apologetic, changing the subject quickly, focusing on the exam. Most assume I don't need an STI screening.

"No, I'd still like one," I correct her.

"Oh! I guess I shouldn't assume just because you're married . . . shame on me."

There is no discussion of lesbian safe-sex practices or lesbian sex practices at all; there is no discussion about whether I am bisexual or pansexual or polyamorous. Am I the only queer woman these doctors see per day? In New York City? I highly doubt it. I've occasionally seen "Do you have sex with men or women" on intake forms, especially at places geared toward servicing the LGBTQ community, but I have, only once, been given information about safer sex as a gay woman.

In 2016 I went to a gynecological clinic in Park Slope, Brooklyn, with a suspected STI. I explained during the intake that I am married to a woman and my wife and I are polyamorous, and we'd recently had sex with another woman together. It turned out that I had BV (bacterial vaginosis). This nurse practitioner explained to me that this mild bacterial infection is not considered an STI within the heterosexual community, but it is among women who have sex with women, since it's "the only STI that can be passed from woman to woman with any regularity." I was stunned. I was 32 and had never been given this information before. BV is caused by an overgrowth of "bad" bacteria in the vagina, which upsets its natural balance. This can happen when sharing sex toys or during manual stimulation, where one woman can throw another woman's vaginal pH out of whack. The treatment is a simple course of antibiotics.

The only reason I knew there was a problem is that I'm very aware of my body and what's "normal" for me. What about other queer women who might not notice? According to this Women's Health Guide, "If left untreated, BV may increase your risk for STDs like herpes, chlamydia, gonorrhea, HIV, and pelvic inflammatory disease, which can lead to infertility" (Bacterial Vaginosis—Women's Health Guide 2015).

I believe queer women deserve better. Now that my wife and I are trying to conceive, my relationship with reproduction and birth control has changed again. I've gone straight to a fertility clinic, since lack of sperm is a pretty huge impediment to conception. If I am not getting proper information in New York City, I can't imagine what's happening in the rest of the country. I feel as though lesbian sex is a mystery to many, even within the medical community itself, the one place where information should always be accurate, available, and openly discussed.

References

"Bacterial Vaginosis—Women's Health Guide." 2015. U.S. Department of Veterans' Affairs. https://www.publichealth

.va.gov/infectiondontpassiton/womens-health-guide/
bacterial-vaginosis.asp. Access on June 17, 2019.

Tao, Guoyu. 2008. "Sexual Orientation and Related Viral
Sexually Transmitted Disease Rates Among US Women
Aged 15 to 44 Years." *American Journal of Public Health.*
98(6): 1007–1009. Available online at https://www.ncbi
.nlm.nih.gov/pmc/articles/PMC2377304/. Accessed on
June 17, 2019.

*Marissa Quenqua is a freelance writer living in Brooklyn. Her
work has been featured by Freerange Nonfiction, and she's written several romance novels under a pseudonym for the publisher
Enamored Ink. Marissa is currently at work on a YA novel about
two queer girls in love and is a writing mentor for high school students through the nonprofit organization Girls Write Now.*

Why We Need Comprehensive Sex Ed
Ilka Sankari

I was in eighth grade when I learned what *first base* meant.
I thought I knew. Then, teen educators from Planned Parenthood's youth leadership program, REV, talked to my class about
consent. The question of how to define "first base" came up, so
I immediately raised my hand and declared it was "just making out." Everyone disagreed, some kids saying it was oral sex,
some saying it was just a kiss. I felt pretty dumb until the high
schoolers told us we'd done a great job: they said our answers
show just how different people's ideas about sex are, which is
why we need to talk about consent.

That moment taught me more than any other sexual education class I've had. And it happened because I live in a state
that mandates comprehensive sex ed. Living in Oregon, I have
received medically accurate, comprehensive sex ed since elementary school. This practice of legally requiring kids be taught
more than just the dangers of sex, which really only instills fear

and doesn't offer a solution, has been linked to huge benefits. States where comprehensive sex ed is mandatory have lower teen pregnancy rates and lower STD rates, and teenagers are able to make informed decisions.

Therefore, what is comprehensive sex ed? The definitions vary, but at its core it is complete, accurate reproductive health education. Advocates for Youth define it as sex ed that "teaches about abstinence as the best method for avoiding STDs and unintended pregnancy, but also teaches about condoms and contraception to reduce the risk of unintended pregnancy and of infection with STDs, including HIV. It also teaches inter-personal and communication skills and helps young people explore their own values, goals, and options" (Sex Education Programs: Definitions & Point-by-Point Comparisons 2001).

As a teenager on the receiving end of public education, this practice is a no-brainer. Our culture in the United States stig-matizes conversations around sex, reproductive health, and even just our own bodies so much. That stigma can make it feel impossible to get accurate, unbiased education about these topics anywhere but the classroom. How many families talk to their kids about the best birth control options, STD preven-tion, and how to practice consent? And even if they wanted to, how many parents/guardians have the knowledge they need to have those conversations? If you're thinking not a lot, you're right. A 2014 Planned Parenthood study found that while 92 percent of parents had talked to their kids about "sexual-ity-related topics," only 43 percent said they felt "very com-fortable" doing so (New Poll: Parents Are Talking with Their Kids About Sex but Often Not Tackling Harder Issues 2016). With this cultural discomfort, where are kids supposed to learn about sex if not school?

But while comprehensive sex ed seems like an obvious best practice to me, many states disagree, so much, in fact, that some states in the United States withhold information under the premise that teaching about sex, contraceptives, or abortion (the list goes on) will encourage these activities. Only 13 states require that sexual education even be medically accurate. Even worse, seven states prohibit educators from discussing LGBTQ+ identities and relationships, with some even requiring that educators frame these topics negatively. This happens because there is no federal standard for sex ed in schools, so it's become a sort of patchwork of policies across the country. It's this approach that allows for personal values to interfere: state and local legislators dictate what can be taught, if anything at all. Sex ed taught this haphazardly typically leads to an incomplete education, if not a downright damaging one.

A 2017 report from the U.S. Centers for Disease Control and Prevention shows that Alabama, Kentucky, Louisiana, Mississippi, and Texas all rank among the top 10 in the nation for the highest teen birth rates (Teen Birth Rate by State 2019). Correspondingly, almost none of those states mandate any sex education (Sex and HIV Education 2016). The key here is that teens are always going to have sex. Withholding information doesn't deter sex; it just makes it more dangerous. No matter a lawmaker, teacher, or parent's personal views, the reality shows that teens are and always will be sexually active. Not teaching us tools for safe sex leaves kids in the dark about how to protect themselves from pregnancy, STDs, and more. Sexual education should not be motivated by trying to stop young people from having sex but by the goal to give us all the tools possible to be safe.

Furthermore, safe sex doesn't end at protection from unwanted pregnancies or STDs. It should include conversations about boundaries, consent, and respect, and schools should teach that. Like my transformative experience with consent education, many kids have never understood what consent really is until someone explains it to them. Unfortunately, I am one of the lucky students who even had consent explained to me instead of learning through personal experience of having it violated. Many students never receive education on what consent and boundaries look like, making it harder for them to identify what healthy sexual relationships are and understand their rights.

Sex ed in this country has a long way to go. In order to lower teen pregnancy rates, STD rates, and cultural discomfort around sexuality, we need to broaden the conversations we have around sex. Teaching abstinence-only is shaming and uninformative. Leaving curriculum decisions up to specific states, districts, and schools leaves dangerous gaps in students' education. We need to move toward comprehensive sex ed for all, which truly informs youth and empowers us to make healthy decisions. Trained professionals from organizations like Planned Parenthood or other local sex ed groups are wonderful resources for providing accurate, unbiased information. It's time young people be treated like adults, not limited to the education a sexually repressed society doles out to us.

References

"New Poll: Parents Are Talking with Their Kids About Sex but Often Not Tackling Harder Issues." 2016. Planned Parenthood Federation of America. https://www .plannedparenthood.org/about-us/newsroom/press-releases/new-poll-parents-talkingtheir-kids-about-sex-often-not-tackling-harder-issues. Accessed on June 13, 2019.

"Sex and HIV Education." 2016. Guttmacher Institute. https://www.guttmacher.org/state-policy/explore/sex-and-hiv-education. Accessed on June 13, 2019.

"Sex Education Programs: Definitions & Point-by-Point Comparisons." 2001. Advocates for Youth. https:// advocatesforyouth.org/resources/fact-sheets/sex-education-programs-definitions-and-point-by-point-comparison/. Accessed on June 13, 2019.

"Teen Birth Rate by State." 2019. Centers for Disease Control and Prevention. https://www.cdc.gov/nchs/pressroom/sosmap/teen-births/teenbirths.htm. Accessed on June 13, 2019.

Ilka Sankari is a 17-year-old high school student in Eugene, Oregon. She's passionate about reproductive justice and is engaged in related activism through her local Planned Parenthood and its youth volunteer group, REV.

4 Profiles

This story of birth control is, to a large extent, the story of individuals and organizations that have believed in, worked for, and promoted the topic for much of their existence. The list of such individuals and organizations is very long, and those entities listed here provide no more than a sample of the many lives that have been devoted to (sometimes for; sometimes against) the role of contraception in human life.

Advocates for Youth

Advocates for Youth (AFY) was founded in 1980, under the name of the Center for Population Options (CPO), by American sociologist Joy Dryfoos. Dryfoos is probably best known for her concept of schools as being "full-service" institutions, where the needs faced by students in all aspects of their lives were considered part of the school's mission. She has also been called the "mother" of the school-based health clinic movement. In 1994, CPO changed its name to Advocates for Youth to better emphasize the organization's primary goal of serving the full range of health issues faced by adolescents.

Gregory Pincus, one of the developers of the oral birth control pill in the 1950s, which contributed to the sexual revolution of the 1960s and the effectiveness of family planning all over the world. Pincus also cofounded the Worcester Foundation for Experimental Biology (WFEB) and was one of its directors for many years. (Bettmann/Getty Images)

One of AFY's first achievements was creation of the International Clearinghouse on Adolescent Fertility, whose purpose it was to disseminate information about pregnancy and childbearing in English, French, and Spanish throughout the world. The program lasted fewer than five years. Over the years, AFY has developed and promoted a variety of programs to promote all aspects of sex education among adolescents, including the Media Project (1980–2005), a program designed to include information about sex education in television programs and other media; Life Planning Education (begun in 1983), offering ways of integrating sex education with vocational and business education programs; Support Center for School-Based Health Care (begun in 1984), promoting the notion of full-service, school-based health centers; the National Conference on AIDS and Adolescents (first conducted in 1987); coproduction of a documentary video on the teaching of sex to young people (1988); a cosponsorship of the First Inter-Africa Conference on Adolescent Reproductive Health (1992); founder of the first Internet intervention for lesbian, gay bisexual, and transgender (LGBT) youth (1998); founder of the Anti-homophobia/Transphobia Project to educate individuals of all ages about homosexuality and transsexuality (2007); cofounder of the Future of Sex Education Initiative (FoSE) (2007); creator of the Great American Condom Campaign (2009); and publisher of Rights, Respect, and Responsibility, a K-12 sex education curriculum that includes all 16 topics recommended by the U.S. Centers for Disease Control and Prevention (2016).

Currently, AFY organizes its work around 13 basic program areas: abortion access; confidentiality in health care; contraceptive access; growth and development; HIV; honest sex education; LGBTQ health and rights; racial justice and intersectionality; reproductive justice; sexual violence; supportive and healthy schools; young people in the Global South; and youth leadership and organizing. The organization makes use of four types of tools to deliver its messages on these topics: fact sheets, health information, newsletters, and policy and advocacy. For example, it offers a pamphlet for trans Muslim individuals called "I'm Muslim and My Gender Doesn't Fit Me." So-called one-pagers are also available on a variety of topics, such as "Professional Learning Standards for Sex Education," which provides a concise but complete description of recent recommendations for curricula in sex education.

AFY publishes two primary online newsletters, *iYAN* (The International Youth Activist Network newsletter) and the *School Health Equity Newsletter*, which provide information and suggestions for professionals in the field on recent developments in the theory and practice of sex education. AFY is also active in the field of policy and advocacy, providing updates for activists and professionals in the field as well as lobbying of decision-makers on important sex education issues. Some typical topics within this category are The Global Health, Empowerment and Rights (HER) Act; Know Your IX State Policy Playbook; One Year In: A Timeline of How the Trump Administration Has Harmed Young People; 2017 Youth Policy Agenda; and The Equal Access to Abortion Coverage in Health Insurance (EACH Woman) Act.

Contraception is a crucial part of the AFY mission, with well over nearly 200 specific items on its website dealing with this topic. Among those offerings are Access to Safe Abortion and Contraception: Vital for Young Women Globally, a Priority for U.S. Foreign Assistance; American Academy of Pediatrics Updates Contraception Recommendations; Young Women and Long-Acting Reversible Contraception; Contraceptive Access; Abortion Access; Reproductive Justice; 1.5 Billion Dollars for U.S. International Family Planning and Reproductive Health Assistance; Trump Rollback of Birth Control Mandate Is an Attack on Young People; and Abstinence-Only-Until-Marriage Peddler Given High Level Position in Trump Administration.

Bill Baird (1932–)

Bill Baird has sometimes been called "the father of the birth control and abortion rights movement in the United States." The encomium arises originally from actions he took in the late

1960s on behalf of an individual's right to obtain contraceptive devices. In 1967, he was invited to give a lecture at Boston University (BU) on the topic of contraception. The invitation had come by way of a petition signed by 679 BU students interested in challenging a portion of the Massachusetts State constitution, the so called Crimes against Chastity clause, which prohibited the distribution of contraceptive devices to unmarried individuals. At the lecture, Baird discussed the arguments for individuals' using various types of contraception and the "absurdity" of the centuries-old "Crimes against Chastity" clause. He also distributed condoms to members of the audience. Baird was arrested immediately following the lecture and charged on two counts of describing and disseminating contraceptive devices.

Baird's case worked its way through the court system. At the state level, the Massachusetts Supreme Judicial Court found him innocent of talking about contraceptives, based on his First Amendment rights but guilty of actually handing them out, based on the "Crimes against Chastity" clause. Eventually, the case reached the U.S. Supreme Court in the matter of *Eisenstadt v. Baird*. In 1972, that court ruled in a 6–1 decision in favor of Baird. In one of the most memorable statements made by the court, Justice William J. Brennan Jr. wrote that "if the right of privacy means anything, it is the right of the individual to be free from unwarranted governmental intrusion into matters so fundamentally affecting a person as to whether to bear or beget a child" (*Eisenstadt v. Baird*, 405 U.S. 438 (1972). https://supreme.justia.com/cases/federal/us/405/438/#tab-opinion-1949625. Accessed on August 12, 2019).

Bill Baird was born into an impoverished family in Brooklyn, New York, on June 20, 1932. He sometimes helped his family meet ends by trolling through garbage cans in the neighborhood. He lost two siblings to malnourishment, one at the age of 12 months and one at 12 years. He eventually attended Brooklyn College, from which he received his bachelor's degree in 1955. He then went to work for EMKO, a company that manufactured birth control devices. On one occasion, he was visiting a hospital in Harlem, New York, when an African American woman was admitted for wounds obtained while attempting to abort her unborn child. She died, and Baird was so overcome by the experience that he decided to devote his life to preventing such events from happening in the future. In 1963, he opened a mobile birth control clinic called the Plan Van, through which he distributed free samples of contraceptives. He also began speaking and writing about the need for birth control and the options available to women and men. (For these actions, he was fired from his job at EMKO.)

Largely regarded as a hero by the birth control movement, he has also been regarded with disdain and hatred by antiabortion individuals. He claims to have been the subject of death threats throughout most of his adult life. In 1976 and 1979 he was lead plaintiff on two other important court cases, both of which were called *Bellotti v. Baird*, attempting to obtain the right of minors to abortion without consent of their parents. He won both cases.

Over the last half century, Baird has supported himself by lecturing and writing about contraceptive issues, often drawing less-than-adequate financial compensation for his work. He continues that effort today, however.

Center for Reproductive Rights

The Center for Reproductive Rights (CRR) was founded in 1992 by attorney Janet L. Benshoof and other interested parties. At the time, Benshoof was director of the Reproductive Freedom Project of the American Civil Liberties Union. She felt a need for a global agency that would focus exclusively on issues of women's reproductive freedom, such as contraception, abortion, and genital mutilation. The new organization was originally called the Center for Reproductive Law and Policy and was organized to work on the issues about which Benshoof was concerned. (The organization changed its name to its present title in 2003.) Today, CRR focuses on abortion, contraception, maternal health, funding for reproductive health care, censorship, and young people's rights. It carries out its work in and through agencies in 50 countries in Africa, Asia, the Caribbean, Europe, Latin America, and the United States. It also works within and through other governmental and nongovernmental agencies, such as the United Nations, Council of Europe, Human Rights Council, Inter-American Commission on Human Rights, and United Nations Population Fund.

The center's work falls into four major categories: through the legal system, at the United Nations, working with policymakers, and reporting on the status of reproductive rights around the world. Some examples of each area in 2019 alone are as follows:

Legal

- Litigation in Ecuador, Guatemala, and Nicaragua dealing with forced pregnancies and sexual abuse in each country.
- A law suit against the U.S. Department of Health and Human Services for the withholding of medical services by providers because of religious or moral beliefs.
- Legal action against the state of Mississippi for unconstitutional and illegal limitations on access to abortion for women in the state.
- Involvement of the center's South Asia Reproductive Justice and Accountability Initiative in a successful case in Pakistan to protect a woman's right to obstetric fistula care.

United Nations

- Publication of a Fact Sheet on violations of reproductive rights among girls in the Caribbean and Latin America.
- Filing of four cases before the United Nations Human Rights Committee abortion laws in Guatemala, Nicaragua, and Ecuador demanding accountability for survivors of

sexual violence and denying adolescent girls and survivors of rape the ability to terminate their pregnancies, as well as laws in Ecuador, Guatemala, and Nicaragua violating the reproductive rights of these girls and others like them.

- Statement opposing the Trump administration's decision to withdraw from the United Nations Human Rights Council.

Engaging Policymakers

- Support for reintroduction in the U.S. Congress of the Women's Health Protection Act of 2019.
- Statements in opposition to restrictive abortion laws in Alabama, Georgia, Mississippi, and other states.
- Along with other reproductive rights groups, a petition to officials of Nairobi County, Kenya, for removal of billboards containing incorrect information about limitations on use of contraceptives among women in the region.

Reporting on Rights

- Fact Sheet on "Perilous Pregnancies: Health Care for Undocumented Migrant Women in the EU."
- Update on the status of abortion for minors who have been raped in India.
- Summary of Trump administration's revised rules on Title X family planning programs.
- Corrections by Lourdes Rivera, senior vice president of U.S. Programs at the Center for Reproductive Rights, about the status of abortion rights laws in the United States and individual states by President Trump.

Min-Chueh Chang (1908–1991)

Anyone familiar with the history of the development of the first oral contraceptive pill will recognize the name of Gregory Pincus. Pincus led the research team that brought that project to a successful conclusion in the late 1950s. A perhaps less familiar name associated with that effort is Chinese American reproductive biologist Min-Chueh Chang. Chang joined the Worcester Foundation for Experimental Biology (WFEB) in 1945, shortly after its founding. His responsibilities at WFEB were perhaps somewhat unclear at first. After having been assigned room for his own research, Chang later said, his main activity was to work as "night watchman." That assessment was almost certainly less than accurate, as he almost immediately delved into the research that had attracted him to the institute in the first place, the development of in vitro fertilization technology initiated by Pincus in the 1930s. Chang's work focused on the fundamental character and relationships of sperm, the egg, and the process of fertilization. He remained at WFEB for the rest of his professional career, retiring from the institution in 1982. At that point, he had authored and coauthored more than 350 scholarly papers on the development of the pill and other fields of his research.

Min-Chueh Chang was born in the village of Dunhou, near the city of Tai Yuan, in Shanxi Province, China, on October 10, 1908. His father was a government official with adequate means to send him to Tsinghua University. There he earned his bachelor's degree in animal physiology in 1933. He then won a scholarship for an overseas fellowship, which he fulfilled by enrolling at Edinburgh University. He spent only a year there, however, as he was unhappy with the unpleasant weather in Edinburgh as well as a perceived bias by some Scots against foreign nationals. After leaving Edinburgh, he accepted an offer to continue his studies at Fitzwilliam College, Cambridge. He narrowed his research interests there to the topic of reproductive biology, a subject to which he was to devote himself for the rest of his life.

After completing his doctoral studies at Cambridge in 1941, Chang found that, because of World War II, he had few options for future research. He was fortunate enough to have been offered lodging and minimal research at Cambridge until the end of the war, when he decided to emigrate to the United States. The only person to respond to his inquiries for work was Pincus, and Chang accepted the offer to join the WFEB research team. He eventually created his own research team that, over the years, produced a series of unusually talented and successful researchers. In recognition of his accomplishments, Chang was awarded a number of honors, including the Albert Lasker Award (1954), Ortho Medal and Award of the American Fertility Society (1961), Hartman Award by the Society for the Study of Fertility (1971), Frances Amory Prize by the American Academy of Arts and Sciences (1975), and the Wippman Scientific Research Award of the Planned Parenthood Federation of America (1987). In 1990, he was elected to membership in the National Academy of Sciences. A year after this honor, Chang died in Worcester on June 5, 1991.

Mary Dennett (1872–1947)

Mary Dennett was a suffragette, peace activist, and outspoken proponent of contraception during the mid-20th century. Her work has been overshadowed by the accomplishments of her contemporary, and perhaps more successful comrade, Margaret Sanger. Although the two agreed on many fundamental principles about the need for easy access to contraceptives among American women, they differed as to the mechanisms for achieving that objective. By the end of the 1910s, many birth control advocates in the United States had given up on the idea of passing federal legislation to repeal the notorious Comstock Laws of 1873. They decided that working in individual states, one at a time, was more likely to produce success in gaining access to birth control information and devices than was lobbying at the federal level.

Dennett disagreed with that philosophy. She was convinced that working through federal officials to achieve this goal, what she called "straight repeal," would bring about desired results more quickly and more universally. ("Straight repeal" meant essentially removing two words from the Comstock Laws, "preventing conception.") She approached a series of federal officials with this suggestion, obtaining some agreement but no actual actions for her cause. In 1919, one U.S. senator, L. Heisler Ball (R-DE), a practicing physician, agreed to introduce a bill on the topic. He never followed up on his promise, however. Dennett also contacted Postmaster General William H. Hays Sr. about her campaign. Hays appeared to be sympathetic to Dennett's cause but resigned his office to become Chairman of the Motion Picture Producers and Distributors of America before he could act on her request. In 1923, she found another ally in Senator Albert B. Cummins (R-IA), but Cummins's bill was never voted upon because of widespread absenteeism by his colleagues when the bill came up for consideration. In 1925, she admitted defeat and discontinued her efforts to get a straight repeal of the Comstock Acts. (Although the Comstock Laws stayed on the books of states and the federal government for many years, they were finally de facto invalidated in 1965.)

Dennett first got into trouble over her birth control activities in 1915 when she wrote a 24-page pamphlet for her sons on human sexuality, "The Sex Side of Life." The pamphlet provided in a clear manner the "facts of life," including detailed information about human reproduction. The pamphlet soon became popular among a number of parents who, like Dennett, had never been able to find this type of information in print. Although warned that her pamphlet was "filthy" and in violation of the Comstock Laws, she continued to distribute the pamphlet until 1928, when she was arrested by postal authorities for her illegal activities. She was tried and found guilty by the district court, a decision that was later overturned by the United States Court of Appeals for the Second Circuit in 1930. Legal authorities note that this decision was the basis of a more reaching verdict in 1936, *United States v. One Package of Japanese Pessaries*, in which the distribution of contraceptive materials between physicians was legalized. (A complete story of the Dennett trials is available at John

M. Craig. 1995. " 'The Sex Side of Life': The Obscenity Case of Mary Ware Dennison." *Frontiers: A Journal of Women's Studies*. 15(3): 145–166. A copy of "The Sex Side of Life" is available on Project Gutenberg, https://www.gutenberg.org/files/31732/31732-h/31732-h.htm.)

Dennett's work on behalf of birth control also included her involvement with Margaret Sanger's American Birth Control League (ABCL). When the two reformers began to disagree on tactics, however, Dennett left the ABCL in 1919 to form her own organization, the Voluntary Parenthood League. Only six years later, the two organizations decided to merge, taking the name of the ABCL, later to become today's Planned Parenthood Federation of America.

Mary Coffin Ware was born in Worcester, Massachusetts, on April 4, 1872. She and her siblings spent much of their early life with their aunt, Lucia Ames Mead, an educator, feminist, and pacifist who lived in Boston. Mary attended elementary and secondary schools in Boston before completing her secondary education at Miss Capens School for Girls in Northampton, Massachusetts. She then continued her studies at the Boston Museum of Fine Arts school. After graduation, she taught decoration and design at the Drexel Institute in Philadelphia. In 1898, she and a sister opened a handicraft shop, where they sold leather products. In 1900, she married architect William Hartley Dennett, a prominent architect. After bearing three children, Mary was told by her physician that she could not have any more children. She and her husband were mystified because, as she later said, "I was utterly ignorant of the control of conception, as was my husband also" (Constance M. Chen. 1996. *"The Sex Side of Life": Mary Ware Dennett's Pioneering Battle for Birth Control and Sex Education*. New York: New Press). The Dennett marriage was doomed in any case, however, because he became enamored of a woman client with whom he was working. The marriage ended in divorce in 1912.

In addition to her work on behalf of birth control education, Dennett was active in other lines of social reform, including pacifism, women's rights, and homeopathy. For example, she helped create a pacifist organization, the World Federalists, of which she served as chair from 1941 to 1944. As her health failed, she moved to a nursing home in Valatie, New York, where she died on July 25, 1947.

Guttmacher Institute

The Guttmacher Institute was founded as a semiautonomous section of Planned Parenthood as the Center for Family Planning Program Development. An important factor in the creation of the institute was the growing concern about family planning issues in the United States and around the world during the early 1960s. The institute was conceived of as a mechanism for carrying out original research on and conveying information about family planning issues, objectives that still guide its program. The institute changed its name to the Alan Guttmacher Institute in 1974 upon the death of obstetrician and gynecologist Alan Guttmacher, who was one its founders and its first president. Three years later, in 1977, the institute became a fully independent organization, although it has continued to maintain a close relationship with Planned Parenthood. In 2005, the institute changed its name once more, to Guttmacher Institute.

One of the institute's first actions was the creation of a scholarly journal for reports on its original work, *Family Planning Perspectives*. In 2002, the journal was renamed *Perspectives on Sexual and Reproductive Health*. *Perspectives* continues as a peer-reviewed medical journal covering topics on reproductive health that has been ranked first in two categories, demography and family studies, by *Journal Citation Reports*. Other publications developed by the institute were a newsletter, *Washington Memo* (1974), later renamed *The Guttmacher Report on Public Policy* (1998), and then *Guttmacher Policy Review* (2006), and *International Family Planning Digest* (1975), later *Family Planning Perspectives* (1978) and then *International Perspectives on*

Sexual and Reproductive Health (2009). In 1970, the institute staff worked with members of Congress and their staff in the development of Title X of the Public Health Service Act. It provided much of the data and background information on which the terms of the act were based.

A primary activity throughout the institute's history has been data collection for policy development and education of professionals in the field and the general public. Some of those projects are as follows:

1973: The first census of abortion providers in the United States

1976: A survey of adolescent sexual activity, summarized in *11 Million Teenagers*

1979: Research on access to contraceptive services among teenagers, reported in "Telling Parents: Clinic Policies and Adolescents' Use of Family Planning and Abortion Services"

1987: First national survey of abortion patients in the United States

1987: First national assessment of harassment of U.S. abortion providers

1989: A report on the teaching of sex education in American schools, "What Public School Teachers Teach about Preventing Pregnancy, AIDS and Sexually Transmitted Diseases"

1994: A report on insurance coverage for contraception, "Uneven and Unequal: Insurance Coverage and Reproductive Health Services"

1998: Research on reproductive health practices in 53 countries worldwide, "Into a New World: Young Women's Sexual and Reproductive Lives"

2002: Two publications of data on men's sexual and reproductive health in the United States and worldwide in "In Their Own Right"

2011: First national survey on unintended pregnancies, by state

2014: The institute's first amicus curiae brief filed in the U.S. Supreme Court case of *Burwell v. Hobby Lobby Stores*

One of the institute's most valuable services for professionals and nonprofessionals alike is the Data Center on its website (https://data.guttmacher.org/regions). The tool allows one to select any nation or region of the world and any one of a number of categories under "abortion" and/or "pregnancy" to generate tables of data on such topics. The abortion and pregnancy categories are also subdivided into several other groupings, such as "abortion rate," "number of abortions," "abortions by marital status," "unintended pregnancies," and "maternal health care provision." Some of the awards, affiliations, and other administrative entities developed to achieve the institution's objectives have been the Darroch Award for research excellence in the field of sexual and reproductive health; the Fred H. Bixby Foundation, which brings one person from a developing country to the Guttmacher Institute for up to two months to collaborate with staff on international projects; the Cory L. Richards Memorial Scholarship, which supports emerging leaders in the field of sexual and reproductive health and rights; the Guttmacher-Lancet Commission on Sexual and Reproductive Health and Rights, for the development of a comprehensive, evidence-based, and actionable agenda for sexual and reproductive health and rights priorities over the next 15 years and beyond; and acknowledgment of the institute as a National Institutes of Health Population Center in 2013.

Frederick Hollick (1818–1900)

Hollick was a British American physician and proponent of forthright sex education for the general public. He was born in Birmingham, England, on December 22, 1818. Various authorities disagree somewhat as to his educational background, some saying that he attended the Birmingham Mechanics Institute and others claiming that he was a "self-educated" mechanic. In any case, he became interested in the work of the British textile manufacturer and social reformer Robert Owen and served as one of his "missionaries" to Glasgow in the early 1840s. When Owen's movement failed, Hollick emigrated to the United States, where he attended the Physio-Medical Institute in Cincinnati, from which he earned his medical degree in 1846. He then moved to Philadelphia, where he began writing and lecturing on sexual topics. His work was based on a philosophy that human sexuality was an issue of predominant importance in individuals' lives, but that instruction in the topic was virtually absent in the lives of most men and women.

One of the most controversial aspects of Hollick's public lectures was his use of a papier-mâché model of a woman's body. He used the model to display and explain the parts of her reproductive system and how they were involved in the act of intercourse and reproduction. At first, his talks caused uneasiness and discomfort among his audiences, although they eventually gained approval from many women because of their answering fundamental questions about sexuality which they had never been taught.

Hollick also wrote three books dealing with human sexuality that, like his lectures, received both strong opposition and enthusiastic support from various parts of society. The books were *The Diseases of Woman, Their Causes and Cure Familiarly Explained: With Practical Hints for Their Prevention and for the Preservation of Female Health* (1847), *The Marriage Guide, or, Natural History of Generation* (1860), and *The Origin of Life and Processes of Reproduction in Plants and Animals* (1878). It was *The Marriage Guide*, with its unvarnished discussions about the facts of pregnancy and reproduction, that was of greatest interest and concern among his readers.

By the mid-1840s, Hollick's work had become sufficiently aggravating for public officials in Philadelphia that he was charged with offenses against public decency, primarily because of the use of the papier-mâché woman in his lectures. He was accused of lectures that bordered on pornographic because of his stark presentations. He was found innocent of those charges but was arrested and charged a second time on similar complaints. Hollick failed to show up for the second trial, became disillusioned about his experiences in Philadelphia, and moved to New York City. Little is known about Hollick's work in New York or the circumstances of his death in 1900.

Kaiser Family Foundation (KFF)

The Kaiser Family Foundation (KFF) is a nonprofit organization focusing on health-care issues in the United States and other parts of the world. It is an offshoot of the philanthropic works created by Henry J. Kaiser and his family over a period of more than 70 years. Kaiser was an American industrialist who made his fortune through the construction of Liberty Ships, cargo ships used during World War II for the movement of materiel needed in the war effort in all parts of the world. To support his shipbuilding activities, Kaiser also created other industrial entities, such as Kaiser Aluminum and Kaiser Steel. In 1945, Kaiser created Kaiser Permanente, a health-care program for employees of his companies. Today, Kaiser Permanente continues to operate in eight states and the District of Columbia, America's largest-managed care system.

KFF was itself created in 1948 to publish research, analysis, polling, and journalism about health-care issues. The role of the United States in developing global health policy is also a major interest of the organization. KFF is especially interested in health-care issues involving persons with low income and individuals who are especially vulnerable to health-care cost, such as the uninsured, those with chronic illnesses, or Medicaid/Medicare recipients. KFF was originally affiliated with Kaiser Permanente but since 1985 does not have any connection with that service.

KFF currently lists 10 areas of interest for its work: disparities policy, global health policy, health costs, health reform, HIV/AIDS, Medicaid, Medicare, private insurance, uninsured, and women's health policy. Specific items dealing with birth control can be found under all 10 of these categories, with women's health policy containing the most entries. Some topics included in this classification are the following:

Fact sheets on Oral Contraception, Emergency Contraception, Medicaid's Role for Women, the U.S. Government and International Family Planning & Reproductive Health: Statutory Requirements and Policies, Potential Impact of *Texas v. U.S. Decision* on Key Provisions of the Affordable Care Act, Sterilization as a Family Planning Method, Coverage of Gynecological Care and Contraception, How Does Where You Work Affect Your Contraceptive Coverage, Contraceptive Use and Methods in the U.S., and the U.S. Government and Global Health.

Reports on Dimensions of New Contraceptives: Norplant and Poor Women, Improving the Use of Contraceptives: The Challenge Continues, and Emergency Contraception in California—Survey Report.

News releases on New Brief Examines the Future of Contraceptive Coverage, Most State Medicaid Programs Cover Prescription Contraceptives, While Coverage of Over-the-Counter Contraceptives Varies, Poll Finds Most Americans Oppose the Trump Administration's Changes to Restrict Title X Family Planning Funds from Clinics That Also Provide or Refer for Abortion, and New Report Analyzes Health Insurance Coverage of Contraceptives.

Issue briefs on New Regulations Broadening Employer Exemptions to Contraceptive Coverage: Impact on Women, The Future of Contraceptive Coverage, Private Insurance Coverage of Contraception, State and Federal Contraceptive Coverage Requirements: Implications for

Women and Employers, and Ask KFF: Alina Salganicoff Answers 3 Questions on Final Title X Regulations for Family Planning Clinics.

Perspectives on Contraceptive-Only Plans: Questions and Answers, Insurance Coverage of Contraceptives, *Zubik v. Burwell*: Contraceptives, Religious Freedom and the Courts, and Health and the 2016 Election: Implications for Women.

Poll findings on Emergency Contraception in California, National Survey on Public Perceptions about Contraception, Women's Health Care Providers' Experiences with Emergency Contraception, National Survey on Public Knowledge and Attitudes on Contraception and Unplanned Pregnancy 1995, and Data Note: Differences in Public Opinion on the ACA's Contraceptive Coverage Requirement, by Gender, Religion, and Political Party.

One of KFF's most useful projects is Kaiser Health News (KHN), a nonprofit health newsroom whose articles are available at no cost at its web page, https://khn.org/. Some of its most recent articles are "Why Some CEOs Figure 'Medicare for All' Is Good for Business," "Legal Promise of Equal Mental Health Treatment Often Falls Short," "Mired in Medical Debt? Federal Plan Would Update Overdue-Bill Collection Methods," and "Did the ACA Create Preexisting Condition Protections for People in Employer Plans?" KHN also provides regular podcasts on health topics of interest, such as "Fetal Tissue Research Is Latest Flashpoint in Abortion Debate," "What Just Happened to the ACA and What Happens Now?," "Health Policy Goes to Court," and "Whither Work Requirements?"

Katharine McCormick (1875–1967)

Major scientific breakthroughs almost always occur because of the vigorous efforts of intelligent, committed scientists (or teams of scientists). But brains and perseverance are not enough to make those discoveries happen. Scientific research has long been an expensive activity that individuals and even small groups of researchers cannot pay for themselves. They need the funding of large corporations, benevolent charities, and/or governmental units (usually some agency of the federal government).

Such was the case in the early days of research on an oral contraceptive pill. At the time, such a device was regarded by funding agencies as a dangerous cause to be avoided at all costs. As of 1950, 30 states still had laws on their books restricting the distribution and use of contraceptives. Given that reputation, chemical corporations and governmental agencies would not even consider the possibility of funding the work of Gregory Pincus and his researchers at the Worcester Foundation for Experimental Biology (WFEB), where work on a possible new oral contraceptive pill was centered.

All that changed in 1953, when a woman by the name of Katharine McCormick came into a large fortune upon the death of her husband, then heir to the International Harvester company. McCormick met with her longtime friend, Margaret Sanger, to discuss the possibility of investing in Pincus's work at WFEB. At the first meeting between the two, McCormick wrote Pincus a check in the amount of $40,000, only the first step in her funding of about $2 million for that project over the next decade. (The exact data on funding amounts are the subject of some dispute.) Without that source of funding, Pincus's work might well have continued for many more years (or decades), with development of the new pill delayed by a similar period of time.

Katharine McCormick was born Katharine Dexter on August 27, 1875, in Dexter, Michigan. Her family moved to Chicago shortly thereafter, where she was raised and educated. Katharine's father was Wirt Dexter, a well-known and very successful attorney. When he died in 1889, Dexter left a considerable fortune to his son, who then died five years later. At that point, the fortune passed to Dexter's wife, Josephine, and to

Katharine. The two were able to live comfortably as members of the upper class for the rest of their lives.

In the meanwhile, Katharine had attended the Massachusetts Institute of Technology (MIT), from which she received her bachelor's degree in biology in 1904. In spite of their wealth, the Dexters had long believed in the value of education for their children and had convinced Katharine to pursue her college degree. At the same time, as members of the upper class, they expected her to find and marry a man with similar credentials. She did so in 1904, when she met and married Stanley Robert McCormick, the youngest son of Cyrus McCormick. The older McCormick had founded International Harvester in 1847 and rapidly realized substantial success. Upon his death in 1885, the International Harvester fortune passed to his son, Stanley. Katharine was thus in line for two very large inheritances upon the death of her husband.

That possibility seemed remote in 1904, however, when the young woman and man were married. But within two years, that situation changed. Stanley McCormick was diagnosed with schizophrenia and sent to a sanitarium in Montecito, California, where his sister had also been in residence for many years. In 1909, Stanley was declared mentally incompetent, and control of the International Harvester assets was transferred to Katharine and her mother. She spent much of the rest of her life funding research projects on mental disorders. For example, she founded the Neuroendocrine Research Foundation at Harvard Medical School in 1927 and funded publication of the journal *Endocrinology* (which had been founded in 1938).

After the original research on the pill had been completed, McCormick turned her attention to other projects. In 1962, for example, she paid for the construction of a new dormitory for women at her alma mater, MIT. The institution had long justified its failure to admit many women because it had inadequate housing facilities for them. McCormick's donation solved that problem. Six years later she made a second donation for another dormitory, both of which became known as

Stanley McCormick halls. She also made a substantial donation to the Santa Barbara Museum of Art that allowed the institution to construct the Stanley McCormick Gallery in 1942. Upon her death in Boston on December 28, 1967, she left a bequest in the amount of $5 million to Stanford University School of Medicine for the support of the education of women physicians and an additional $5 million to Planned Parenthood Federation of America, which used the money to build the Katharine Dexter McCormick Library in New York City. She also left a million dollars to the WFEB and a half million dollars to the Chicago Art Institute.

Gregory Pincus (1903–1967)

Among the many contributions made by Margaret Sanger to the early birth control movement was her vision of a "magic pill" that women could take to avoid pregnancy. She had heard of primitive societies around the world that had discovered herbal products that could be used for such a purpose. And she hoped that the American scientific community could eventually discover a synthetic product that could achieve a similar result. But her hopes for a magic pill remained unfulfilled for more than two decades.

Then, in 1951, a chance encounter at a dinner party in London changed the trajectory of that search. Sanger was introduced to American biologist Gregory Pincus, who had been working since the early 1930s on the mammalian reproductive system. Among his breakthroughs was one of the first successful uses of in vitro fertilization to produce a baby rabbit. His discovery made headlines in several of the nation's newspapers and magazines. The *New York Times* and *Colliers* magazine both characterized his research by calling him Dr. Frankenstein. And the general public reacted with concern, at least partly because Pincus's research was conducted at about the same time that Aldous Huxley's *Brave New World* was published (1932). To many people, the horrors described in Huxley's book appeared to be just around the corner because of Pincus's research. These reactions were too much for Harvard University, where Pincus was then serving as assistant professor of biology. He was not offered a new contract, and his professional career appeared to be over.

Quite the opposite was true, although the road to his greatest success was not an easy one. When he met Sanger, she described to him her hope for a magic pill. "Do you think," she asked him, "it would be possible to develop an efficient contraceptive that would be easy to take, for example, a cheap pill?" ("Margaret Sanger and the Pill." 2012. Margaret Sanger Papers Project. https://sangerpapers.wordpress.com/2012/11/21/margaret-sanger-and-the-pill/. Accessed on June 8, 2019). Such a project sounded like a dream come true to Pincus, since it fell neatly within the rubric of his ongoing research hopes: the role of hormones in the process of reproduction among mammals.

By that time, Pincus had moved from Harvard to Clark University, in Worcester, Massachusetts, where he had cofounded the WFEB. Sanger's project sounded like a perfect fit for his new institution except for one problem: he didn't have enough money to begin such a project. Sanger herself solved that problem for Pincus in 1952 when she introduced Pincus to Sanger's friend and philanthropist Katharine McCormick, heir to the International Harvester fortune. A year later, McCormick pledged a donation of $100,000 a year for research on the pill, later to be increased to $180,000 annually. Her total contribution to the WFEB project was in excess of $2 million.

Within a year, Pincus and his research team developed a pill ready to be tested among humans. By 1957, that pill had been approved by the U.S. Food and Drug Administration (FDA), although not for contraceptive use. That step occurred three years later when the FDA added that use of the pill to its approval decision. Sanger's magic pill had at last become a reality.

Gregory Goodwin Pincus was born in Woodbine, New Jersey, on April 9, 1903. His father was a graduate of Storrs

(Connecticut) Agricultural College, teacher, and editor of a farm journal. His mother came from a family also involved in agricultural research and teaching. Pincus at one time credited this familial background in agriculture to his own interest in biology. He attended both elementary and high school in New York City, where he served as president of both the literary and debating clubs at Morris High School. He then enrolled at Cornell where he earned his bachelor's degree in agriculture in 1924. While at Cornell, he founded and edited the *Cornell Literary Review*.

Pincus was accepted by Harvard University for his graduate studies. There he was awarded his MS and ScD degrees in genetics in 1927. He then continued his studies at Cambridge University in England and the Kaiser Wilhelm Institute for Biology in Berlin. In 1930, he accepted an appointment as instructor in general physiology at Harvard, after which he was promoted to assistant professor in 1931.

Having lost his job at Harvard, Pincus began searching for a new position, no small task in the midst of the Great Depression. In 1938, however, he was offered a position as visiting professor of experimental zoology at Clark University in Worcester, Massachusetts. He held that post until 1945, by which time the WFEB had become sufficiently successful for him to devote all of his time there. From 1946 to 1950 Pincus also held the title of titular professor of physiology at Tufts University and, from 1950 to his death in 1967, a similar post at Boston University. (The title means "in name only," awarded Pincus simply to allow his students at WFEB to work for their doctoral degrees at Tufts or Boston at the institute rather than those universities.)

Pincus received a number of honors and awards for his research, including the Oliver Bird Prize (1957), the Albert D. Lasker Award in Planned Parenthood (1960), the Sixth Annual Julius A. Koch Award (1962), the Modern Medicine Award for Distinguished Achievement (1964), the City of Hope National Medical Center Award (1964), the Cameron Prize in Practical

Therapeutics from the University of Edinburgh (1966), and the Scientific Achievement Award of the American Medical Association (1967). He was also awarded an honorary professorship by the San Marcos University, Lima, Peru. He was elected a fellow of the American Academy of Arts and Sciences (1939), a member of the National Academy of Sciences (1965), and president of the Endocrine Society (1951–1952). Pincus died of a rare blood disease, myeloid metaplasia, in Boston on August 22, 1967.

Planned Parenthood

The Planned Parenthood Federation of America, more commonly known simply as Planned Parenthood, is a 501(c)(3) tax-exempt corporation that provides reproductive health services through more than 600 clinics in the United States. The organization had its origins in the earliest days of the birth control movement in this country. In 1916, birth control pioneer Margaret Sanger, along with her sister and registered nurse, Ethel Byrne, and fellow activist, feminist, and translator, Fania Mindell, opened the nation's first birth control clinic in the Brownsville section of Brooklyn, New York.

The clinic distributed a pamphlet describing its work, saying, "Mothers! Can you afford to have a large family? Do you want any more children? If not, why do you have them? Do not kill, Do not take life, but Prevent. Safe, Harmless Information can be obtained of trained Nurses at 46 Amboy Street . . . All Mothers Welcome" ("Flyer for 46 Amboy Street Birth Control Clinic," Sophia Smith Collection, Smith College, N.Y., n.d. https://sangerpapers.wordpress.com/tag/brownsville-clinic/. Accessed on June 6, 2019). About 140 women visited the clinic on the first day it was open, and attendance jumped to more than 450 women at the end of the first week.

The clinic was, however, illegal since existing federal law prohibited the description and/or distribution of any form of contraceptive device or method. Sanger and her companions were arrested, charged, and convicted of violating these laws. Their case went on for months, with Sanger ending up with a 30-day sentence in the local workhouse prison. The publicity accompanying these trials made the Brownsville clinic even better known and more popular among the lower-class population of the area. By 1921, Sanger had decided to create a nationwide project with goals similar to those of the Brownsville clinic, the American Birth Control League. It was created as a joint effort of several state birth control groups in British Columbia, Colorado, Connecticut, Indiana, Massachusetts, Michigan, Ohio, and Pennsylvania. By 1941, the League had 222 centers that served nearly 50,000 clients. A year later, the organization adopted its new name, the Planned Parenthood Federation of America.

Today, Planned Parenthood clinics offer a variety of reproductive health services. Testing and treatment for sexually transmitted infections constitute the large portion of those services, accounting for 48.7 percent of all clinic activities. Other services include contraception (27.1 percent of all services), cancer screening and prevention (6.3 percent), abortion services (3.4 percent), and other women's health and miscellaneous services (13.4 percent and 1.1 percent, respectively). Altogether, Planned Parenthood provided about 9.6 million discrete sessions for about 2.4 million women visiting its clinics in 2017.

In 1952, at a meeting in Bombay (now Mumbai), India, Planned Parenthood was one of the founding organizations of the International Planned Parenthood Federation. Today that organization has 134 associate members in 134 countries in addition to 26 partner organizations located in 21 additional countries. In 2017, the organization provided a total of 208.6 million discrete reproductive health services to its clients. The organization's most recent annual report is available at https://www.ippf.org/sites/default/files/2018-07/APR2017_WEB.pdf.

Planned Parenthood also carries out a program of political action through a separate arm, the Planned Parenthood Action

Fund. The purpose of that entity is to ensure that reproductive health services are available to all who need them by promoting laws that promote such services and fighting against laws that tend to reduce access. Specific activities sponsored by the organization include developing and implementing programs to educate and organize the general public; inform and mobilize voters on issues related to reproductive health; lobby for federal, state, and local policies that ensure access to health care; work for political candidates who advocate for reproductive rights; and stand in solidarity with social justice partners to fight against hate and discrimination.

Legal and political activities are also a major part of the agendas of state chapters of Planned Parenthood. One of the most famous court cases involving reproductive health issues in the United States was *Planned Parenthood v. Casey*, in which the Southeast Pennsylvania chapter of Planned Parenthood filed suit against Pennsylvania governor Robert Casey that resulted in striking down state law requiring women to notify their husbands of their plans to have an abortion. Other state cases include *Planned Parenthood of Central Missouri v. Danforth* (1976), involving various aspects of state law with regard to reproductive health; *Planned Parenthood Association of Kansas City v. Ashcroft* (1983), concerning threats made to abortion doctors made by protestors; *Ayotte v. Planned Parenthood of Northern New England* (2006), regarding parental notification policies in the state of New Hampshire; *Box v. Planned Parenthood of Indiana and Kentucky* (2018), asking for reconsideration of an Indiana law limiting abortion on the basis of sex, race, color, disability, or other factors; and *Planned Parenthood of Greater Ohio. v. Hodges* (2019), responding to a state law preventing the state from providing any federal funds to any agency that provides abortion services.

From the moment of its creation in 1916, Planned Parenthood, in all its manifestations, has been the subject of strong opposition among certain elements of society. In many cases, these objections have been expressed in the form of reasoned debate and discussion about topics such as the beginning of life, the role of contraception in birth control, and the legitimacy of abortion as a method of birth control. In other cases, opponents have made use of more violent ways of expressing their objections to Planned Parenthood services. In one report, the National Abortion Federation noted that, since 1977, there had been 176,000 instances of picketing at Planned Parenthood clinics (with 34,000 arrests); 16,000 cases of hate mail to clinics; 1,500 cases of vandalism; 400 death threats; and 200 bombings. Among the most extreme of these measures have been the murder and wounding of clinic employees, such as Dr. David Gunn (1993), Dr. John Bayard Britton (1994), Dr. Barnett Slepian (1998), and Dr. George Tiller (2009), as well as other clinic employees and police officers killed as incidental victims in such acts.

Power to Decide

In 2017, an exciting new website dealing with unintended pregnancies among teens appeared on the Internet, Power to Decide, except that it wasn't really all that new. Power to Decide was the new name for an organization that had existed since 1996: The National Campaign to Prevent Teen and Unplanned Pregnancy or, more simply, The National Campaign. The goal of the organization was to reduce the rate of teenage pregnancy by one-third by 2005. It decided on a two-pronged effort to achieve that goal: (1) to create and develop a grassroots movement to better educate men and women of all ages about the problems of unplanned pregnancies among teens and (2) to change cultural values about teenage pregnancy by working with the media, religious groups, and other influential organizations in society. The campaign achieved significant success in this effort, distributed 10 million pieces of informational material and hosted more than 30 million viewers on its web page. The organization also created a National Day to Prevent Teen Pregnancy on May 7 annually, accompanied by the National Day Quiz about teen pregnancy.

Power to Decide has essentially continued the traditional activities of The National Campaign. Its new long-term goals are to reduce teen pregnancy by 50 percent by 2026; to reduce pregnancy among women aged 18–29 by 25 percent during the same period; and to reduce disparities among racial, ethnic, socioeconomic, and other groups by 25 percent by 2026. An important new feature of Power to Decide's work is called Select360, a consulting service that provides "customized support to help build innovative solutions at the national, state, and local levels so that we can continue to ensure that young people have what they need to decide their futures" (The National Campaign Announces New Select360 Consulting Services. 2017. Cision. https://www.prweb.com/releases/2017/10/prweb14808798.htm. Accessed on June 7, 2019). The elements of Select360 are as follows:

One Key Question, which helps professionals who work with teenagers to respond effectively to the question as to if, when, and under what circumstances young women want to get pregnant. The program has currently been adopted by health-care workers and social service providers in 30 states at the local, state, regional, and national levels.

Strategic Communications & Audience Management, which takes advantage of The National Campaign/Power to Decide's long history of creating and implementing methods of reaching out to and educating a diverse range of organizations important in dealing with unplanned pregnancies. The program involves methods such as working with entertainment and other forms of mass media, online and on-air advertising, and social marketing campaigns.

Program Design & Measurement, a campaign to help individuals and organizations build their own programs for dealing with teen pregnancy issues. Examples of such programs are Better Birth Control, Campus Sexual Health, and Family Court Systems.

Policy & Advocate Strategy makes use of experts in a variety of fields to help clients develop state and national strategies for dealing with issues of teenage pregnancy.

Licensed Content includes access to the organization's vast database of materials on teenage pregnancy, such as methods of birth control, first-person stories and videos, animated cartoons, news segments, photographs and videos, and a large database of statistics.

Two of the organization's subsidiary units of special interest are Bedsider and Stay Teen. The former program has been described as the "girlfriend's guide" to information about birth control. The goal of Bedsider is "to help women find the method of birth control that's right for them, to learn how to use birth control consistently and effectively, and to gradually encourage women to consider using more effective forms of birth control over time" (Select360 Counseling. 2019. Power to Decide. https://powertodecide.org/select360-consulting#tab-1. Accessed on June 7, 2019). Stay Teen is designed to be a complete source of information about all things related to birth control, with separate sections on advice, sex, relationships, myths versus facts, and abstinence. Other sections of the website contain clever illustrated explanations of birth control–related topics, games and quizzes, and a section called "Ask Us Anything," the questions and answers for which are changed on a regular basis. An important feature of the Power to Decide website is its summary of polling on birth control issues. Some polls recently reviewed cover the topics of unplanned pregnancy and the zika virus, the role of trust among teenagers and adults, attitudes of adult Americans about advances in birth control, and levels of support for various birth control programs.

Margaret Sanger (1879–1966)

Sanger is arguably the most famous person associated with the birth control movement in the United States in the mid-20th century. She is said to have come to her interest in the topic when her mother died at the age of 50 as a result of bearing 11 children. Some records state that she accused her father of her mother's death prior to the latter's funeral when she said, "You caused this. Mother is dead from having too many children" ("People and Events. 2001." PBS. http://www.shoppbs.pbs .org/wgbh/amex/pill/peopleevents/p_sanger.html. Accessed on August 12, 2019).

Sanger was born Margaret Louis Higgins on September 14, 1879, in Corning, New York. Her father was Michael Hennessey Higgins, who had emigrated to the United States from Ireland when he was 14 years of age. He served as a drummer in the Civil War a year later and briefly considered becoming a doctor. Instead, he took up masonry. Sanger's mother, Ann Purcell Higgins, had also emigrated from Ireland during the Great Potato Famine of 1845–1849. She eventually became pregnant 18 times over a period of 22 years, delivering 11 live children, the sixth of whom was Margaret.

Sanger attended St. Mary's grade school in Corning. In 1895, her sisters Mary and Anna then scraped together enough money to send her to a boarding school, Claverack College and Hudson River Institute. A Dutch Protestant institution, Claverack's aim was to provide training in moral, physical and social development. Sanger was forced to leave Claverack in 1897, prior to her graduation, in order to care for her mother, already suffering from exhaustion and tuberculosis. After her mother's death, she was able to resume her education, this time at the White Plains Hospital, in Westchester, New York, where she earned her nursing degree in 1902. In the same year, she met and married her husband, architect William Sanger. The two were to work together in the birth control movement during the rest of their lives together.

For nearly a decade, the Sangers lived a comfortable life in a house built by William in Hastings-on-Hudson, New York. In 1910, however, they abandoned that lifestyle to move to New York and become active in the city's progressive movement.

Margaret took a job as nurse in a slum neighborhood and soon became interested in the host of health issues her clients faced there. A chance occasion during the period began to change the focus of her work. She was asked by a friend to fill in for a lecturer unable to fulfill a speaking commitment to a small group of members of the Socialist Party. At the last minute, she decided to change the topic of her lecture from labor to health issues. When she was asked to give a follow-up speech on the topic, her audience increased from 10 to 75.

By this time, Sanger had begun a vigorous program of self-education on birth control issues and sharing her newfound knowledge with those who needed it most: poor women looking for relief from their often never-ending series of pregnancies, miscarriages, and childbirth. In 1912, she began writing a series of columns for the *New York Call* newspaper on "What Every Mother Should Know." Most of her work was constrained, however, by the nefarious Comstock Laws of 1873, which prohibited the distribution of birth control information and devices. In 1916, she decided to test these laws by opening a birth control clinic, the first one in the United States, in the Brownsville section of Brooklyn. Nine days into the clinic's operation, Sanger was arrested and charged for distributing "obscene materials" under the Comstock Laws. She was found guilty, assessed a fine, and released. She then returned to the clinic, where she was arrested and charged again. This event resulted in a court hearing, *People v. Sanger*, in which she was found guilty once again and sentenced to 30 days in the Queens County Penitentiary. This pattern of intentional breaking of the law, arrest, and conviction was repeated a total of eight times in Sanger's career.

Sanger's legal problems did not interfere with her increasingly aggressive efforts to make birth control available to women who needed it most in New York. In the midst of her first trial, for example, she started publishing a new magazine called *Birth Control Review*, which focused not on birth control methodology but on the birth control movement. She also wrote a book on the role of birth control as a part of the women's rights movement, published at the end of the trial. In 1921, she founded the American Birth Control League, a predecessor of the modern-day Planned Parenthood organization.

Almost certainly the most serious blot on Sanger's career was her embrace of the eugenics movement. A popular philosophy at the time, eugenics was an idea that the quality of the human race could be greatly improved by the government's controlling those individuals who should be allowed to reproduce and those who should be prevented from doing so, even if it had to be done involuntarily. This goal could be achieved by preventing the reproduction of the mentally and physically disabled. The list of scientists, researchers, and other individuals supporting and promoting eugenics in the first third of the 20th century is impressive. And at the peak of the movement's history, more than 30 states had laws permitting eugenic programs. In what must almost certainly have seemed like a praiseworthy objective for the birth control movement, Sanger also became a fervent supporter of eugenics. At one point, for example, she recommended "a stern and rigid policy of sterilization and segregation to that grade of population whose progeny is tainted, or whose inheritance is such that objectionable traits may be transmitted to offspring" (Margaret Sanger. 1932. "My Way to Peace." https://www.nyu.edu/projects/sanger/webedition/app/documents/show.php?sangerDoc=129037.xml. Accessed on June 4, 2019).

In 1936, Sanger became involved in one of the classic court cases about contraception in U.S. history: *United States v. One Package of Japanese Pessaries*. In that case, the court ruled that the government could not interfere with the shipment of contraceptive materials ordered and/or shipped by a qualified physician. With that issue resolved, Sanger decided to move to Tucson, Arizona, and discontinue her work in the birth control movement. She was not very successful in that objective, continuing to write and speak on the topic even in her new Tucson home. Perhaps her most important achievement toward the end of her life was her role in the development of the first oral contraceptive pill, a goal achieved in 1960. She died six years later, on September 6, 1966, at her home in Tucson.

Sexuality Information and Education Council of the United States (SIECUS)

SIECUS was founded in 1964 by Dr. Mary Calderone and a group of like-minded activists in the field of human sexuality. At the time, Calderone was medical director of Planned Parenthood. She and her cofounders created the new organization because of their concern that both adults and adolescents were not getting enough accurate information about sexuality. They took as their guiding principle the fact that "sexuality is a fundamental part of being human, one worthy of dignity and respect." They chose as part of their mission to "ensure social justice inclusive of sexual and reproductive rights" ("About Us." 2019. SIECUS. https://siecus.org/about-siecus/. Accessed on June 5, 2019). Other founding members of the organization were Wallace Fulton, Reverend William Genne, Lester Kirkendall, Dr. Harold Lief, and Clark Vincent.

In January 1965, SIECUS held a press conference in New York City to announce its creation, followed a month later by publication of its first newsletter, *SIECUS Newsletter*. Within a matter of weeks, there were more than 1,000 requests for the newsletter, the majority of educational institutions (349) and physicians (250). The organization also published its first three study guides on sexuality, on the topics of homosexuality, masturbation, and sex education. It had also received a grant from the U.S. Office of Education to convene a national conference on "Sex, the Individual, and Society: Implications for Education." With each new year, SIECUS added another achievement to its list of accomplishments: its first text for professionals, *The Individual, Sex, and Society* in 1969; its first national conference, "New Findings in Human Sexuality" in 1970; and study guides in 14 areas of human sexuality in 1971.

By 1972, SIECUS had also expanded its newsletter into a full professional journal, *SIECUS Reports.*

From it very beginnings, SIECUS was the subject of intense attack by conservative and religious organizations, such as the Christian Crusade, Focus on the Family, the John Birch Society, Moral Majority, Family Research Council, and special interests groups such as Sanity on Sex, Mothers for Moral Stability, and People against Unconstitutional Sex Education. Objections were raised about both the content of the SIECUS program and the very concept of sex education in schools itself. At one point, for example, Robert Welch, founder of the John Birch Society, called the idea of sex education in schools "a filthy Communist plot." (For more on this topic, see Luther G. Baker. 1969. "The Rising Furor over Sex Education." *The Family Coordinator.* 18(3): 210–217.) These attacks, while a distraction from SIECUS's work, did not in the end impede its everyday efforts to promote education about human sexuality.

A major change in SIECUS's focus came in the mid-1980s with the growth of the HIV/AIDS epidemic. The organization was one of the most active in providing information on the disease and its impact on everyday life in America. Its first article on the disease "What Does AIDS Mean?" appeared in the November 1982 issue of *SIECUS Reports.* It also published the first national bibliography on AIDS education in 1984 and the first pamphlet for adults who were counseling their children about the disease a year later. Also in 1984, SIECUS joined with Gay Men's Health Crisis to sponsor a conference in New York City on "AIDS and Sexuality: A Dialogue."

Comprehensive sex education has also been an ongoing major concern of SIECUS. One of its most accomplishments in this area came in 1990 when SIECUS convened a meeting of the National Guidelines Task Force, a group of experts in the field of sex education. The task force eventually produced a report, *Guidelines for Comprehensive Sexuality Education— Kindergarten—12th Grade*, released in 1991. The guidelines included suggested ways in which communities could develop new sex education programs and/or evaluate existing programs. The four major elements of such programs were providing accurate information about sexuality, helping young people develop positive attitudes about sexuality, learning skills of communication about topics relating to sexuality, and guiding young people in making good choices on sexual matters.

Today, SIECUS's work is focused on eight major topics: sex education, cultural competency in sex education, consent and healthy relationships, sexual and reproductive health, unintended pregnancy, sexual orientation and gender identity, sexual rights, and abstinence. This work is described and summarized in a variety of formats, including fact sheets, policy briefings, state profiles, technical assistance, and other types of publications. For example, the state profiles are published annually and provide information on state laws and policies, data on sexual health and behavior, and federal funding for programs in the states. (For the most recent profiles, see https://siecus .org/state-profiles-2018/.) The organization's publications fall into three general categories: historical publications (33 volumes of articles, opinion pieces, and other works from 1972 through 2005); standards and guidelines; and special reports. (For a list of publications, see https://siecus.org/publications/.) The SIECUS website also contains a valuable collection of articles on topics of current interest, such as reauthorization of the PREP program, abortion laws in states, new administrative rules by the Trump administration, sex education as a vehicle for racial justice, sexual abuse of migrant children, and government policies for trans people.

Marie Stopes (1880–1958)

Marie Charlotte Carmichael Stopes was a paleobotanist, author, birth control advocate, and women's rights activist. She was born on October 15, 1880, in Edinburgh, Scotland, to Henry Stopes and Charlotte Carmichael Stopes. Her mother was a Shakespearean scholar and an activist for women's suffrage, and her father was an architect, brewer, and amateur paleontologist. He gained considerable fame in the last of these categories, having collected and classified the largest collection of artifacts available in Great Britain at the time. The couple had met at a meeting of the British Association for the Advancement of Science, of which they were both members.

The Stopes left Scotland when Marie was only six weeks old, moving first to Colchester, in England, and then to London. At first, she was home-schooled but later attended St. George's School for Girls, in Edinburgh, and the North London Collegiate School. In 1900, she matriculated at the University of London, where she gained first-class honors in botany and geology in her first year. She was then awarded her BSc a year later. After a year of research in the London area, Stopes entered the University of Munich, where she earned her PhD in 1904. She then returned to England, where she was granted her DSc in paleobotany from University College London, the youngest person ever to have earned a doctorate in the country.

Stopes continued her research and teaching at University College London until 1920 and the University of Manchester from 1904 to 1910. She was in demand by various governmental agencies to conduct studies of specific topics of geological interest. In 1907, for example, Stopes visited Japan where she spent 18 months at Tokyo's Imperial University. There she conducted a study of fossilized plants extracted from coal mines on the northern island of Hokkaido. A second expedition took place in 1910, when the Canadian government commissioned her to conduct a study of the Fern Ledges at St. John, New Brunswick. There was a controversy as to the exact dating of the structure, and Stopes was chosen to resolve the issue. While working in Canada, she met her future husband, Reginald Gates. The couple was married in England in 1911, but the marriage was annulled a year later on the basis of Gates's impotence.

During this period, Stopes published several books and articles on various subjects in her field, including *Botany, or, the*

Modern Study of Plants (1912); *Catalogue of the Mesozoic Plants in the British Museum (Natural History): The Cretaceous Flora: Part I–II* (1913); *The "Fern Ledges" Carboniferous Flora of St. John, New Brunswick* (1914); and *On the Four Visible Ingredients in Banded Bituminous Coal: Studies in the Composition of Coal* (1918). She also wrote about her nongeological experiences in Japan in books on various cultural topics, such as *A Journal from Japan* (1910); *Plays of Old Japan* (1913); and *Plays of Old Japan: The "No"* (1927).

Stopes's unhappy marriage caused her to begin thinking about a topic far removed from her field of paleobotany: the nature of sex in human relationships. Her interest in the topic became so intense that by 1920 she had largely abandoned her professional activities in geology to write, speak, and work on behalf of birth control issues. The first fruit of that effort was a book she published in 1918, *Married Love*. She had actually completed the book five years earlier but had been unable to find a publisher willing to print the manuscript. The book proved to be an instant success, going through five editions in its first year. She then followed up with a second book in the same year, *Wise Parenthood: A Book for Married People*. A year later, she published an abbreviated version of *Married Love*, a 16-page pamphlet "A Letter to Working Mothers on How to Have Healthy Children and Avoid Weakening Pregnancies." The pamphlet was offered at no charge to less affluent women and couples who had previously largely been ignored by birth control advocates.

Stopes's "radical" ideas about birth control produced controversy, even hysteria, among health-care professionals and many ordinary citizens who were repulsed by discussions of such a "dirty" topic. That debate carried over into her own life when she delivered a stillborn child in 1919, an event for which she blamed her doctor's unwillingness to follow her own instincts about methods of delivery.

By 1920, Stopes had become committed to the birth control movement and resigned her post at University College

London. She and her second husband, Humphrey Verdon Roe, decided to pursue an effort of considerable interest to both of them: a birth control clinic for poor women in London. Roe had attempted to establish such an entity for a number of years but had been unable to find a sponsor for the clinic. By 1920, Stopes had decided to create an organization, the Society for Constructive Birth Control and Racial Progress, around which to rally support for the clinic. Those efforts were eventually successful, and the Mothers' Clinic for Constructive Birth Control was opened in London in 1921. The clinic was open only to married women and did not perform abortions, largely because of Stopes's and Roe's objections to the procedure. Lacking such an option, Stopes became even more interested in contraceptive methods that could be taught to women who visited the clinic.

A peak in the controversy over Stopes's work came in 1922 when British physician Halliday Sutherland published *Birth Control: A Statement of Christian Doctrine against the Neo Malthusians*. In his book, Sutherland tied Stopes, her work, and her birth control movement to the science of eugenics. He argued that birth control was just another way of trying to winnow out the poor and lower class by limiting their rate of reproduction. He specifically referred to Stopes as "a doctor of German philosophy" who was imposing on her clients "the most harmful method [of contraception] of which I have had experience" ("Marie Stopes." 2019. Genetic Matrix. https://www.geneticmatrix.com/stopes-marie-human-design-chart.html. Accessed on August 12, 2019). Stopes sued Sutherland for libel, a case she lost in the first court in which it was heard. She then appealed and won a judgment against Sutherland. Sutherland then took the case to the House of Lords, where he won once again. Some years later, the controversy was renewed when it was Sutherland this time who sued Stopes for libel in an article she wrote for her newsletter *Birth Control News*. This time it was Sutherland who lost the case.

The Sutherland battles, those with other opponents, and the work of the clinic itself proved a burden for Stopes, and in 1923 she purchased a home on the Isle of Portland, Dorset. There she was able to renew her work on paleobotany and eventually founded the Portland Museum, which specialized not only in paleobotanical objects but also in archeological topics, shipwrecks, and the history of the island itself. Stopes died on October 2, 1948, at her home in Dorking, Surrey. She left her clinic assets to the Eugenics Society.

5   Data and Documents

Data

Table 5.1   Current Contraceptive Status among Women Aged 15–49: United States, 2015–2017. Percentage Currently Using Any Contraceptive Method. *This table provides a summary of the percentage of women between the ages of 15 and 49 using any type of contraception by age, race, and educational level.*

Characteristic	Number (1000s)	Percentage
Total	72,218	64.9
Age group (years)		
15–19	9,454	37.2
20–29	21,334	61.9
30–39	21,079	72.0
40–49	20,351	73.7
Hispanic origin and race		
Hispanic	14,597	64.0
Non-Hispanic white	40,662	67.0
Non-Hispanic black	9,715	59.9
Education		
No high school diploma or GED*	5,589	75.6
High school diploma or GED	13,336	70.3
Some college, no bachelor's degree	18,529	68.2
Bachelor's degree or higher	21,677	70.2

*general education diploma

Source: Daniels, Kimberly, and Joyce C. Abma. 2018. "Current Contraceptive Status among Women Aged 15–49: United States, 2015–2017." Data Brief 327. National Center for Health Statistics. https://www.cdc.gov/nchs/data/databriefs/db327-h.pdf. Accessed on April 16, 2019.

Health Education teacher Leticia Jenkins speaks to her class of ninth graders at James Monroe High School in North Hills, California, on May 18, 2018. (Frederic J. Brown/AFP/Getty Images)

Table 5.2 Percentage Distribution of Women Aged 15–49, by Current Contraceptive Status: United States, 2015–2017.

This table provides a summary of the fraction of women using each of several types of contraceptive methods over the period 2015–2017.

Characteristic	Percentage
All women	100
Not using contraception	35.1
Surgically sterile—female (noncontraceptive)	0.2
Nonsurgically sterile—female or male	2.5
Pregnant or postpartum	3.7
Seeking pregnancy	3.8
Other nonuse	
Never had intercourse	10.2
No intercourse in three months before interview	6.8
Had intercourse in three months before interview	7.9
Using contraception	64.9
Female sterilization	18.6
Male sterilization	5.9
Oral contraceptive pill	12.6
Long-acting reversible contraception	10.3
Intrauterine device	7.9
Implant	2.3
Three-month injectable (Depo-Provera)	2.1
Contraceptive ring or patch	1.2
Diaphragm	0.0
Condom	8.7
Periodic abstinence—calendar rhythm	1.3
Periodic abstinence—natural family planning	0.2
Withdrawal	3.9
Other methods	0.2

Source: Daniels, Kimberly, and Joyce C. Abma. 2018. "Current Contraceptive Status among Women Aged 15–49: United States, 2015–2017." Data Brief 327. National Center for Health Statistics. https://www.cdc.gov/nchs/data/databriefs/db327-h.pdf. Accessed on April 16, 2019.

Table 5.3   Condom Use in the United States by Certain Characteristics, 2011–2015.
This table lists the frequency with which certain groups of individuals used condoms over the period from 2011 to 2015.

Characteristic	Number[1]	Used a Condom with a Partner for Sexual Intercourse				
		Every Time	Most of the Time	About Half the Time	Some of the Time	None of the Time
		Percentage Distribution				
All women aged 15–44						
Total, 2002	48,777	12.9	9.4	4.3	12.2	61.2
Total, 2006–2010	48,964	15.9	9.1	3.9	13.5	57.6
Total, 2011–2015	48,211	14.8	9.0	3.8	12.6	59.9
Age group (years)						
15–19	3,697	35.6	23.0	7.6	18.0	15.7
20–24	8,357	17.9	14.4	5.3	20.6	41.8
25–44	36,157	11.9	6.2	3.1	10.2	68.6
25–34	17,379	12.8	8.0	3.4	13.1	62.7
35–44	17,379	10.9	4.3	2.7	7.1	74.9
Education						
No high school diploma or GED	4,228	12.6	6.4	2.6	8.5	69.9
High school diploma or GED	9,948	10.5	5.0	3.4	10.9	70.3
Some college, no bachelor's degree	12,622	11.6	7.2	3.7	11.7	65.7
Bachelor's degree or higher	14,449	14.3	7.8	3.4	12.3	62.3
Hispanic origin and race						
Hispanic or Latina	9,564	14.9	9.4	4.4	12.1	59.3

(Continued)

Table 5.3 Continued

Characteristic	Number[1]	Used a Condom with a Partner for Sexual Intercourse				
		Every Time	Most of the Time	About Half the Time	Some of the Time	None of the Time
		Percentage Distribution				
Not Hispanic or Latina						
White, single race	27,491	13.3	7.8	3.5	12.8	62.6
Black or African American, single race	4,654	20.8	11.2	4.7	12.8	50.4
Relationship with last sexual partner at last sex						
Cohabiting, engaged, or married	16,951	10.1	4.4	2.7	10.4	72.4
Going with him or going steady	4,459	25.8	15.4	7.3	19.7	31.7
Casual relationship[2]	2,427	26.7	20.0	6.9	20.0	26.5
Number of opposite-sex sexual partners in past 12 months						
One partner	41,718	14.4	7.2	3.0	10.3	65.1
Two or more partners	6,493	16.8	20.4	8.9	27.7	26.3
All men aged 15–44						
Total, 2002	48,249	nd	Nd	nd	nd	nd
Total, 2006–2010	48,541	nd	Nd	nd	nd	nd
Total, 2011–2015	47,782	19.0	14.4	5.2	14.1	47.3
Age group (years)						
15–19	3,947	53.5	20.5	8.3	10.8	6.9
20–24	7,941	29.5	27.4	7.4	15.4	20.4
25–44	35,893	13.0	10.9	4.4	14.1	57.7
25–34	18,431	16.2	14.2	5.9	17.6	46.1
35–44	17,463	9.4	7.5	2.8	10.4	70.0

Education

No high school diploma or GED	5,293	11.8	8.4	4.1	15.2	60.4
High school diploma or GED	11,668	13.0	12.7	5.0	14.3	54.9
Some college, no bachelor's degree	12,078	16.3	15.4	4.2	13.4	50.8
Bachelor's degree or higher	11,897	15.9	12.7	5.7	14.0	51.7

Hispanic origin and race

Hispanic or Latino	10,107	20.5	15.0	5.0	15.6	43.8

Not Hispanic or Latino

White, single race	27,026	17.2	12.9	5.2	12.5	52.3
Black or African American, single race	6,010	22.1	20.8	5.0	17.0	35.1

Relationship with last sexual partner at last sex

Cohabiting, engaged, or married	31,141	8.9	8.7	3.7	14.2	64.5
Going with her or going steady	8,967	35.9	22.3	8.4	16.3	17.1
Casual relationship[2]	7,047	41.5	29.2	7.7	10.7	10.9

Number of opposite-sex sexual partners in past 12 months

One partner	38,381	16.3	10.2	4.1	13.3	56.0
Two or more partners	9,401	29.9	31.6	9.7	16.9	11.9

n.d., no data.

[1] In thousands.

[2] Going out once in a while/just friends/had just met him.

Source: Copen, Casey E. 2017. "Condom Use during Sexual Intercourse among Women and Men Aged 15–44 in the United States: 2011–2015 National Survey of Family Growth." National Health Statistics Report. https://www.cdc.gov/nchs/data/nhsr/nhsr105.pdf. Accessed on April 17, 2019.

Table 5.4 Reported Abortions, by Known Age Group and Year, United States, 2006–2015.*
This table summarizes the percentage of women of various age groups who had abortions over the period from 2006 to 2015.

Age Group	2006	2007	2008	2009	2010	2011	2012	2013	2014	2015
<15	0.5	0.5	0.5	0.5	0.5	0.4	0.4	0.3	0.3	0.3
15–19	16.5	16.5	16.1	15.5	14.6	13.5	12.2	11.4	10.4	9.8
20–24	32.7	32.7	32.7	32.7	32.9	32.9	32.8	32.7	32.1	31.1
25–29	24.1	24.2	24.4	24.4	24.5	24.9	25.4	25.9	26.8	27.6
30–34	14.2	14.1	14.3	14.8	15.3	15.8	16.4	16.8	17.2	17.7
35–39	8.8	8.8	8.8	8.8	8.9	8.9	9.1	9.2	9.7	10.0
≥40	3.1	3.2	3.1	3.3	3.4	3.6	3.7	3.6	3.6	3.6

*Percentage of all abortions.
Source: "Abortion Surveillance—United States, 2015." *Surveillance Summaries.* November 23, 2018. 67(13): 1–45, Table 4.

Table 5.5 Reported Abortions, by Known Weeks of Gestation and Year (Percentage).
This table reports on the known number of abortions by time of gestation for females of age less than 13 years to more than 21 years.

Weeks of Ges- tation	Year									
	2006	2007	2008	2009	2010	2011	2012	2013	2014	2015
≤13	91.5	91.5	91.5	91.9	91.9	91.5	91.4	91.6	91.0	91.0
≤8	63.5	63.7	64.2	65.3	65.9	65.7	65.8	65.9	64.8	65.4
9–13	28.0	27.8	27.3	26.6	26.0	25.8	25.6	25.7	26.2	25.6
>13	8.4	8.5	8.5	8.2	8.2	8.5	8.6	8.5	9.0	9.0
14–15	3.3	3.4	3.4	3.3	3.3	3.4	3.5	3.4	3.5	3.5
16–17	1.8	1.9	1.9	1.8	1.8	1.8	1.9	1.9	2.2	2.1
18–20	1.9	1.9	1.9	1.8	1.8	1.9	1.9	1.9	1.9	2.0
≥21	1.4	1.3	1.3	1.3	1.3	1.3	1.3	1.3	1.4	1.4
Total (number)	536,848	530,632	533,302	510,891	501,176	474,584	449,983	429,825	418,587	407,877

Source: Jatlaoui, Tara C., et al. "Abortion Surveillance—United States, 2015." 2018. *MMWR Surveillance Summaries*. 67(No. SS-13): 1–45, Table 8. https://www.cdc.gov/mmwr/volumes/67/ss/ss6713a1.htm#T8_down. Accessed on April 30, 2019.

Table 5.6   Reasons for Having Sterilization as a Method of Birth Control.

This table lists reasons for a woman's having an abortion as reported by both women and men.

Sterilization (Female)

Reason (Women's Responses)	2006–2010	2011–2015
She had all the children she wanted	63.7%	66.6%
Her husband or partner had all the children he wanted	4.5%	6.9%
Medical reasons for the tubal ligation	23.8%	21.5%
Problems with other methods of birth control	3.0%	1.7%
Some other reason	5.1%	3.3%

Source: "Sterilization (Female)." 2017. National Center for Health Statistics. https://www.cdc.gov/nchs/nsfg/key_statistics/s.htm#sterilizationfemale. Accessed on April 30, 2019.

Sterilization (Male)

Reason (Men's Responses)	2002	2006–2010	2011–2015
She had all the children she wanted	47.0%	38.8%	40.2%
Her husband or cohabiting partner had all the children he wanted	36.4%	42.3%	38.1%
Medical reasons	5.0%	4.8%	12.1%
Problems with other methods of birth control	0.5%	3.1%	1.5%
Some other reason	11.1%	11.1%	8.1%

Source: "Vasectomy." 2017. National Center for Health Statistics. https://www.cdc.gov/nchs/nsfg/key_statistics/v.htm#prevalence. Accessed on April 30, 2019.

Table 5.7   Percentage of Schools in Which Teachers Taught Specific Human Sexuality Topics as Part of Required Instruction, by School Level.

This table summarizes the relative amount of attention given to 18 possible topics in a sex education class at elementary-, middle-, and high-school levels.

Topic	Total	Elementary Schools	Middle Schools	High Schools
Abstinence as the most effective method to avoid pregnancy, HIV, and other STDs	37.0	7.2	49.6	76.3
Condom efficacy (i.e., how well condoms work and do not work)	46.2	NA	26.7	65.7
Dating and healthy relationships	35.3	5.4	48.8	73.8

(Continued)

Table 5.7 Continued

Topic	Total	Elementary Schools	Middle Schools	High Schools
How students can influence, support, or advocate for others to make healthy decisions related to sexual behaviors	32.3	3.9	44.8	69.4
How to correctly use a condom	22.8	NA	10.4	35.3
How to obtain condoms	33.6	NA	17.0	50.3
Human development issues (e.g., reproductive anatomy and puberty)	39.5	20.6	45.3	66.4
Marriage and commitment	27.9	6.1	29.7	64.0
Resisting peer pressure to engage in sexual behavior	35.5	6.4	46.8	74.8
Risks associated with having multiple sexual partners	55.8	NA	38.5	73.2
Sexual identity and sexual orientation	36.5	NA	21.5	51.5
Social or cultural influences on sexual behavior	30.0	1.5	41.4	68.3
The importance of using a condom at the same time as another form of contraception to prevent both STDs and pregnancy	40.4	NA	25.9	54.9
The importance of using condoms consistently and correctly	39.4	NA	19.0	59.9
The influence of families on sexual behavior	27.0	1.5	36.6	61.7
The influence of peers on sexual behavior	34.9	6.6	45.0	74.3
The influence of the media on sexual behavior	32.4	5.6	42.6	68.8
The relationship among HIV, other STDs, and pregnancy	33.2	3.6	44.3	73.5
The relationship between alcohol or other drug use and risk for HIV, other STDs, and pregnancy	34.1	3.8	44.7	76.1

NA, question not asked in elementary school.

Source: "Results from the School Health Policies and Practices Study 2014." 2015. U.S. Department of Health and Human Services. Centers for Disease Control and Prevention, Table 1.19. https://www.cdc.gov/healthyyouth/data/shpps/pdf/shpps-508-final_101315.pdf. Accessed on May 8, 2019.

Documents

Comstock Law of 1873

One of the most important events in the history of birth control in the United States occurred in the adoption by the U.S. Congress of the Comstock Act in 1873. That act made it illegal to use the U.S. Postal Service to transmit material on several topics, including contraceptives, abortion, sexual toys, and any other subject related to birth control. The law applied to all interstate traffic as well as traffic within the District of Columbia and U.S. territories. It was soon followed, however, by "little Comstock Laws" in most of the individual states. The act was a clear expression of the attitudes of the American people (or, at least, their elected representatives) on the evils of birth control practice in the nation. The Comstock Act was later expanded, with more severe penalties, before losses in the courts began to chip away at its effectiveness. (For example, the act was amended in 1909 to include traffic by railroad and other "express" methods of delivery.) Although many little Comstock Laws remain on the books in some states today, and it has never officially been repealed at the federal level, it no longer has any practical effect on birth control devices and information today.

CHAP. CCLVIII.—An Act for the Suppression of Trade in, and Circulation of, obscene Literature and Articles of immoral Use.

Be it enacted by the Senate and House of Representatives of the United Penalty for, in States of America in Congress assembled, That whoever, within the District of Columbia or any of the Territories of the United States, or other place within the exclusive jurisdiction of the United States, shall sell, or the United States, lend, or give away, or in any manner exhibit, or shall offer to sell, or to lend, or to give away, or in any manner to exhibit, or shall otherwise publish or offer to publish in any manner, or shall have in his possession, for any such purpose or purposes, any obscene book, pamphlet, paper, writing, advertisement, circular, print, picture, drawing or other representation, figure, or image on or of paper or other material, or any cast, instrument, or other article of an immoral nature, or any drug or medicine, or article whatever, for the prevention of conception, or for causing unlawful abortion, or shall advertize the same for sale, or shall write or print, or cause to be written or printed, any card, circular, book, pamphlet, advertisement, or notice of any kind, stating when, where, how, or of whom, or by what means, any of the articles in this section hereinbefore mentioned, can be purchased or obtained, or shall manufacture, draw, or print, or in any wise make any of such articles, shall be deemed guilty of a misdemeanor, and, on conviction thereof in any court of the United States having criminal jurisdiction in the District of Columbia, or in any Territory or place within the exclusive jurisdiction of the United States, where such misdemeanor shall have been committed; and on conviction thereof, he shall be imprisoned at hard labor in the penitentiary for not less than six months nor more than five years for each offense, or fined not less than one hundred dollars nor more than two thousand dollars, with costs of court.

Source: *An Act for the Suppression of Trade in, and Circulation of, Obscene Literature and Articles of Immoral Use.* March 3, 1873, ch. 258, § 2, 17 Stat. 599.

United States v. One Package of Japanese Pessaries (1936)

The Comstock Law of 1873 and succeeding amendments and court actions placed a powerful ban on the transmission of contraceptive information through the U.S. mail, by railroad, and by other means. The law was extraordinarily effective for nearly 60 years, with courts largely upholding the law's provisions and, in some cases, extending those provisions. The first real success in ameliorating the effects of the law came in 1936, when the United States Court of Appeals for the Second Circuit ruled that shipments of contraceptive materials and information from doctors and/or to doctors did not violate the law. The case arose when

Dr. Hannah Stone, working at one of Margaret Sanger's birth control clinics, requested and received a shipment of a new type of diaphragm from a Japanese physician. Federal officials seized the shipment, declaring it was a violation of the Comstock Act. Dr. Hannah sued the government in an effort to overturn its actions in the case and was successful at the lower court level. When the government appealed to the court of appeals, that judgment was affirmed, largely resulting in the first major breakthrough in opposition to Comstock provisions. The court's decision was written by Judge Augustus Noble Hand, who wrote the following (asterisks as in original).

The question is whether physicians who import such articles as those involved in the present case in order to use them for the health of their patients are excepted by implication from the literal terms of the statute. Certainly they are excepted in the case of an abortive which is prescribed to save life, for section 305 (a) of the Tariff Act only prohibits the importation of articles for causing "unlawful abortion." This was the very point decided in *Bours v. United States*, 229 F. 960 (C.C.A.7), where a similar statute (Cr.Code, § 211 [18 U.S.C.A. § 334 and note]) declaring nonmailable "every article or thing designed, adapted, or intended for preventing conception or producing abortion, or for any indecent or immoral use," was held not to cover physicians using the mails in order to say that they will operate upon a patient if an examination shows the necessity of an operation to save life. And this result was reached even though the statute in forbidding the mailing of any article "intended for * * * producing abortion" did not, as does section 305(a) of the Tariff Act, qualify the word "abortion" by the saving adjective "unlawful."

. . .

It is true that in 1873, when the Comstock Act was passed, information now available as to the evils resulting in many cases from conception was most limited, and accordingly it is argued that the language prohibiting the sale or mailing of contraceptives should be taken literally and that Congress intended to bar the use of such articles completely. While we may assume that section 305(a) of the Tariff Act of 1930 (19 U.S.C.A. § 1305(a)) exempts only such articles as the act of 1873 excepted, yet we are satisfied that this statute, as well as all the acts we have referred to, embraced only such articles as Congress would have denounced as immoral if it had understood all the conditions under which they were to be used. Its design, in our opinion, was not to prevent the importation, sale, or carriage by mail of things which might intelligently be employed by conscientious and competent physicians for the purpose of saving life or promoting the well being of their patients. The word "unlawful" would make this clear as to articles for producing abortion, and the courts have read an exemption into the act covering such articles even where the word "unlawful" is not used. The same exception should apply to articles for preventing conception. While it is true that the policy of Congress has been to forbid the use of contraceptives altogether if the only purpose of using them be to prevent conception in cases where it would not be injurious to the welfare of the patient or her offspring, it is going far beyond such a policy to hold that abortions, which destroy incipient life, may be allowed in proper cases, and yet that no measures may be taken to prevent conception even though a likely result should be to require the termination of pregnancy by means of an operation. It seems unreasonable to suppose that the national scheme of legislation involves such inconsistencies and requires the complete suppression of articles, the use of which in many cases is advocated by such a weight of authority in the medical world.

Source: *United States v. One Package of Japanese Pessaries*, 86 F.2d 737 (2d Cir. 1936).

Griswold v. Connecticut (1965)

By the mid-1950s, the Comstock Law (1873) had become little more than a historic artifact in the story of contraceptive use in the United States. Although it had not been officially repealed by the U.S. Congress, the law had essentially lost its effectiveness as a result of court rulings. In addition, only two states, Massachusetts and Connecticut, had retained "little Comstock Laws" on their books, although they were hardly ever enforced. Griswold v. Connecticut *arose when Planned Parenthood League of Connecticut opened a birth control clinic in New Haven on November 1, 1961. Clinic director Estelle Griswold and resident gynecologist C. Lee Buxton were arrested, tried, convicted, and fined $100 each. They appealed their case to the Appellate Division of the Circuit Court and the Connecticut Supreme Court, losing at both levels. They then appealed to the U.S. Supreme Court, which overturned the lower courts' rulings by a 7–2 vote. The key issue underlying the decision was whether the U.S. Constitution includes a "right to privacy" provision for U.S. citizens. The Constitution contains no clear, specific statement of such a right, but Justice William O. Douglas, writing for the majority, said that such a right was present in certain "penumbras" and "emanations" to be found in other parts of the document. Concurring and dissenting opinions by other justices indicated that that issue was not enthusiastically supported, although there was sufficient agreement to rule in favor of the appellants. (Omitted references are indicated by triple asterisks, ***.)*

The association of people is not mentioned in the Constitution nor in the Bill of Rights. The right to educate a child in a school of the parents' choice—whether public or private or parochial—is also not mentioned. Nor is the right to study any particular subject or any foreign language. Yet the First Amendment has been construed to include certain of those rights.

By *Pierce v. Society of Sisters, supra,* the right to educate one's children as one chooses is made applicable to the States by the force of the First and Fourteenth Amendments. By *Meyer v. Nebraska, supra,* the same dignity is given the right to study the German language in a private school. In other words, the State may not, consistently with the spirit of the First Amendment, contract the spectrum of available knowledge. The right of freedom of speech and press includes not only the right to utter or to print, but the right to distribute, the right to receive, the right to read ***, and freedom of inquiry, freedom of thought, and freedom to teach (***)—indeed the freedom of the entire university community. *** Without those peripheral rights the specific rights would be less secure.

. . .

The foregoing cases suggest that specific guarantees in the Bill of Rights have penumbras, formed by emanations from those guarantees that help give them life and substance. ***. Various guarantees create zones of privacy. The right of association contained in the penumbra of the First Amendment is one, as we have seen. The Third Amendment in its prohibition against the quartering of soldiers "in any house" in time of peace without the consent of the owner is another facet of that privacy. The Fourth Amendment explicitly affirms the "right of the people to be secure in their persons, houses, papers, and effects, against unreasonable searches and seizures." The Fifth Amendment in its Self-Incrimination Clause enables the citizen to create a zone of privacy which government may not force him to surrender to his detriment. The Ninth Amendment provides: "The enumeration in the Constitution, of certain rights, shall not be construed to deny or disparage others retained by the people."

. . .

The present case, then, concerns a relationship lying within the zone of privacy created by several fundamental constitutional guarantees. And it concerns a law which, in forbidding the use of contraceptives rather than regulating their manufacture or sale, seeks to achieve its goals by means having a maximum destructive impact upon that relationship. Such a law cannot stand in light of the familiar principle, so often applied by this Court, that a "governmental purpose to control or prevent activities constitutionally subject to state regulation may not be achieved by means which sweep unnecessarily broadly and thereby invade the area of protected freedoms."

*** Would we allow the police to search the sacred precincts of marital bedrooms for telltale signs of the use of contraceptives? The very idea is repulsive to the notions of privacy surrounding the marriage relationship. We deal with a right of privacy older than the Bill of Rights—older than our political parties, older than our school system. Marriage is a coming together for better or for worse, hopefully enduring, and intimate to the degree of being sacred. It is an association that promotes a way of life, not causes; a harmony in living, not political faiths; a bilateral loyalty, not commercial or social projects. Yet it is an association for as noble a purpose as any involved in our prior decisions.

Reversed.

Source: *Griswold v. Connecticut*, 381 U.S. 479 (1965).

Title X of the Public Health Service Act of 1970

After a century of promoting a program of opposition to birth control services in the United States, the U.S. Congress in 1970 finally adopted some of the earliest and most consequential legislation dealing with the topic. In that year, President Richard M. Nixon submitted to the Congress his plan for a Public Health Service with a wide range of duties and responsibilities. Among those charges was the creation of a program for financial support of family planning programs for low-income and other unserved members of the U.S. population. Those provisions were collected largely in Title X of the act and are summarized here.

Project Grants and Contracts for Family Planning Services

SEC. 1001. [300] (a) The Secretary is authorized to make grants to and enter into contracts with public or nonprofit private entities to assist in the establishment and operation of voluntary family planning projects which shall offer a broad range of acceptable and effective family planning methods and services (including natural family planning methods, infertility services, and services for adolescents). To the extent practicable, entities which receive grants or contracts under this subsection shall encourage family participation in projects assisted under this subsection.

. . .

Formula Grants to States for Family Planning Services

SEC. 1002. [300a] (a) The Secretary is authorized to make grants, from allotments made under subsection (b), to State health authorities to assist in planning, establishing, maintaining, coordinating, and evaluating family planning services. No grant may be made to a State health authority under this section unless such authority has submitted, and had approved by the Secretary, a State plan for a coordinated and comprehensive program of family planning services.

. . .

Training Grants and Contracts

SEC. 1003. [300a–1] (a) The Secretary is authorized to make grants to public or nonprofit private entities and to enter into contracts with public or private entities and individuals to provide the training for personnel to carry out family planning service programs described in section 1001 or 1002.

. . .

Research

SEC. 1004. [300a-2] The Secretary may—

(1) conduct, and
(2) make grants to public or nonprofit private entities and enter into contracts with public or private entities and individuals for projects for,

research in the biomedical, contraceptive development, behavioral, and program implementation fields related to family planning and population.

. . .

Informational and Educational Materials

SEC. 1005. [300a–3] (a) The Secretary is authorized to make grants to public or nonprofit private entities and to enter into contracts with public or private entities and individuals to assist in developing and making available family planning and population growth information (including educational materials) to all persons desiring such information (or materials).

Source: Population Research and Voluntary Family Planning Programs, Title X, Public Health Service Act. Public Law 91-572 (1970).

Eisenstadt v. Baird (1972)

The most recent case of consequence to the Comstock Law of 1873 was Eisenstadt v. Baird, *decided by the U.S. Supreme Court in 1972. The case involved an action taken by William Baird, sometimes referred to as the "father" of the birth control movement in the United States, after a lecture at Boston University. Baird offered a condom and a package of contraceptive foam to a 19-year-old student in order to be arrested under Massachusetts law prohibiting the distribution of birth control devices to unmarried women or men. Baird was arrested, as he expected, and eventually found guilty of violating the state law by the Massachusetts Supreme Judicial Court. He appealed to the U.S. Supreme Court and, in 1972, the early decision was reversed. In his opinion, Justice William J. Brennan Jr. explained that the court's ruling was based on the Equal Protection Clause of the U.S. Constitution, which guaranteed the same rights to all individuals, regardless of (among others) their marital status. The court voted 6–1 (with two empty seats) in favor of the decision. (Omitted citations are indicated by triple asterisks, ***.)*

1. If, as the Court of Appeals held, the statute under which appellee was convicted is not a health measure, appellee may not be prevented, because he was not an authorized distributor, from attacking the statute in its alleged

discriminatory application to potential distributees. Appellee, furthermore, has standing to assert the rights of unmarried persons denied access to contraceptives because their ability to obtain them will be materially impaired by enforcement of the—[sic] statute. ***

2. By providing dissimilar treatment for married and unmarried persons who are similarly situated, the statute violates the Equal Protection Clause of the Fourteenth Amendment. ***.

   (a) The deterrence of fornication, a 90-day misdemeanor under Massachusetts law, cannot reasonably be regarded as the purpose of the statute, since the statute is riddled with exceptions making contraceptives freely available for use in premarital sexual relations and its scope and penalty structure are inconsistent with that purpose. ***

   (b) Similarly, the protection of public health through the regulation of the distribution of potentially harmful articles cannot reasonably be regarded as the purpose of the law, since, if health were the rationale, the statute would be both discriminatory and overbroad, and federal and state laws already regulate the distribution of drugs unsafe for use except under the supervision of a licensed physician. ***

   (c) Nor can the statute be sustained simply as a prohibition on contraception per se, for whatever the rights of the individual to access to contraceptives may be, the rights must be the same for the unmarried and the married alike. If under Griswold, supra, the distribution of contraceptives to married persons cannot be prohibited, a ban on distribution to unmarried persons would be equally impermissible, since the constitutionally protected right of privacy inheres in the individual, not the marital couple. If, on the other hand, Griswold is no bar to a prohibition on the distribution of contraceptives, a prohibition limited to unmarried persons would be underinclusive and invidiously discriminatory.

Source: *Eisenstadt v. Baird*, 405 U.S. 438 (1972).

Roe v. Wade (1973)

Probably the single most important court case dealing with birth control issues in the United States was Roe v. Wade, *a case decided by the U.S. Supreme Court on January 22, 1973. The case was brought on behalf of Norma McCorvey, who, for purposes of the case, was referred to as Jane Roe. It arose out of McCorvey's efforts to obtain an abortion in Texas which, at the time, allowed abortions only in the case of rape or incest. Proponents of a woman's right to obtain an abortion selected this case as a test of the state and the nation's abortion laws. Those laws were generally restrictive, allowing abortions only under such extreme conditions as rape, incest, or severe health issues for the pregnant woman. The court ultimately decided that the Fourteenth Amendment of the U.S. Constitution contained an implicit right to privacy for all Americans and that that right to privacy validated a woman's choice to have an abortion. At the same time, the Court recognized that states have a legitimate interest in "safeguarding health, in maintaining medical standards, and in protecting potential life." The Court resolved this conflict by prohibiting bans on abortion during the first two trimesters of pregnancy but allowing states to impose appropriate restrictions on an abortion during the third trimester. Relevant portions of the court's decision are as follows:*

To summarize and to repeat:

1. A state criminal abortion statute of the current Texas type, that excepts from criminality only a lifesaving procedure on behalf of the mother, without regard to pregnancy stage and

without recognition of the other interests involved, is violative of the Due Process Clause of the Fourteenth Amendment.

(a) For the stage prior to approximately the end of the first trimester, the abortion decision and its effectuation must be left to the medical judgment of the pregnant woman's attending physician.

(b) For the stage subsequent to approximately the end of the first trimester, the State, in promoting its interest in the health of the mother, may, if it chooses, regulate the abortion procedure in ways that are reasonably related to maternal health.

(c) For the stage subsequent to viability, the State in promoting its interest in the potentiality of human life may, if it chooses, regulate, and even proscribe, abortion except where it is necessary, in appropriate medical judgment, for the preservation of the life or health of the mother.

. . .

This holding, we feel, is consistent with the relative weights of the respective interests involved, with the lessons and examples of medical and legal history, with the lenity of the common law, and with the demands of the profound problems of the present day. The decision leaves the State free to place increasing restrictions on abortion as the period of pregnancy lengthens, so long as those restrictions are tailored to the recognized state interests. The decision vindicates the right of the physician to administer medical treatment according to his professional judgment up to the points where important state interests provide compelling justifications for intervention. Up to those points, the abortion decision in all its aspects is inherently, and primarily, a medical decision, and basic responsibility for it must rest with the physician. If an individual practitioner abuses the privilege of exercising proper medical judgment, the usual remedies, judicial and intra-professional, are available.

[In support of its stand on a person's right to privacy, the Court cited an opinion by Mr. Justice John Marshall Harlan in Griswold v. Connecticut *in 1965:]*

"[T]he full scope of the liberty guaranteed by the Due Process Clause cannot be found in or limited by the precise terms of the specific guarantees elsewhere provided in the Constitution. This 'liberty' is not a series of isolated points pricked out in terms of the taking of property; the freedom of speech, press, and religion; the right to keep and bear arms; the freedom from unreasonable searches and seizures; and so on. It is a rational continuum which, broadly speaking, includes a freedom from all substantial arbitrary impositions and purposeless restraints . . . and which also recognizes, what a reasonable and sensitive judgment must, that certain interests require particularly careful scrutiny of the state needs asserted to justify their abridgment."

Source: *Roe v. Wade*, 410 U.S. 113 (1973).

Carey v. Population Services International (1977)

This case involves a challenge to a New York State law dealing with the sale and advertising of contraceptives in the state. The law specifically prohibited

(1) the sale or distribution of any contraceptive of any kind to a minor under the age of 16 years;

(2) the distribution of contraceptives by anyone other than a licensed pharmacist to any person 16 years of age or older; and

(3) the advertising or display of contraceptives by any entity, including licensed pharmacists.

The law was challenged by a North Carolina—based company, Population Services International, which advertised its products in New York and sold them to residents of the state, without regard to the age of the purchaser. The U.S. Supreme Court found the New York law to be unconstitutional for the reasons given here.

. . .

2. Regulations imposing a burden on a decision as fundamental as whether to bear or beget a child may be justified only by compelling state interests, and must be narrowly drawn to express only those interests.

3. The provision prohibiting distribution of nonmedical contraceptives to persons 16 or over except through licensed pharmacists clearly burdens the right of such individuals to use contraceptives if they so desire, and the provision serves no compelling state interests. It cannot be justified by an interest in protecting health insofar as it applies to nonhazardous contraceptives or in protecting potential life, nor can it be justified by a concern that young people not sell contraceptives, or as being designed to serve as a quality control device or as facilitating enforcement of the other provisions—of the statute.

4. The prohibition of any advertisement or display of contraceptives that seeks to suppress completely any information about the availability and price of contraceptives cannot be justified on the ground that advertisements of contraceptive products would offend and embarrass those exposed to them and that permitting them would legitimize sexual activity of young people. These are classically not justifications validating suppression of expression protected by the First Amendment, and here the advertisements in question merely state the availability of products that are not only entirely legal but constitutionally protected.

Source: *Carey v. Population Services International*, 431 U.S. 678 (1977).

Hyde Amendment (1976, et seq.)

One long-standing principle of birth control supported by the U.S. Congress is opposition to the spending of any federal funds for any aspect of abortion. The principle was first expressed in a bill introduced by Representative Henry Hyde (R-IL) on September 30, 1976. The bill was proposed as a response by the Congress to the U.S. Supreme Court's decision on abortion as expressed in Roe v. Wade *in 1973. The Hyde Amendment has been included in annual congressional appropriation bills in every Congress since its first passage in 1976. Wording of the amendment has changed somewhat over the years, primarily with regard to possible exceptions to the limitation. A recent version of the bill is as follows.*

SEC. 506. (a) None of the funds appropriated in this Act, and none of the funds in any trust fund to which funds are appropriated in this Act, shall be expended for any abortion.

(b) None of the funds appropriated in this Act, and none of the funds in any trust fund to which funds are appropriated in this Act, shall be expended for health benefits coverage that includes coverage of abortion.

(c) The term "health benefits coverage" means the package of services covered by a managed care provider or organization pursuant to a contract or other arrangement.

SEC. 507. (a) The limitations established in the preceding section shall not apply to an abortion—

(1) if the pregnancy is the result of an act of rape or incest; or

(2) in the case where a woman suffers from a physical disorder, physical injury, or physical illness, including a life-endangering physical condition caused by or arising from the pregnancy itself, that would, as certified by a physician, place the woman in danger of death unless an abortion is performed.

(b) Nothing in the preceding section shall be construed as prohibiting the expenditure by a State, locality, entity, or private person of State, local, or private funds (other than a State's or locality's contribution of Medicaid matching funds).

(c) Nothing in the preceding section shall be construed as restricting the ability of any managed care provider from offering abortion coverage or the ability of a State or locality to contract separately with such a provider for such coverage with State funds (other than a State's or locality's contribution of Medicaid matching funds).

(d)(1) None of the funds made available in this Act may be made available to a Federal agency or program, or to a State or local government, if such agency, program, or government subjects any institutional or individual health care entity to discrimination on the basis that the health care entity does not provide, pay for, provide coverage of, or refer for abortions.

(2) In this subsection, the term "health care entity" includes an individual physician or other health care professional, a hospital, a provider-sponsored organization, a health maintenance organization, a health insurance plan, or any other kind of health care facility, organization, or plan.

Source: "Consolidated Appropriations Act, 2018." 2018. Washington, DC: U.S. Government Printing Office. https://www.govinfo.gov/content/pkg/CPRT-115HPRT29457/pdf/CPRT-115HPRT29457.pdf. Accessed on April 17, 2019.

Hazelwood School District v. Kuhlmeier (1988)

An ongoing issue for young adults in the United States over recent decades has been the extent to which sexual issues, such as birth control, can be openly discussed in a school setting. The courts have

taken a variety of positions on this question, of which Hazelwood
v. Kuhlmeier *is one of the most famous. The case arose when school
principal Robert Eugene Reynolds prevented members of the staff of
the school newspaper,* Spectrum, *from including two articles in an
issue of the paper, one on pregnancy and one on divorce. A group of
the students involved sued the Hazelwood School Board for violating their First Amendment rights of free speech. The District Court
held for the school board, the Appeals Court for the students, and
the U.S. Supreme Court (in this decision) for the school board. The
role that sexual issues played a part in the Supreme Court's decision
is of interest not only for this but also for other related cases. (Triple
asterisks, ***, indicate omitted references.)*

From the majority:
We have nonetheless recognized that the First Amendment
rights of students in the public schools "are not automatically
coextensive with the rights of adults in other settings," ***, and
must be "applied in light of the special characteristics of the
school environment." *** A school need not tolerate student
speech that is inconsistent with its "basic educational mission,"
*** even though the government could not censor similar
speech outside the school. Accordingly, we held in Fraser that
a student could be disciplined for having delivered a speech
that was "sexually explicit" but not legally obscene at an official
school assembly, because the school was entitled to "disassociate itself" from the speech in a manner that would demonstrate
to others that such vulgarity is "wholly inconsistent with the
'fundamental values' of public school education."
. . .
Educators are entitled to exercise greater control over this second form of student expression to assure that participants learn
whatever lessons the activity is designed to teach, that readers or
listeners are not exposed to material that may be inappropriate
for their level of maturity, and that the views of the individual
speaker are not erroneously attributed to the school. Hence, a
school may in its capacity as publisher of a school newspaper or

producer of a school play "disassociate itself," *** not only from speech that would "substantially interfere with [its] work . . . or impinge upon the rights of other students," *** but also from speech that is, for example, ungrammatical, poorly written, inadequately researched, biased or prejudiced, vulgar or profane, or unsuitable for immature audiences. A school must be able to set high standards for the student speech that is disseminated under its auspices standards that may be higher than those demanded by some newspaper publishers or theatrical producers in the "real" world—and may refuse to disseminate student speech that does not meet those standards. In addition, a school must be able to take into account the emotional maturity of the intended audience in determining whether to disseminate student speech on potentially sensitive topics, which might range from the existence of Santa Claus in an elementary school setting to the particulars of teenage sexual activity in a high school setting. A school must also retain the authority to refuse to sponsor student speech that might reasonably be perceived to advocate drug or alcohol use, irresponsible sex, or conduct otherwise inconsistent with "the shared values of a civilized social order."

From the dissenting minority:

The case before us aptly illustrates how readily school officials (and courts) can camouflage viewpoint discrimination as the "mere" protection of students from sensitive topics. Among the grounds that the Court advances to uphold the principal's censorship of one of the articles was the potential sensitivity of "teenage sexual activity." *** Yet the District Court specifically found that the principal "did not, as a matter of principle, oppose discussion of said topi[c] in Spectrum." *** That much is also clear from the same principal's approval of the "squeal law" article on the same page, dealing forthrightly with "teenage sexuality," "the use of contraceptives by teenagers," and "teenage pregnancy," *** If topic sensitivity were the true basis of the principal's decision, the two articles should have been equally objectionable. It is much more likely that the objectionable article was objectionable because of the viewpoint it expressed: It might have been read (as the majority apparently does) to advocate "irresponsible sex."

Source: *Hazelwood School District v. Kuhlmeier*, 484 U.S. 260 (1988).

Planned Parenthood of Southeastern Pennsylvania v. Casey (1992)

Many of the issues surrounding birth control have their basis in the way female and male roles are traditionally defined. More specifically, women throughout history have been defined as inferior beings who owe at least their allegiance, and often their whole lives, to the man or men in their lives. It is hardly surprising, then, that some governmental entities have adopted legislation in the past that formalized this relationship on matters of birth control. As one frequently mentioned example, the state of Pennsylvania has long had a law on its books requiring a woman to notify her husband if she planned to have an abortion. She had to obtain written notice from him that she had his permission for the procedure, a document that had to be shown to the attending physician before the operation could be performed. In the case of Planned Parenthood of Southeastern Pennsylvania v. Casey, *decided by the U.S. Supreme Court in 1992, that provision of the law was found to be unconstitutional. The relevant portion of the court's decision in that case is as follows. (The law remains on the books in Pennsylvania, although it is no longer enforceable.) (Triple asterisks,* ***, *indicate the omission of certain citations.)*

There was a time, not so long ago, when a different understanding of the family and of the Constitution prevailed. In *Bradwell v. State*, 16 Wall. 130 (1873), three Members of this Court reaffirmed the common-law principle that "a woman had no legal existence separate from her husband, who was regarded as her head and representative in the social state; and, notwithstanding some recent modifications of this civil status, many of the special rules of law flowing from and dependent upon this cardinal principle still exist in full force in most States." *** Only one generation has passed since this Court observed that "woman is still regarded as the center of home and family life," with attendant "special responsibilities" that precluded full and independent legal status under the Constitution. *** These views, of course, are no longer consistent with our understanding of the family, the individual, or the Constitution.

In keeping with our rejection of the common-law understanding of a woman's role within the family, the Court held in Danforth that the Constitution does not permit a State to require a married woman to obtain her husband's consent before undergoing an abortion. *** The principles that guided the Court in Danforth should be our guides today. For the great many women who are victims of abuse inflicted by their husbands, or whose children are the victims of such abuse, a spousal notice requirement enables the husband to wield an effective veto over his wife's decision. Whether the prospect of notification itself deters such women from seeking abortions, or whether the husband, through physical force or psychological pressure or economic coercion, prevents his wife from obtaining an abortion until it is too late, the notice requirement will often be tantamount to the veto found unconstitutional in Danforth. The women most affected by this law—those who most reasonably fear the consequences of notifying their husbands that they are pregnant—are in the gravest danger.

The husband's interest in the life of the child his wife is carrying does not permit the State to empower him with this troubling degree of authority over his wife. The contrary view leads to consequences reminiscent of the common law. A husband has no enforceable right to require a wife to advise him before she exercises her personal choices. If a husband's interest in the potential life of the child outweighs a wife's liberty, the State could require a married woman to notify her husband before she uses a postfertilization contraceptive. Perhaps next in line would be a statute requiring pregnant married women to notify their husbands before engaging in conduct causing risks to the fetus. After all, if the husband's interest in the fetus' safety is a sufficient predicate for state regulation, the State could reasonably conclude that pregnant wives should notify their husbands before drinking alcohol or smoking. Perhaps married women should notify their husbands before using contraceptives or before undergoing any type of surgery that may have complications affecting the husband's interest in his wife's reproductive organs. And if a husband's interest justifies notice in any of these cases, one might reasonably argue that it justifies exactly what the Danforth Court held it did not justify—a requirement of the husband's consent as well. A State may not give to a man the kind of dominion over his wife that parents exercise over their children.

Section 3209 embodies a view of marriage consonant with the common-law status of married women but repugnant to our present understanding of marriage and of the nature of the rights secured by the Constitution. Women do not lose their constitutionally protected liberty when they marry. The Constitution protects all individuals, male or female, married or unmarried, from the abuse of governmental power, even where that power is employed for the supposed benefit of a member of the individual's family. These considerations confirm our conclusion that § 3209 is invalid.

Source: *Planned Parenthood of Southeastern Pennsylvania v. Casey,* 505 U.S. 833 (1992).

Abstinence-Only-Until-Marriage Education Funding (1996)

Some individuals and organizations have argued that the only certain method of birth control is abstinence and that that form of birth control is, therefore, the only one that governmental agencies should *recommend and support financially. As far back as 1981, the U.S. government had adopted that principle in its funding for birth control practices in the nation. The earliest of these actions occurred shortly after the inauguration of President Ronald Reagan, with adoption of the Adolescent Family Life Act. The act included provisions for grants to individual states for the promotion and practice of abstinence-only-until-marriage (AOUM). Some form of that act has been reintroduced and adopted ever since. Federal funding has ranged from as low as $9 million in 1997 to $177 million in 2008. Throughout this period of time, but more so at some than others, critics have pointed out that research on AOUM has clearly demonstrated that the program is ineffective in preventing teenage pregnancy and out-of-wedlock births. Yet the Congress continues to fund the program, with an allotment of $110 million in 2019 for AOUM projects. The following first excerpt summarizes the rationale and definition for AOUM, while the second excerpt contains a section from a recent effort to discontinue this program.*

"(b)(1) The purpose of an allotment under subsection (a) to a State is to enable the State to provide abstinence education, and at the option of the State, where appropriate, mentoring, counseling, and adult supervision to promote abstinence from sexual activity, with a focus on those groups which are most likely to bear children out-of-wedlock.

"(2) For purposes of this section, the term 'abstinence education' means an educational or motivational program which—

"(A) has as its exclusive purpose, teaching the social, psychological, and health gains to be realized by abstaining from sexual activity;

"(B) teaches abstinence from sexual activity outside marriage as the expected standard for all school age children;

"(C) teaches that abstinence from sexual activity is the only certain way to avoid out-of-wedlock pregnancy, sexually transmitted diseases, and other associated health problems;

"(D) teaches that a mutually faithful monogamous relationship in context of marriage is the expected standard of human sexual activity;

"(E) teaches that sexual activity outside of the context of marriage is likely to have harmful psychological and physical effects;

"(F) teaches that bearing children out-of-wedlock is likely to have harmful consequences for the child, the child's parents, and society;

"(G) teaches young people how to reject sexual advances and how alcohol and drug use increases vulnerability to sexual advances; and

"(H) teaches the importance of attaining self-sufficiency before engaging in sexual activity."

Source: "Public Law 104–193. 104th Congress." 1996. https://www.congress.gov/104/plaws/publ193/PLAW-104publ193.pdf. Accessed on April 17, 2019.

Real Education for Healthy Youth Act of 2017 (2017)

The following bill begins with a recitation of the role of abstinence education in health education programs for children and teenagers in the United States. It then concludes with provisions for repeal of the original legislation on the topic (Section 510 of the Social Security Act [42 U.S.C. 710 et seq.]).

A Bill

To provide for the overall health and well-being of young people, including the promotion of lifelong sexual health and healthy relationships, and for other purposes.

. . .

(c) SENSE OF CONGRESS.—It is the sense of Congress that—

> (1) federally funded sex education programs should aim to—
>
>> (A) provide information about a range of human sexuality topics, including—

. . .

>>> (ii) sexual behavior including abstinence;

. . .

> (2) CONTENTS OF COMPREHENSIVE SEX EDUCATION PROGRAMS.—The comprehensive sex education programs funded under this section shall include instruction and materials that address—

. . .

(d) abstinence, delaying age of first sexual activity, the use of condoms, preventive medication, vaccination, birth control, and other sexually transmitted infection prevention measures, and pregnancy, including—

> (i)   the importance of effectively using condoms, preventive medication, and applicable vaccinations to protect against sexually transmitted infections, including HIV;
>
> (ii)   the benefits of effective contraceptive and condom use in avoiding unintended pregnancy;
>
> (iii) the relationship between substance use and sexual health and behaviors; and
>
> (iv)   information about local health services where students can obtain additional information and services related to sexual and reproductive health and other related care;

. . .

(e) Authorized Activities.—

  (1) REQUIRED ACTIVITY.—Each eligible entity receiving a grant under this section shall use grant funds for professional development and training of relevant faculty, school administrators, teachers, and staff, in order to increase effective teaching of comprehensive sex education students.

  (2) PERMISSIBLE ACTIVITIES.—Each eligible entity receiving a grant under this section may use grant funds to—

    (A) provide research-based training of teachers for comprehensive sex education for adolescents as a means of broadening student knowledge about issues related to human development, healthy relationships, personal skills, and sexual behavior, including abstinence, sexual health, and society and culture;

. . .

(d) Reprogramming Of Abstinence Only Until Marriage Program Funding.—The unobligated balance of funds made available to carry out section 510 of the Social Security Act (42 U.S.C. 710) (as in effect on the day before the date of enactment of this Act) are hereby transferred and shall be used by the Secretary to carry out this Act. The amounts transferred and made available to carry out this Act shall remain available until expended.

(e) Repeal Of Abstinence Only Until Marriage Program.—Section 510 of the Social Security Act (42 U.S.C. 710 et seq.) is repealed.

Source: "S.1653—Real Education for Healthy Youth Act of 2017." 2017. Congress.gov. https://www.congress.gov/bill/115th-congress/senate-bill/1653/text. Accessed on April 17, 2019.

Affordable Care Act (and Subsequent Rules) (2010)

The U.S. Congress does not have a very strong record of support-ing birth control practices and programs in the nation. Possibly the most important exception to that history was adoption of the Affordable Care Act (ACA) of 2010, also known as "Obamacare" after President Barack H. Obama, who introduced the plan. Although the act itself said very little about requirements for the support of contraceptive practices, a series of rule-making activities based on the act did just that. An overview of those requirements is provided here. Following that excerpt, a section on certain excep-tions to the act is provided. These exceptions allow organizations with opposition to the contraceptive provisions in the ACA and later rules based on the act to be excused from abiding by those pro-visions. (The administration of President Donald Trump has taken a quite different view of this issue and has implemented significant changes in the original ACA rules.)

The Women's Preventive Services Initiative recommends that adolescent and adult women have access to the full range of female-controlled contraceptives to prevent unintended preg-nancy and improve birth outcomes. Contraceptive care should include contraceptive counseling, initiation of contraceptive use, and follow-up care (e.g., management, and evaluation as well as changes to and removal or discontinuation of the con-traceptive method). The Women's Preventive Services Initiative recommends that the full range of female-controlled U.S. Food and Drug Administration-approved contraceptive methods, effective family planning practices, and sterilization procedures be available as part of contraceptive care.

The full range of contraceptive methods for women currently identified by the U.S. Food and Drug Administration include: (1) sterilization surgery for women, (2) surgical sterilization via implant for women, (3) implantable rods, (4) copper intrauterine devices, (5) intrauterine devices with progestin (all durations and doses), (6) the shot or injection, (7) oral contraceptives (combined pill), (8) oral contraceptives (progestin only, and), (9) oral contraceptives (extended or continuous use), (10) the contraceptive patch, (11) vaginal contraceptive rings, (12) diaphragms, (13) contraceptive sponges, (14) cervical caps, (15) female condoms, (16) spermicides, and (17) emergency contraception (levonorgestrel), and (18) emergency contraception (ulipristal acetate), and additional methods as identified by the FDA. Additionally, instruction in fertility awareness-based methods, including the lactation amenorrhea method, although less effective, should be provided for women desiring an alternative method.

. . . *[Re: Exceptions]*

(1) These Guidelines do not provide for or support the requirement of coverage or payments for contraceptive services with respect to a group health plan established or maintained by an objecting organization, or health insurance coverage offered or arranged by an objecting organization, and thus the Health Resources and Service Administration exempts from any Guidelines requirements issued under 45 CFR 147.130(a)(1)(iv) that relate to the provision of contraceptive services:

    (i) A group health plan and health insurance coverage provided in connection with a group health plan to the extent the non-governmental plan sponsor objects as specified in paragraph (I)(a)(2) of this note. Such non-governmental plan sponsors include, but are not limited to, the following entities:

        (A) A church, an integrated auxiliary of a church, a convention or association of churches, or a religious order;

        (B) A nonprofit organization;

        (C) A closely held for-profit entity;

        (D) A for-profit entity that is not closely held; or

        (E) Any other non-governmental employer;

(ii) An institution of higher education as defined in 20 U.S.C. 1002 in its arrangement of student health insurance coverage, to the extent that institution objects as specified in paragraph (I)(a)(2) of this note. In the case of student health insurance coverage, section (I) of this note is applicable in a manner comparable to its applicability to group health insurance coverage provided in connection with a group health plan established or maintained by a plan sponsor that is an employer, and references to "plan participants and beneficiaries" will be interpreted as references to student enrollees and their covered dependents; and

(iii) A health insurance issuer offering group or individual insurance coverage to the extent the issuer objects as specified in paragraph (I)(a)(2) of this note. Where a health insurance issuer providing group health insurance coverage is exempt under this paragraph (I)(a)(1)(iii), the plan remains subject to any requirement to provide coverage for contraceptive services under these Guidelines unless it is also exempt from that requirement.

(2) The exemption of this paragraph (I)(a) will apply to the extent that an entity described in paragraph (I)(a)(1) of this note objects to its establishing, maintaining, providing, offering, or arranging (as applicable) coverage, payments, or a plan that provides coverage or payments for some or all contraceptive services, based on its sincerely held religious beliefs.

Source: "Women's Preventive Services Guidelines." 2016. Health Resources and Services Administration. https://www.hrsa.gov/womens-guidelines-2016/index.html. Accessed on April 16, 2019.

Burwell v. Hobby Lobby (2014)

The Affordable Care Act of 2010 recognized that some of its provisions, such as those dealing with contraception, might violate the religious, moral, philosophical, or other beliefs of individuals or corporations. Authors of the act included, therefore, provisions by which such entities could ask to be excluded from those provisions of the law. In fact, a whole section of the law deals with such instances (https://www.govinfo.gov/content/pkg/ FR-2017-10-13/pdf/2017-21851.pdf). The first major test of this part of the law came when a closely held private company, Hobby Lobby, contested the government's requirement that it provide the type of contraceptive coverage mentioned in the law. The Supreme Court agreed with the complainants, although it pointed out that its decision related specifically and exclusively to "closely held private corporations." The precedent set by the decision may, however, have broader implications for future court cases on similar issues. Some important elements of the Court's decision are provided here.

The Religious Freedom Restoration Act of 1993 (RFRA) prohibits the "Government [from] substantially burden[ing] a person's exercise of religion even if the burden results from a rule of general applicability" unless the Government "demonstrates that application of the burden to the person—(1) is in furtherance of a compelling governmental interest; and (2) is the least restrictive means of furthering that compelling governmental interest."

. . .

At issue here are regulations promulgated by the Department of Health and Human Services (HHS) under the Patient Protection and Affordable Care Act of 2010 (ACA), which, as relevant here, requires specified employers' group health plans to furnish "preventive care and screenings" for women without "any cost sharing requirements," 42 U. S. C.

§300gg—13(a)(4). Congress did not specify what types of preventive care must be covered; it authorized the Health Resources and Services Administration, a component of HHS, to decide.

. . .

[Some of the main points made in the Court's decisions are as follows:]

(1) HHS argues that the companies cannot sue because they are for-profit corporations, and that the owners cannot sue because the regulations apply only to the companies, but that would leave merchants with a difficult choice: give up the right to seek judicial protection of their religious liberty or forgo the benefits of operating as corporations.

. . .

(3) Finally, HHS contends that Congress could not have wanted RFRA to apply to for-profit corporations because of the difficulty of ascertaining the "beliefs" of large, publicly traded corporations, but HHS has not pointed to any example of a publicly traded corporation asserting RFRA rights, and numerous practical restraints would likely prevent that from occurring.

. . .

(b) HHS's contraceptive mandate substantially burdens the exercise of religion.

(1) It requires the Hahns and Greens [additional complainants] to engage in conduct that seriously violates their sincere religious belief that life begins at conception. If they and their companies refuse to provide contraceptive coverage, they face severe economic consequences: about $475 million per year for Hobby Lobby, $33 million per year for Conestoga, and $15 million per year for Mardel. And if they drop coverage altogether, they could face penalties of roughly $26 million for Hobby Lobby, $1.8 million for Conestoga, and $800,000 for Mardel.

. . .

(3) HHS argues that the connection between what the objecting parties must do and the end that they find to be morally wrong is too attenuated because it is the employee who will

choose the coverage and contraceptive method she uses. But RFRA's question is whether the mandate imposes a substantial burden on the objecting parties' ability to conduct business in accordance with their religious beliefs. The belief of the Hahns and Greens implicates a difficult and important question of religion and moral philosophy, namely, the circumstances under which it is immoral for a person to perform an act that is innocent in itself but that has the effect of enabling or facilitating the commission of an immoral act by another. It is not for the Court to say that the religious beliefs of the plaintiffs are mistaken or unreasonable.

. . .

(c) The Court assumes that the interest in guaranteeing cost-free access to the four challenged contraceptive methods is a compelling governmental interest, but the Government has failed to show that the contraceptive mandate is the least restrictive means of furthering that interest.

. . .

(3) This decision concerns only the contraceptive mandate and should not be understood to hold that all insurance-coverage mandates, e.g., for vaccinations or blood transfusions, must necessarily fall if they conflict with an employer's religious beliefs. Nor does it provide a shield for employers who might cloak illegal discrimination as a religious practice. *United States v. Lee*, 455 U. S. 252, which upheld the payment of Social Security taxes despite an employer's religious objection, is not analogous. It turned primarily on the special problems associated with a national system of taxation; and if Lee were a RFRA case, the fundamental point would still be that there is no less restrictive alternative to the categorical requirement to pay taxes. Here, there is an alternative to the contraceptive mandate.

. . .

Reversed and remanded

Source: *Burwell v. Hobby Lobby*, 573 U.S. _682__ (2014).

Religious Exemptions and Accommodations for Coverage of Certain Preventive Services under the Affordable Care Act (2017)

Actions taken by the administration of President Donald Trump with regard to contraceptive policies associated with the Affordable Care Act of 2010 are summarized here.

Our reconsideration of these issues has also led us to conclude, consistent with the rulings in favor of religious employee plaintiffs in <u>Wieland</u> and <u>March for Life</u> cited above, that the Mandate imposes a substantial burden on the religious beliefs of individual employees who oppose contraceptive coverage and would be able to obtain a plan that omits contraception from a willing employer or issuer (as applicable), but cannot obtain one solely because of the Mandate's prohibition on that employer and/or issuer providing them with such a plan. Consistent with our conclusion earlier this year after the remand of cases in Zubik and our reviewing of comments submitted in response to the 2016 RFI, the Departments believe there is not a way to satisfy all religious objections by amending the accommodation. Accordingly, the Departments have decided it is necessary and appropriate to provide the expanded exemptions set forth herein.

2. Compelling Interest

Although the Departments previously took the position that the application of the Mandate to certain objecting employers was necessary to serve a compelling governmental interest, the Departments have now concluded, after reassessing the relevant interests and for the reasons stated below, that it does not. Under such circumstances, the Departments are required by law to alleviate the substantial burden created by the Mandate. Here, informed by the Departments' reassessment of the relevant interests, as well as by our desire to bring to a close the more than 5 years of litigation over RFRA challenges to the Mandate, the Departments have determined that the appropriate administrative response is to create a broader exemption, rather than simply adjusting the accommodation process.

. . .

For all of these reasons, and as further explained below, the Departments now believe it is appropriate to modify the scope of the discretion afforded to HRSA [Health Resources and Services Administration] in the July 2015 final regulations to direct HRSA to provide the expanded exemptions and change the accommodation to an optional process if HRSA continues to otherwise provide for contraceptive coverage in the Guidelines. As set forth below, the expanded exemption encompasses non-governmental plan sponsors that object based on sincerely held religious beliefs, and institutions of higher education in their arrangement of student health plans. The accommodation is also maintained as an optional process for exempt employers, and will provide contraceptive availability for persons covered by the plans of entities that use it (a legitimate program purpose).

. . .

Exemption for Objecting Individuals Covered by Willing Employers and Issuers

As noted above, some individuals have brought suit objecting to being covered under an insurance policy that includes coverage for contraceptives. See, for example, *Wieland v. HHS*, 196 F. Supp. 3d 1010 (E.D. Mo. 2016); *Soda v. McGettigan*, No. 15-cv-00898 (D. Md.). Just as the Departments have determined that the Government does not have a compelling interest in applying the Mandate to employers that object to contraceptive coverage on religious grounds, we have also concluded that the Government does not have a compelling interest in requiring individuals to be covered by policies that include contraceptive coverage when the individuals have sincerely held religious objections to that coverage. The Government does not have an interest in ensuring the provision of contraceptive coverage to individuals who do not wish to have such coverage.

Source: "Religious Exemptions and Accommodations for Coverage of Certain Preventive Services under the Affordable Care Act." 2017. Departments of the Treasury, Labor, and Health and Human Services. https://www.federalregister.gov/documents/2017/10/13/2017-21851/religious-exemptions-and-accommodations-for-coverage-of-certain-preventive-services-under-the. Accessed on April 16, 2019.

Iowa Fetal Heartbeat Act (2018)

There has not been a time since the U.S. Supreme Court's decision in Roe v. Wade *(1973) that opponents of abortion have not explored mechanisms by which that decision could be overturned. One approach has been a two-step process that involves, first, the selection of antiabortion individuals to the Supreme Court and, then, resubmission of a case that would prompt the court to reconsider its decision in* Roe v. Wade. *One of the most recent efforts in that direction has been the passage of so-called fetal heartbeat bills at the state level. These bills say essentially that abortions can occur only under very restrictive terms at any time after a fetal heartbeat can be detected. Even proponents of such acts acknowledge that they are almost certainly unconstitutional under the* Roe v. Wade *ruling. But they hope that challenges to the act will bring the question once more to the attention of the court with, they hope, a more favorable outcome. The following text is extracted from a fetal heartbeat bill passed by the Iowa legislature and signed by Governor Kim Reynolds in 2019.*

146C.2 Abortion prohibited—detectable fetal heartbeat.

1. Except in the case of a medical emergency or when the abortion is medically necessary, a physician shall not perform an abortion unless the physician has first complied with the prerequisites of chapter 146A and has tested the pregnant woman as specified in this subsection, to determine if a fetal heartbeat is detectable.

a. In testing for a detectable fetal heartbeat, the physician shall perform an abdominal ultrasound, necessary to detect a fetal heartbeat according to standard medical practice and including the use of medical devices, as determined by standard medical practice and specified by rule of the board of medicine.

b. Following the testing of the pregnant woman for a detectable fetal heartbeat, the physician shall inform the pregnant woman, in writing, of all of the following:

(1) Whether a fetal heartbeat was detected.

(2) That if a fetal heartbeat was detected, an abortion is prohibited.

c. Upon receipt of the written information, the pregnant woman shall sign a form acknowledging that the pregnant woman has received the information as required under this subsection.

2. a. A physician shall not perform an abortion upon a pregnant woman when it has been determined that the unborn child has a detectable fetal heartbeat, unless, in the physician's reasonable medical judgment, a medical emergency exists, or when the abortion is medically necessary.

b. Notwithstanding paragraph "a," if a physician determines that the probable postfertilization age, as defined in section 146B.1, of the unborn child is twenty or more weeks, the physician shall not perform an abortion upon a pregnant woman when it has been determined that the unborn child has a detectable fetal heartbeat, unless in the physician's reasonable medical judgment the pregnant woman has a condition which the physician deems a medical emergency, as defined in section 146B.1, or the abortion is necessary to preserve the life of an unborn child.

Source: Iowa State Law 146C.2. 2019. https://www.legis.iowa.gov/docs/code/146C.2.pdf. Accessed on April 18, 2019.

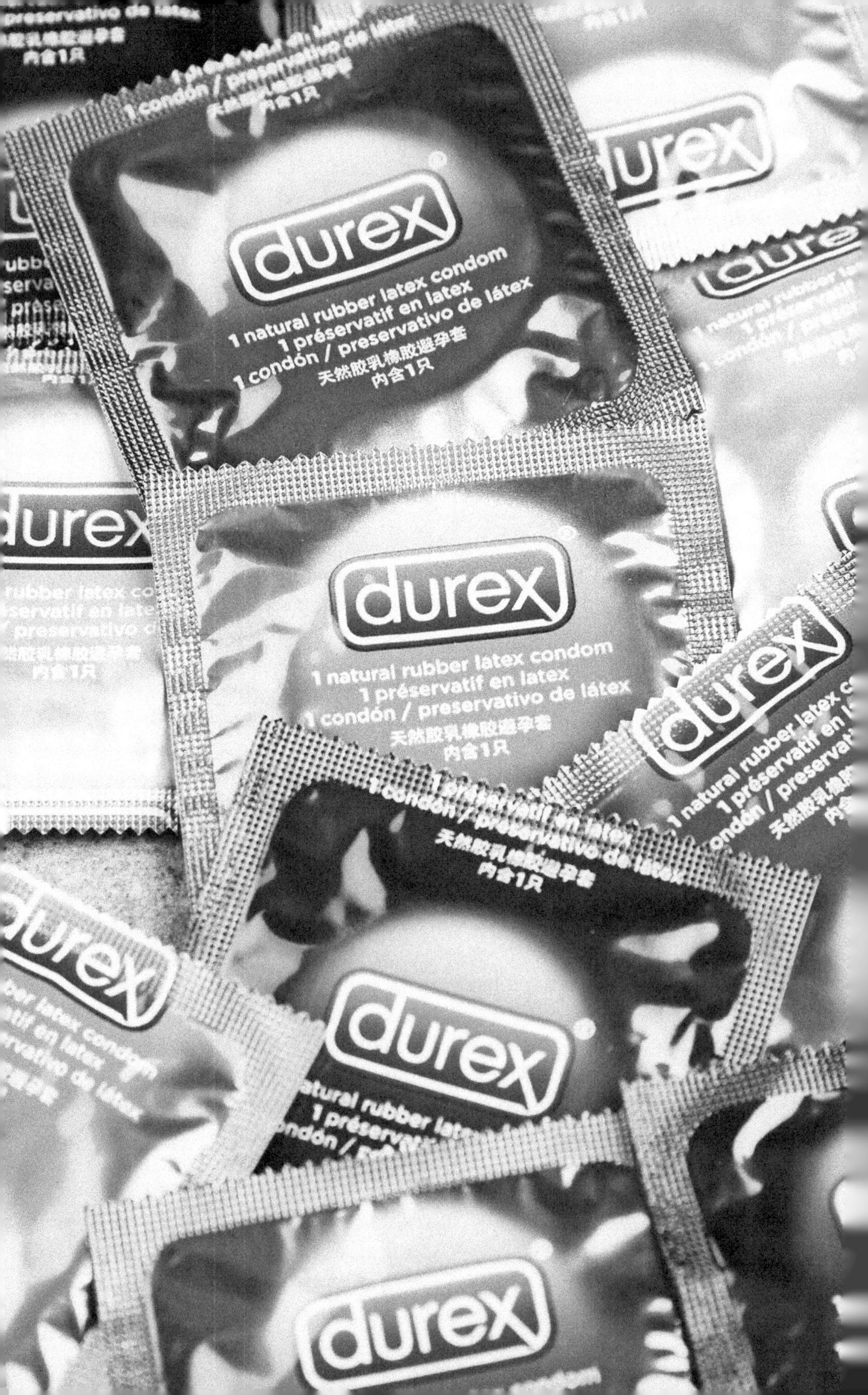
durex
1 natural rubber latex condom
1 préservatif en latex
1 condón / preservativo de látex
天然胶乳橡胶避孕套
内含1只

The books, articles, reports, and Internet sources listed here are no more than a sample of the voluminous literature on the topic of birth control. Because of ongoing controversies, some of the resources listed here may go out of date just before or after publication of the book. Mention of those resources, however, will provide a hint as to publications from which even more up-to-date information about these controversies may be available.

In some cases, a resource may be available in two different formats, printed article and online version of the article, for example. In such cases, the availability of the resource in both media is indicated in the citation. In addition to the items listed here, the reader is encouraged to review the resources listed at the end of Chapters 1 and 2 to find suggestions for additional readings.

Books

Alghrani, Amel. 2018. *Regulating Assisted Reproductive Technologies: New Horizons.* Cambridge, UK; New York: Cambridge University Press.

Products of Durex, a brand of condoms originally developed and produced in the United Kingdom by SSL International. (Monticelllo/Dreamstime.com)

The topic of assisted reproductive technologies is, by its very nature, subject to a host of social, ethical, political, economic, and other issues. As the technology has increased in popularity and complexity, additional questions have arisen, questions about which this book is based.

Brown, Jenny. 2019. *Birth Strike: The Hidden Fight over Women's Work*. Oakland, CA: PM Press.

This book explores the not-always-obvious conflict between the state and individuals over a woman's reproductive rights. The author explains why many U.S. governmental authorities and other critics are arguing for increasing the nation's birthrate and why they should make such demands.

Bruess, Clint E., and Elizabeth Schroeder. 2018. *Sexuality Education: Theory and Practice*, 7th ed. Scotts Valley, CA: ETR.

This popular textbook covers just about every imaginable topic in the field of sex education.

Carlson, Allan C. 2017. *Godly Seed: American Evangelicals Confront Birth Control, 1873–1973*. Abingdon, UK: Routledge.

Attitudes of evangelical Christians about birth control have received possibly less attention than is the case with Roman Catholics. Carlson explores the evolution of evangelical attitudes on the topic from early Christianity to the present day.

Coffin, Patrick. 2018. *The Contraception Deception: Catholic Teaching on Birth Control*. Steubenville, OH: Emmaus Road Publishing.

Pope Paul VI's 1968 encyclical dealt with moral issues of contraception from the standpoint of Roman Catholic theology. Coffin devotes this book to a review of the place of the work, *Humanae Vitae*, in the history of Catholicism, current understandings of Paul's teachings, and what can be learned by a review of the church's position today.

Cohen, Adam. 2016. *Imbeciles: The Supreme Court, American Eugenics, and the Sterilization of Carrie Buck.* New York: Penguin Press.

> Cohen tells the story and comments on one of the most infamous events in the history of modern eugenics, the involuntary sterilization of a young African-American girl labeled as an "imbecile."

Daar, Judith. 2017. *The New Eugenics: Selective Breeding in an Era of Reproductive Technologies.* New Haven, CT: Yale University Press.

> New reproductive technologies have made possible opportunities for childbearing that have seldom, if ever, existed before and that create new issues for ethicists and other specialists in the field. The author here claims that the availability of such technologies creates an environment for a new form of the eugenics movement of previous generations.

Debenham, Clare. 2014. *Birth Control and the Rights of Women: Post-suffrage Feminism in the Early Twentieth Century.* New York: I. B. Tauris.

> The author notes that the history of the suffragette movement and the rise of feminism has been thoroughly studied and documented. Such is not the case, however, with the history of the birth control movement. She provides her own review of that history in the United Kingdom and develops a Collective Biography that focuses on the personality and accomplishments of important individuals involved in the early movement.

Debenham, Clare. 2018. *Marie Stopes' Sexual Revolution and the Birth Control Movement.* Cham, Switzerland: Palgrave Macmillan.

> Marie Stopes was an important activist for contraceptive and family planning causes in the United Kingdom in the period between the two world wars. This book provides a

biographical sketch of her life, along with a review of her ideas and actions during this period.

Eig, Jonathan. 2015. *The Birth of the Pill: How Four Crusaders Reinvented Sex and Launched a Revolution*. New York: W. W. Norton.

Eig reviews the stages in the development of the first hormonal oral contraceptive pill by describing the contributions of four key figures in that story: Margaret Sanger, John Rock, Gregory Pincus, and Katharine McCormick.

Engelman, Peter. 2011. *A History of the Birth Control Movement in America*. Santa Barbara, CA: Praeger.

This excellent book consists of four chapters, "Before 'Birth Control,'" "Birth Control and Free Speech," "Birth Control Clinics," and "Birth Control and Public Acceptance." The book contains a very large number of notes and references on each of these topics: an excellent guide for pursuing one's study on this topic.

Foote, Edward B. 1870. *Medical Common Sense Applied to the Causes, Prevention and Cure of Chronic Diseases; and Plain Home Talk about the Sexual Organs: The Natural Relation of the Sexes; Society Civilization; and Marriage*. New York: Author. Available online at https://archive.org/details/63570670R.nlm.nih.gov/page/n5. Accessed on May 29, 2019.

This book is an example of the type of contraceptive advice being given by the medical profession in the last quarter of the 19th century. Of special interest is the description of a "womb veil," a primitive diaphragm or cervical cap. See page 380.

Gentile, Katie, ed. 2016. *The Business of Being Made: Assisted Reproductive Technologies, Time, Bodies*. New York: Routledge.

This anthology includes chapters by authors from a variety of occupations, including psychologists, clinicians, researchers in the field, and psychiatrists. It is said to be "the first book to critically analyze assisted reproductive technologies (ARTs) from a transdisciplinary perspective."

Greslé-Favier, Claire. 2009. *"Raising Sexually Pure Kids": Sexual Abstinence, Conservative Christians and American Politics.* Amsterdam; New York: Rodopi.

Abstinence-only sex education has been a topic of severe controversy in the United States over the past half century. That controversy involves elements that go far beyond issues of birth control, including theological and political arguments at the core of American society. This book explores the roots and evolution of that controversy.

Grigg-Spall, Holly. 2013. *Sweetening the Pill: Or How We Got Hooked on Hormonal Birth Control.* Winchester, UK; Washington, DC: Zero Books.

Grigg-Spall suggests that American women have become addicted to the birth control pill almost without realizing what was happening. She explores how this has happened and what there is about the pill that women don't know and/or should be concerned about.

Guillebaud, John 2019. *Contraception Today*, 9th ed. Boca Raton, FL: CFC Press.

This very popular book provides a general overview of the types of contraception available.

Hajo, Cathy Moran. 2010. *Birth Control on Main Street: Organizing Clinics in the United States, 1916–1939*. Urbana: University of Illinois Press.

Rather than focusing on national patterns and trends, the author writes about individual birth control clinics in cities around the nation. Her book is based on research in the records of more than 600 such clinics over the indicated time.

Hatcher, Robert A., et al., eds. 2018. *Contraceptive Technology*, 21st edition. New York, NY: Ayer Company Publishers, Inc.
This very popular reference book covers all types of contraception, the ways in which they work, possible side effects, their efficacy, and their advantages and disadvantages.

Haussman, Melissa. 2013. *Reproductive Rights and the State: Getting the Birth Control, RU-486, Morning-after Pills, and the Gardasil Vaccine to the U.S. Market*. Santa Barbara, CA: Praeger.
The author explores the political and regulatory issues involved in introducing four new contraceptive technologies to the United States from a feminist point of view.

Hitchcock, James. 2016. *Abortion, Religious Freedom, and Catholic Politics*. New Brunswick, NJ: Transaction Publishers.
The author analyzes the way in which these three fields have interacted with each other over time with regard to the legitimacy and place of abortion in American society.

Hopwood, Nick, Rebecca Flemming, and Lauren Kassell, eds. 2018. *Reproduction: Antiquity to the Present Day*. New York: Cambridge University Press.
The 40+ essays in this book discuss a variety of specific events relating to contraception throughout history, such as "Women and Doctors in Ancient Greece," "Managing Childbirth and Fertility in Medieval Europe," "Man-Midwifery Revisited," Infertility," and "Modern Ignorance."

Irvine, Janice M. 2004. *Talk about Sex: The Battles over Sex Education in the United States*. Berkeley: University of California Press.
This award-winning book traces the rise and evolution of the debate over the role of sex education in the United States. The author shows how technical issues regarding sex education became embroiled in the conservative wing of American politics and how that connection still

plays out today. This book was the subject of a number of thoughtful and helpful reviews, such as Keith Bates. 2004. "Book Review: Talk about Sex: The Battles over Sex Education in the United States." *Journal of the History of Sexuality.* 13(1): 107–110; Amy Binder. 2003. "Book Review: Talk about Sex: The Battles over Sex Education in the United States." *Contemporary Sociology.* 32(5): 593–595; Jeffrey P. Moran. 2003. "Sex Education and the Rise of the New Right." *Reviews in American History.* 31(2): 283–289; Vanessa Woog. 2005. "Book Review: Talk about Sex: The Battles over Sex Education in the United States." *Culture, Health & Sexuality.* 7(1): 78–80.

Jensen, Robin E. 2010. *Dirty Words: The Rhetoric of Public Sex Education, 1870–1924.* Urbana: University of Illinois Press.

The evolution of public sex education in the United States during the Progressive Era was a slow and contentious process. This book follows the progress of that event and reviews in particular the role that specific women and women's groups played in the evolution of formal sex education programs during the period.

Kaul, Paritosh, Maria Trent, and Krishna K. Upadhya. 2019. *Adolescent Medicine: State of the Art Reviews Adolescent Contraception: Basics and Beyond.* Itasca, IL: American Academy of Pediatrics. Section on Adolescent Health.

The 14 essays in this book cover almost every aspect of adolescent contraceptive theory and practice, including a review of the current status of contraception among U.S. teenagers, the counseling of individual adolescents about contraceptive issues, new methods of contraception, and a review of current use of condoms.

Ladd-Taylor, Molly. 2017. *Fixing the Poor: Eugenic Sterilization and Child Welfare in the Twentieth Century.* Baltimore, MD: Johns Hopkins University Press.

Sterilization of the mentally and physically challenged, as well as those simply deemed to be "unfit" in society, was a common practice in the first four decades on the 20th century. Thirty-two states had laws and programs designed to carry out this process. The author reviews this history, focusing on the state of affairs in Minnesota in the 1920s and 1930s.

Lewis, Sophie. 2019. *Full Surrogacy Now: Feminism Against Family*. London; New York: Verso.

The author provides a very useful introduction to the topic of surrogacy and discusses its place in modern society. She then presents arguments that have been offered for and against the practice and decides that it is time to take a radical new approach to the subject, one that she outlines in the book.

MacNamara, Trent. 2018. *Birth Control and American Modernity: A History of Popular Ideas*. New York: Cambridge University Press.

Ideas about contraception in the United States developed over well over a century of discussion and debate over the practice that was strongly influenced by a variety of moral, religious, social, political, economic, and other factors. This extraordinary book provides an excellent review of that history.

Massa, Mark Stephen. 2018. *The Structure of Theological Revolutions: How the Fight over Birth Control Transformed American Catholicism*. New York: Oxford University Press.

The premise of this book is that Pope Paul VI's 1968 encyclical on birth control, *Humane Vitae*, not only led to a schism in the church over the issue of contraception but also started a revolution in the way in which many Catholics thought about the fundamental structure of the church and its teachings themselves.

McManis, John T. 2012. *Ella Flagg Young and a Half-century of the Chicago Public Schools*. Charleston, SC: Nabu Press.

This book is a reprint of a 1916 biography of Ella Flagg Young and her tenure as superintendent of the Chicago Public School system.

Murray, Melissa, Katherine Shaw, and Reva B. Siegel, eds. 2019. *Reproductive Rights and Justice Stories*. St. Paul, MN: Foundation Press.

This collection of essays discusses in conversational style 12 important essays in the field of reproductive rights.

Nathan, J. 2017. *Our Choice: Ignore Science or Provide and Use Contraception Everywhere—Religiously*. Tigard, OR: Inkwater Press.

The author places the question of contraception into the larger issue of population control and concludes that the best legacy for parents is "Love all your children, but create no more than one or two if none."

Noonan, John T., Jr. 1986. *Contraception: A History of Its Treatment by the Catholic Theologians and Canonists*. Cambridge, MA: Belknap Press of Harvard University Press.

This book considers in great detail a very specific aspect of contraception, namely, the way it which the topic has been dealt with over the centuries by the Roman Catholic church.

Rainwater, Lee. 2017. *Family Design: Marital Sexuality, Family Size, and Contraception*. Abingdon, UK: Routledge.

The author explores a range of issues relating to the question of contraception among married couples, such as family size preferences, rationales for family size, motivations for large and small families, family limitations and contraceptive methods, and effective and ineffective contraceptive methods.

Rice, Charles E. 2014. *Contraception and Persecution*. South Bend, IN: St. Augustine's Press.

> The author, a professor of law at Notre Dame University, argues that the current debate over birth control and abortion is not about sex but about religion and its place in society. He argues that the state, using sexuality as its surrogate, is taking over the role once played by religion in the modern world.

Riddle, John M. 1992. *Contraception and Abortion from the Ancient World to the Renaissance*. Cambridge, MA: Harvard University Press.

Riddle, John M. 1997. *Eve's Herbs: A History of Contraception and Abortion in the West*. Cambridge, MA: Harvard University Press.

> These two books provide detailed and well-researched reviews of the use of contraception during the early centuries of human society: two essential resources for research on this topic.

Rogers, Barbara. 2018. *A Matter of Life and Death: Women and the New Eugenics*. Bath, UK: Brown Dog Books.

> This book focuses on the connection between birth control and population control. The author argues that "population growth would not be a problem if all women had access to safe and effective contraception." She says that efforts to withhold birth control information and technology from women in developing countries constitutes a modern-day form of eugenics.

Sasser, Jade S. 2018. *On Infertile Ground: Population Control and Women's Rights in the Era of Climate Change*. New York: NUY Press.

> Several authors have expressed the opinion that one important way of reducing climate change is through population control. Sasser argues that this recommendation

is the wrong approach since it will continue to place an undue burden on women in developing nations in particular. She suggests that the approach is a way of "repackaging of failed narratives."

Shoupe, Donna, and Siri L. Kjos. 2016. *The Handbook of Contraception: A Guide for Practical Management.* Cham: Humana Press.
   This book is intended primarily for health care practitioners, but it has a great deal of valuable, up-to-date information on most forms of contraception.

Silliman, Jael Miriam, et al. 2016. *Undivided Rights: Women of Color Organize for Reproductive Justice*, 2nd ed. Chicago: Haymarket Books.
   The founding and evolution of the Reproductive Justice movement is a fascinating story of an increasing level of consciousness and activity by otherwise ignored and/or underserved women who are dealing with reproductive issues. This book is an excellent general introduction to that story.

Smith, Janet E., ed. 2018. *Why Humanae Vitae Is Still Right.* San Francisco: Ignatius Press.
   The 11 essays in this book are grouped under general headings of "Consequences," "Theology of the Body," "Saint John Paul II and the Krakow Report," "Philosophical Defenses," "Sensus Fidelium and Conscience," and "New Initiatives."

Sobo, Elisa Janine, and Sandra Bell. 2001. *Celibacy, Culture, and Society: The Anthropology of Sexual Abstinence.* Madison: University of Wisconsin Press.
   Celibacy occurs and has occurred in many cultures throughout human history. The authors describe and discuss specific examples of the phenomenon worldwide and throughout history.

Stone, Geoffrey R. 2017. *Sex and the Constitution: Sex, Religion, and Law from America's Origins to the Twenty-first Century.* New York: Liveright Publishing Corporation.

> After a brief review of the status of birth control in the ancient world, the Middle Ages, and the Enlightenment, the author focuses on the place that sexual issues in general, and contraception in particular, have played in six major periods of American history. He focuses in particular on legal issues around sexuality as expressed in significant court cases.

Stott, Jessica. 2017. *Natural Birth Control: Intro to the Sympto-Thermal Method of Fertility Awareness.* Los Gatos, CA: Smashwords Edition.

> The symptothermal form of birth control is a type of natural fertility awareness. The author explains the process in this book and describes how a woman can put the method into practice.

Tross, Susan, and Theresa Exner. 2017. "Female Condoms." In Thomas J. Hope, Douglas Richman, and Mario Stevenson, eds. *Encyclopedia of AIDS.* New York: Springer. Available online at https://link.springer.com/content/pdf/10.100 7%2F978-1-4614-9610-6_88-1.pdf. Accessed on May 29, 2019.

> This chapter is one of the best available descriptions of the female condom, its uses, and its advantages and disadvantages.

Van Sickle-War, Rachel, and Keven Wallsten. 2019. *The Politics of the Pill: Gender, Framing and Policymaking in the Battle over Birth Control.* New York: Oxford University Press.

> The invention and eventual widespread use of the oral contraceptive pill was far more than a simple development in contraceptive technology. The availability of the pill brought with it a host of political, social, personal, and other problems that are still of concern today. This book

opens with a detailed history of the pill's development and the status of contraception nationally and statewide during this period. It then concludes with a series of chapters on media issues and public opinion relating to use of the pill.

Whelpton, Pascal Kidder, Arthur A. Campbell, and John E. Patterson. 2016. *Fertility and Family Planning in the United States*. Princeton, NJ: Princeton University Press.
   This book discusses a number of aspects of the topics described in its title, with useful chapters on ideal, desired, and expected family size; fecundity impairments; the control of fertility; family planning; and methods and effectiveness of contraceptives.

Wilde, Melissa J. 2019. *Birth Control Battles: How Race and Class Divided American Religion*. Berkeley: University of California Press.
   The author makes the argument that the fight over birth control beginning in the 1930s has never been about "sex, women's rights, or privacy but [has been] actually about race, class, and white supremacist concerns about undesirable fertility."

Wilson, Aimee Armande. 2016. *Conceived in Modernism: The Aesthetics and Politics of Birth Control*. New York: Bloomsbury.
   The author explores the ways in which changing views of contraception in the United States and Great Britain were affected by and, in turn, affected the development of literary modernism.

Articles

Some of the journals that focus almost entirely or largely on birth control are the following:

   BMJ Sexual and Reproductive Health: ISSN: 2515-1991 (print); 2515-2009 (online)

Contraception: ISSN: 0010-7824 (print)

Contraception and Reproductive Medicine: ISSN: 2055-7426 (online)

Contraceptive Technology Update: ISSN: 0274-726X (online)

Current Obstetrics and Gynecology Reports: ISSN: 2161-3303 (online)

The European Journal of Contraception and Reproductive Health Care: ISSN: 1362-5187 (print); 1473-0782 (online)

International Perspectives on Sexual and Reproductive Health: ISSN: 1944-0391 (print); 1944-0405 (online)

Perspectives on Sexual and Reproductive Health: ISSN: 1538-6341 (print); 1931-2393 (online)

Studies in Family Planning: ISSN: 1728-4465 (online)

Women's Health Issues: ISSN: 1049-3867 (print); 1878-4321 (online)

Alton, Katie, and Jeffrey Jensen. 2018. "Update on Permanent Contraception for Women." *Current Obstetrics and Gynecology Reports*. 7(4): 163–171.

The authors review the current status of permanent contraceptive options, along with a discussion of controversies relating to the technologies.

Beauchamp, Andrew, and Catherine R. Pakaluk. 2019. "The Paradox of the Pill: Heterogeneous Effects of Oral Contraceptive Access." *Economic Inquiry*. 57(2): 813–831. Available online at https://onlinelibrary.wiley.com/doi/epdf/10.1111/ecin.12757. Accessed on May 31, 2019.

Some benefits of the oral contraceptive pill have been explained and widely accepted. However, other consequences of pill use have also been identified, as in this article, and they are not always as positive. This study, for example, shows that the greater availability of the pill has led to an increase in the number of nonmarital births and a reduction in high school graduation rates. These patterns were observed primarily in women of lower social economic status and within minority groups.

Bhatia, Kalsang, et al. 2011. "Surrogate Pregnancy: An Essential Guide for Clinicians." *The Obstetrician & Gynaecologist*. 11: 49–54.

This article provides a concise introduction to the topic of surrogacy, along with mention of legal, ethical, economic, social, and personal issues associated with the process.

Brackman, Anita, et al. 2017. "Condom Availability in Schools: A Practical Approach to the Prevention of Sexually Transmitted Infection/HIV and Unintended Pregnancy." *Journal of Adolescent Health*. 60(6): 754–757. Available online at https://www.adolescenthealth.org/SAHM_Main/media/Advocacy/Positions/Condom-availability-in-school.pdf. Accessed on May 31, 2019.

This position paper gives the opinion of the Society for Adolescent Health and Medicine on the question of condom accessibility programs in schools. It concludes that schools should "make condoms available to students as part of efforts to decrease rates of STIs and unplanned pregnancy in adolescents and young adults."

Brougher, Cynthia. 2014. "Free Exercise of Religion by Closely Held Corporations: Implications of Burwell v. Hobby Lobby Stores, Inc." Library of Congress. Congressional Research Service. Washington, D. C.: Congressional Research Service.

The author reviews the legal issues raised by the *Burwell v. Hobby Lobby* Supreme Court decision and suggests some possible ways of dealing with the future consequences of that decision.

Buckles, Kasey S., and Daniel M. Hungerman. 2018. "The Incidental Fertility Effects of School Condom Distribution

Programs." *Journal of Policy Analysis and Management.* 37(3): 464–492. Available online at https://www3.nd.edu/~kbuckles/mga60204/Buckles_Hungerman_condoms.pdf. Accessed on May 31, 2019.

> The authors claim that this paper reports on the first research on the question as to how access to condoms affects fertility. They say that, in contrast to other types of contraceptives, condom availability increases fertility rate of users by about 12 percent. They attribute this somewhat surprising result to the tendency of some schools to provide condoms to students without offering accompanying instruction and counseling.

Campo-Engelstein, Lisa. 2012. "Contraceptive Justice: Why We Need a Male Pill." *Virtual Mentor.* 14(2): 146–151. Available online at https://journalofethics.ama-assn.org/article/contraceptive-justice-why-we-need-male-pill/2012-02. Accessed on June 2, 2019.

> The author argues that the current state of affairs, in which women have a choice of about 18 methods of contraception and men only a handful of options, must be changed. She notes that the current situation places virtually all of the economic and personal choices about birth control on the woman in a relationship, a reality that would change if a male contraceptive pill were available.

Drake, M. J., I. W. Mills, and D. Cranston. 1999. "On the Chequered History of Vasectomy." *BJU International.* 84: 475–481.

> Vasectomy has been used for both legitimate medical purposes as well as less desirable social and political purposes. This article reviews the history of the procedure, with a discussion of both aspects of its applications.

Du Toit, M. 2018. "Involuntary Sterilisation of HIV-positive Women in South Africa: A Current Legal Perspective." *South African Journal of Bioethics and Law.* 11(2): 80–84. Available online at http://www.sajbl.org.za/index.php/sajbl/article/view/591/573. Accessed on May 28, 2019.

Some people may believe that involuntary sterilization is an unpleasant event of past history. This article reveals that such is not the case and that such procedures are still in use in at least some countries.

Elia, John P., and Jessica Tokunaga. 2015. "Sexuality Education: Implications for Health, Equity, and Social Justice in the United States." *Health Education*. 115(1): 105–120.

The authors argue that sex education in the United States has traditionally been biased against students of color, LGBTQ+ individuals, and those with disabilities. They find some progress in correcting these deficiencies and recommend additional actions that can be taken in the future.

English, Abigail, and Carol A. Ford. 2004. "The HIPAA Privacy Rule and Adolescents: Legal Questions and Clinical Challenges." *Perspectives on Sexual and Reproductive Health*. 36(2): 80–86. Available online at https://www.guttmacher .org/journals/psrh/2004/hipaa-privacy-rule-and-adoles-cents-legal-questions-and-clinical-challenges. Accessed on May 31, 2019.

The rights of patients with regard to their medical records is guaranteed in the Health Insurance Portability and Accountability Act of 1996 (HIPAA). Questions may arise as to the circumstances, if any, under which HIPAA rules also apply to minor children. This article provides a detailed analysis of that issue.

Glass, Daniel J. 2015. "Not in My Hospital: The Future of State Statutes Requiring Abortion Providers to Maintain Admitting Privileges at Local Hospitals." *Akron Law Review*. 49(1): 249–285. Available online at https://ideaexchange.uak ron.edu/akronlawreview/vol49/iss1/7/. Accessed on May 30, 2019.

One of the strategies used by opponents of abortion to reduce access to such services is to require abortion providers to have admitting privileges at some (usually nearby) hospital. This article explores the legal rationale for such laws and finds that they are likely to be unconstitutional.

Grady, William R. 1996. "Men's Perceptions of Their Roles and Responsibilities Regarding Sex, Contraception and Childrearing." *Family Planning Perspectives*. 28(5): 221–226. Available online at https://www.guttmacher.org/journals/psrh/1996/09/mens-perceptions-their-roles-and-responsibilities-regarding-sex-contraception. Accessed on June 2, 2019.

Interestingly enough, this article is one of the few that deals with the question of men's roles in pregnancy, birth control, and related issues. Although now quite dated, it provides some of the rare information as to how men themselves answer this question.

Greasley, Kate. 2017. "Taking Abortion Rights Seriously: Whole Woman's Health v Hellerstedt." *Modern Law Review*. 80(2): 325–338.

In the case cited here, the U.S. Supreme Court ruled that two so-called TRAP abortion-limiting laws in Texas were unconstitutional because they placed a "substantial obstacle" on a woman's ability to obtain an abortion in the state.

Guiahi, Maryam. 2018. "Catholic Health Care and Women's Health." *Obstetrics & Gynecology*. 131(3): 534–537.

Some researchers have asked about the nature and quality of contraceptive services at clinics owned and/or operated by the Roman Catholic church. The church has specific and rigorous policies about the use of contraception by church members, and these researchers are interested in knowing how church policies affects the types of services offered by such clinics. This article reviews the data on this subject and includes the author's views on those data. For an example of the type of research that has been done on the question, also see Maryam Guiahi, et al. 2017. "What Are Women Told When Requesting Family Planning Services at Clinics Associated with Catholic Hospitals? A Mystery Caller Study." *Perspectives on Sexual and Reproductive Health.* 49(4): 207–212.

Hall, Kelli Stedham, et al. 2017. "Ongoing Implementation Challenges to the Patient Protection and Affordable Care Act's Contraceptive Mandate." *American Journal of Preventive Medicine.* 52(5): 667–670. Available online at https://www.ncbi.nlm.nih.gov/pmc/articles/PMC5401649/. Accessed on May 31, 2019.

The authors explain how provisions of the contraceptive mandate in the Affordable Care Act of 2010 have made contraception available to millions of women who would otherwise not have had access to these products. They then examine possible consequences on women who need birth control devices of Trump administration policies to roll back those provisions.

Hopkins, Keith. 1965. "Contraception in the Roman Empire." *Comparative Studies in Society and History.* 8(1): 124–151.

The author provides an excellent review of contraceptive practices in the Roman Empire.

Huber, Valerie J., and Michael W. Firmin. 2014. "A History of Sex Education in the United States Since 1900." *International Journal of Educational Reform.* 23(1): 25–51. Available online at https://www.loveandfidelity.org/wp-content/uploads/2014/10/Huber-Published-Sex-Ed-article.pdf. Accessed on May 30, 2019.

This article is one of the most complete and informational sources about the history of sex education in the United States generally available to the average reader.

Jensen, Robin. 2007. "Using Science to Argue for Sexual Education in U.S. Public Schools." *Science Communication*. 29(2): 217–241.

> The author provides an excellent review and discussion of Dr. Ella Flagg Young's efforts to introduce sex education in the curriculum of the Chicago Public Schools in the early 1910s.

Jones, Bonnie S., Sara Daniel, and Lindsay K. Cloud. 2018. "State Law Approaches to Facility Regulation of Abortion and Other Office Interventions." *American Journal of Public Health*. 108(4): 486–492. Available online at https://www.ncbi.nlm.nih.gov/pmc/articles/PMC5844403/. Accessed on May 30, 2019.

> The authors reviewed a variety of health laws comparable to those designed to limit abortions in particular (so-called TRAP laws) and found that the latter are based on different and more stringent standards than are the former.

Khan, Fhad, et al. 2013. "The Story of the Condom." *Indian Journal of Urology*. 29(1): 12–15. Available online at https://www.ncbi.nlm.nih.gov/pmc/articles/PMC3649591/. Accessed on May 26, 2019.

> This article provides a comprehensive, if somewhat abbreviated, history of condoms from the earliest civilizations to the present day.

Kimport, Katrina. 2018. "More than a Physical Burden: Women's Mental and Emotional Work in Preventing Pregnancy." *The Journal of Sex Research*. 55(9): 1096–1105.

> Decisions about contraception and actual use of birth control technology is almost entirely an issue for women. This study finds that emotional and other related aspects of contraception also fall disproportionally on women also.

Liao, Pamela Verma. 2012. "Half a Century of the Oral Contraceptive Pill: Historical Review and View to the Future." *Canadian Family Physician*. 58(12): e757–e760. Available online at https://www.ncbi.nlm.nih.gov/pmc/articles/PMC3520685/. Accessed on May 28, 2019.

> The author surveys the evolution of pill use in the 50 years following its first release. It also focuses on social changes that have occurred because of the pill's availability, concerns about possible adverse effects, a comparison of risks and benefits, and possible future directions on oral contraceptives.

Liles, Iyanna, et al. 2016. "Contraception Initiation in the Emergency Department." *Southern Medical Journal*. 109(5): 300–304. Available online at https://www.researchgate.net/publication/301791407_Contraception_Initiation_in_the_Emergency_Department_A_Pilot_Study_on_Providers'_Knowledge_Attitudes_and_Practices. Accessed on May 28, 2019.

> Many young women at risk for unintended pregnancy appear at hospital emergency departments seeking help for unrelated issues. This situation provides an opportunity for attending health care workers to initiate a conversation about contraception practices. This study found that such individuals are willing to consider such an option but that they tend to be poorly informed about contraceptive options.

Lloyd, Alison L., and Jackie Waterfield. 2016. "Men's Perspectives of Male Hormonal Contraception." *International Journal of Reproduction, Contraception, Obstetrics and Gynecology*. 5(8): 2546–2552.

> Research on possible male hormonal contraceptives is now well-advanced. But few studies have been conducted as to the way in which such products would be accepted by the general public. This study finds that males tend to

be as open toward male hormonal contraceptives as they are to female versions of the product.

Lord, Alexandra M. 2003. "Models of Masculinity: Sex Education, the United States Public Health Service, and the YMCA, 1919–1924." *Journal of the History of Medicine and Allied Sciences.* 58(2): 123–152.

By the end of World War I, U.S. public health officials had come to the conclusion that it was no longer a question as to *whether* young men would learn about sex but how they would do so. In 1919, the U.S. Public Health Service joined with the Young Men's Christian Association (YMCA) to create the "Keeping Fit" sex education program, one of the earliest such programs in American history.

Maksut, Jessica L., and Lisa A. Eaton. 2015. "Female Condoms=Missed Opportunities: Lessons Learned from Promotion-centered Interventions." *Women's Health Issues.* 25(4): 366–376.

The authors point out that female condoms are generally very effective as contraceptives and in the transmission of sexually transmitted infections. However, they appear to be underutilized. In this study they explore factors that may explain this fact and offer suggestions for extending the use of the technology.

Moore, Alia, Sarah Ryan, and Carol Stamm. 2019. "Seeking Emergency Contraception in the United States: a Review of Access and Barriers." *Women & Health.* 59(4): 364–374.

The authors take note of increasing acceptance of emergency contraception in the United States over the past three decades but ask how easy it is to obtain the product in a pharmacy. They found that the product was unavailable in 31 percent of cases, largely because of "low demand" (30 percent of cases), being "out of stock" (21 percent), personal objections by staff (9 percent), and "store policy" (10 percent).

Murtagh, Chloe, et al. 2018. "Exploring the Feasibility of Obtaining Mifepristone and Misoprostol from the Internet." *Contraception* 97(4): 287–291.

The authors conducted a survey to determine the accessibility of mifepristone and misoprostol from online providers, along with the purity of products they obtained from those sites. They concluded that "some people for whom clinic-based abortion is not easily available or acceptable may consider self-sourcing pills from the internet to be a rational option."

Peragallo Urrutia, Rachel, et al. 2018. "Effectiveness of Fertility Awareness—Based Methods for Pregnancy Prevention." *Obstetrics & Gynecology*. 132(3): 581–604.

The authors conducted an extensive review of fertility awareness programs in an effort to determine the efficacy of this type of contraception. They found that there were so few studies of sufficient quality to draw any overall conclusions on the question, suggesting that more and better research on the topic is needed. For a discussion of this report, also see "Better Studies Needed on Effectiveness of Fertility Awareness-based Methods for Contraception." 2018. Medical Xpress. https://medicalxpress.com/news/2018-08-effectiveness-fertility-awareness-based-methods-contraception.html. Accessed on May 29, 2019.

Peter, Christina R., Timothy B. Tasker, and Stacey S. Horn. "Parents' Attitudes toward Comprehensive and Inclusive Sexuality Education." *Health Education*. 115(1): 71–92.

These researchers asked a sample of parents about two popular forms of sex education in the schools. Although respondents were not well-informed about the types mentioned, they tended to prefer a sex education program that deals with a wide range of sex-related topics.

Ross, Loretta, and Rickie Solinger. 2017. *Reproductive Justice: An Introduction*. Oakland: University of California Press.

Two founders of the Reproductive Justice movement explain the philosophical premise on which the movement is based and provide an overview of the history of the organization's development.

Santelli, John S., et al. 2017. "Abstinence-Only-Until-Marriage: An Updated Review of U.S. Policies and Programs and Their Impact." *Journal of Adolescent Health.* 61: 273–280. Available online at https://www.jahonline.org/article/S1054-139X(17)30260-4/pdf. Accessed on May 28, 2019.

This article offers the latest research on the efficacy of abstinence-only-until-marriage sex education programs. The authors conclude that "[p]olicies or programs offering abstinence as a single option for unmarried adolescents are scientifically and ethically flawed. AOUM programs have little demonstrated efficacy in helping adolescents to delay intercourse, while prompting health-endangering gender stereotypes and marginalizing sexual minority youth."

Sayegh, Anthony, Sharon Rose, and Naomi A. Schapiro. 2012. "Condom Availability in Middle Schools: Evidence and Recommendations." *Journal of Pediatric Health Care.* 26: 471–475. Available online at https://nursing.ucsf.edu/sites/nursing.ucsf.edu/files/inline-files/condom_avalability_in_middle_school.pdf. Accessed on May 29, 2019.

The issue of condom availability programs at the middle school level poses issues that may not be raised for older students, at the high school level. This report summarizes existing evidence on the nature of such programs and their impacts on students. It concludes with recommendations for the greater use of such programs.

Schivone, Gillian, Laneta Dorflinger, and Vera Halpern. 2016. "Injectable Contraception: Updates and Innovation." *Current Opinion in Obstetrics and Gynecology.* 28(6): 504–509.

The authors review recent development in the field of injectable contraceptives and discuss their role in contraceptive practices in the future.

Smith, Lesley. 2011. "The Kahun Gynaecological Papyrus: Ancient Egyptian Medicine." *Journal of Family Planning and Reproductive Health Care.* 37: 54–55. Available online at https://pdfs.semanticscholar.org/fc44/fdb65cf46c2b6536228a83ed9b0b261899a1.pdf. Accessed on May 27, 2019.

This very interesting paper reviews what we know about contraception in ancient Egypt from an important papyrus recovered from the time.

Smith, Steven D., and Caroline Mala Corbin. 2013. "Debate: The Contraception Mandate and Religious Freedom." *University of Pennsylvania Law Review Online.* http://www.pennlawreview.com/online/Steven-DSmith-Caroline-Mala-Corbin-161-U-Pa-L-Rev-261.pdf. Accessed on May 27, 2019.

Two law professors present opposing views of the developing conflict between the contraception mandate and new regulations extending the right of refusal of service on the basis of religious beliefs.

Strong, Bryan. 1972. "Ideas of the Early Sex Education Movement in America, 1890–1920." *History of Education Quarterly.* 12(2): 129–161.

The birth of formal sex education instruction in the United States can be dated to the last decade of the 19th century. The movement grew rapidly over the next three decades, a period in history examined by this excellent article.

Swartzendruber, Andrea, et al. 2018. "Sexual and Reproductive Health Services and Related Health Information on Pregnancy Resource Center Websites: A Statewide Content Analysis." *Women's Health Issues.* 28(1): 14–20.

Pregnancy resource centers are nonprofit organizations with a primary mission of encouraging pregnant women to proceed with childbirth. This study analyzed 64 websites of such organizations. Researchers found that more than half of websites (58 percent) did not mention abortion as a birth control option and an almost equal number (53 percent) contained false or misleading statements about pregnancy and/or contraception.

Trenholm, Christopher, et al. 2008. "Impacts of Abstinence Education on Teen Sexual Activity, Risk of Pregnancy, and Risk of Sexually Transmitted Diseases." *Journal of Policy Analysis and Management.* 27(2): 255–276.

This study is one of the most frequently cited items by opponents of abstinence-only sex education. The four programs, involving more than 2,000 students, were found to have "no significant impact on teen sexual activity, no differences in rates of unprotected sex, and some impacts on knowledge of STDs and perceived effectiveness of condoms and birth control pills."

Wang, Timothy, et al. 2018. "The Effects of School-Based Condom Availability Programs (CAPs) on Condom Acquisition, Use and Sexual Behavior: A Systematic Review." *AIDS and Behavior.* 22(1): 308–320. Available online at https://www.ncbi.nlm.nih.gov/pmc/articles/PMC5758683/. Accessed on May 29, 2019.

The authors review a number of studies on the effects of condom acquisition and use and sexual behaviors for schools with condom availability programs (CAPs). They conclude that "school-based CAPs are likely to be effective at increasing the acquisition and use of condoms, school-based CAPs should be considered as one part of a comprehensive, multi-component strategy to prevent STIs and unwanted pregnancy among adolescents."

Waters, Jessica L., and Leandra N. Carrasco. 2018. "Untangling the Reproductive Rights and Religious Liberty Knot." *Yale Journal of Law & Feminism.* 26(2): 3. Available online at https://digitalcommons.law.yale.edu/yjlf/vol26/iss2/3/. Accessed on May 31, 2019.

> The so-called contraceptive mandate created by the Affordable Care Act of 2010 (Obamacare) has, from the outset, created conflicts between the demands of that act and religious and moral beliefs of individuals and businesses that oppose that mandate. This article provides a detailed look at this controversy.

Watkins, Elizabeth Siegel. 2012. "How the Pill Became a Lifestyle Drug: The Pharmaceutical Industry and Birth Control in the United States Since 1960." *American Journal of Public Health.* 102(8): 1462–1472. Available online at https://www.ncbi.nlm.nih.gov/pmc/articles/PMC3464843/. Accessed on May 28, 2019.

> The marketing and use of the birth control pill has changed significantly from its first release in 1960 to the present day. At first, it was conceived of as a product intended for women who simply wished to have greater control over their own family planning hopes. It has now become a so-called *lifestyle drug*, whose primary purpose it is to improve the lifestyle of women who choose to use the product.

Young, Michael, and Tina Penhollow. 2006. "The Impact of Abstinence Education." *American Journal of Health Education.* 37(4): 194–202. Available online at https://files.eric.ed.gov/fulltext/EJ795898.pdf. Accessed on May 30, 2019.

> The authors undertake to review all existing studies on the effectiveness of abstinence-only sex education programs, along with other commentaries and reviews on the topic. They conclude that such programs tend to undervalue or ignore evaluation studies, making it difficult to assess

their true effectiveness. Proponents of the approach also seem to be least enthusiastic about programs that are most effective.

Reports

Abma, Joyce C., and Gladys Martinez. 2017. "Sexual Activity and Contraceptive Use among Teenagers in the United States, 2011–2015." Hyattsville, MD: U.S. Department of Health & Human Services. Centers for Disease Control and Prevention. National Center for Health Statistics.

This report is derived from the federal government's National Survey of Family Growth. It provides data and statistics on several factors relating to adolescent sexuality in the United States between 2011 and 2015.

"Access to Contraception." 2015. Committee Opinion No. 615. American College of Obstetricians and Gynecologists. *Obstetrics and Gynecology.* 125: 250–255. Available online at https://www.acog.org/Clinical-Guidance-and-Publications/ Committee-Opinions/Committee-on-Health-Care-for-Underserved-Women/Access-to-Contraception. Accessed on May 31, 2019.

This position statement from the American College of Obstetricians and Gynecologists consists of several recommendations on access to contraception in the United States, along with comments on unintended pregnancy rates in the United States, knowledge deficits on the subject, restrictive legal and legislative issues, cost and insurance coverage, objections to contraception, unnecessary medical practices, institutional and economic barriers, and health care inequities.

"Birth Control Use." 2019. Child Trends. https://www .childtrends.org/indicators/birth-control-pill-use. Accessed on May 31, 2019.

This website contains statistical data on a variety of topics relating to birth control, such as this web page plus additional web pages on teen pregnancy, sexual activity among teens, and condom use.

Branum, Amy M., and Jo Jones. 2015. "Trends in Long-acting Reversible Contraception Use among U.S. Women Aged 15–44." National Center for Health Statistics.
The use of long-acting reversible contraceptives increased nearly fivefold between 2002 and 2011–2013. This report follows this trend among women in general and among subgroups based on age, race, and other characteristics.

Brener, Nancy D. 2017. "School Health Profiles 2016. Characteristics of Health Programs Among Secondary Schools." U.S. Department of Health and Human Services. Centers for Disease Control and Prevention. https://www.cdc.gov/healthyyouth/data/profiles/pdf/2016/2016_Profiles_Report .pdf. Accessed on May 26, 2019.
This publication provides data and statistics of virtually every aspect of school health programs in the United States. Very interesting and useful information on sexual health programs is included.

"Contraceptive Use." 2016. Centers for Disease Control and Prevention. https://www.cdc.gov/nchs/fastats/contraceptive .htm. Accessed on May 31, 2019.
This website provides links to several statistical studies that have been done on the use of contraceptive devices in the United States.

"Contraceptive Use in the United States." 2018. Guttmacher Institute. https://www.guttmacher.org/fact-sheet/contracep tive-use-united-states. Accessed on May 26, 2019.
The chapters in this report include "Who Needs Contraceptives?" "Who Uses Contraceptives?" "Which Methods

Do Women Use?" "Adolescent Contraceptive Use," "Contraceptive Effectiveness," "The Broad Benefits of Contraceptive Use," "Emergency Contraception," and "Who Pays for Contraception?"

Daniels, Kimberley, and Joyce C. Abma. 2018. "Current Contraceptive Status among Women Aged 15–49: United States, 2015–2017." Hyattsville, MD: National Center for Health Statistics. https://www.cdc.gov/nchs/data/databriefs/db327-h .pdf. Accessed on May 31, 2019.
This brochure reviews the latest data available on contraceptive use by American women between 2015 and 2017.

Kantor, Leslie, and Nicole Levitz. 2017. "Parents' Views on Sex Education in Schools: How Much Do Democrats and Republicans Agree?" Public Library of Science. Available online at https://doi.org/10.1371/journal.pone.0180250. Accessed on May 31, 2019.
Numerous studies have shown widespread support for sex education in the schools. These researchers ask if that support is consistent across political leanings by respondents. They find that the answer to that question is "yes, it does."

Second International Congress on Male Contraception. 2018. International Consortium for Male Contraception. http:// www.ic-mc.info/past-conferences/2nd-icmc-international-congress-paris-2018/. Accessed on June 2, 2019.
This website contains a list of presentations made at the Second International Conference on Male Contraception. Abstracts for most of those presentations are available on the website. The topics listed provide an overview of a topic rarely discussed in the United States, namely, what is the role of men in birth control issues.

Selected Practice Recommendations for Contraceptive Use, 3rd ed. 2016. Reproductive Health and Research. Geneva: World

Health Organization. https://www.who.int/reproductivehe
alth/publications/family_planning/SPR-3/en/. Accessed on
May 28, 2019.

This publication is a regular report from the World Health
Organization designed for policy makers and family planning program managers at the national level. It contains
several recommendations for the implementation and
conduct of contraceptive programs at all levels.

"Sex Education: A National Survey on Support among
Likely Voters." 2018. Planned Parenthood. https://www
.plannedparenthood.org/uploads/filer_public/7a/ac/7aacf0ad-
fd1c-4dcc-b65f-47e3c3754e0d/sex_education_-_a_national_
survey_on_support_among_likely_voters_logo.pdf. Accessed
on May 31, 2019.

Researchers continue to ask the general public about their
views on sex education. This report is one of the most recent
of those studies, largely reaffirming the findings reported
in earlier studies, namely, a very widespread support for
comprehensive sex education programs in the schools

Stewart-Cousins, Andrea, and Jeff Klein. 2018. "Pricey Pre-
dicament: Access to Affordable Emergency Contraception."
New York State Senate Democratic Conference. https://
www.nysenate.gov/sites/default/files/press-release/attachm
ent/380492674-pricey-predicament-access-to-affordable-eme
rgency-contraception.pdf. Accessed on May 29, 2019.

The Democratic Conference of the New York state senate was curious as to the cost and availability of emergency contraception in the state. It studied the question
and produced this report. The report includes very useful
information about emergency contraception in general,
along with the results of its search for costs for the product. It found that a single pill could cost a patient as much
as $60, which the authors of the report thought to be
unacceptably high.

"Trends in Contraceptive Use Worldwide 2015." 2015. United Nations, Department of Economic and Social Affairs, Population Division. https://www.un.org/en/development/ desa/population/publications/pdf/family/trendsContracep tiveUse2015Report.pdf. Accessed on May 31, 2019.

    This report covers almost every aspect of contraceptive use worldwide, by region, and in well over 100 specific countries.

Witwer, Elizabeth, Rachel Jones, and Laura Lindberg. 2018. "Sexual Behavior and Contraceptive and Condom Use among U.S. High School Students, 2013–2017." New York: Guttm- acher Institute. Available online at https://www.guttmacher .org/sites/default/files/report_pdf/sexual-behavior-contracep tive-condom-use-us-high-school-students-2013-2017.pdf. Accessed on May 29, 2019.

    The authors of this report examine trends in condom use among adolescents to determine how, if at all, these trends will affect the high rate of unintended pregnancies in the United States. The report has a large amount of very use- ful statistical information on the question. This report is one of the essential references about condom use among adolescents in American schools today.

Internet

"Abstinence." 2019. SexInfo. Online. http://www.soc.ucsb .edu/sexinfo/article/abstinence. Accessed on May 28, 2019.

    This website provides one of the most complete and thoughtful overviews of all aspects of sexual abstinence as an option in birth control.

"Abstinence Education Programs: Definition, Funding, and Impact on Teen Sexual Behavior." 2018. Henry J. Kaiser Family Foundation. https://www.kff.org/womens-health-policy/fact- sheet/abstinence-education-programs-definition-funding-and- impact-on-teen-sexual-behavior/. Accessed on May 28, 2019.

Abstinence-only education has been the subject of ongoing controversy for more than a half century in the United States. This website provides all of the essential information that one needs to understand that controversy.

Adams, Cydney. 2019. "America's Sex Ed Controversy: Can You Teach Consent?" CBSN Originals. https://www.cbsnews.com/news/sex-education-consent-abstinence-cbsn-originals/. Accessed on May 30, 2019.

The author discusses the need for teaching about consent in sexual relationships and the apparent failure of many sex education programs to include the topic in their curriculum.

"All about Hormones." 2017. Bedsider. https://www.bedsider.org/features/317-all-about-hormones. Accessed on May 29, 2019.

Hormonal contraceptives work by changing the character of a woman's menstrual cycle. This article provides a simplified version of that process with some helpful illustrations.

Allen, Samantha. 2015. "Should Sex Ed Be Mandatory?" The Daily Beast. https://www.thedailybeast.com/should-sex-ed-be-mandatory. Accessed on May 30, 2019.

The author discusses arguments for and against requiring sex education courses for all students in the United States and compares the situation in America today with that of other countries around the world.

"The Ancient World's 'Birth Control Pill': Silphion." 2010. Sister Zeus. http://www.sisterzeus.com/Silphio.htm. Accessed on May 27, 2019.

Silphion was one of the most commonly used contraceptives by ancient women. This article provides an overview of the herb.

Bentsianov, Sari. 2016. "Why Confidentiality Is Crucial." Mount Sinai Adolescent Health Center. https://teenhealthcare

.org/blog/why-confidentiality-is-crucial/. Accessed on May 31, 2019.

The author of this web page explains why confidentiality is essential to discussing an adolescent's sexual behaviors.

"Birth Control Failures." 2019. American Pregnancy Association. https://americanpregnancy.org/preventing-pregnancy/birth-control-failure/. Accessed on May 31, 2019.

This website offers a very helpful chart containing information on the failure rate for several common contraceptives, along with side effects and risks associated with each device or procedure.

"Birth Control Pharmacies." 2019. https://www.birthcontrol pharmacies.com/. Accessed on May 26, 2019.

Some states now allow pharmacists to prescribe birth control paraphernalia and then issue such materials and devices to customers. This website outlines the process involved in such transactions and provides links to pharmacies that participate in this program.

"The Birth Control Pill: A History." 2015. Planned Parenthood. https://www.plannedparenthood.org/files/1514/3518/7100/Pill_History_FactSheet.pdf. Accessed on May 26, 2019.

This pamphlet provides an excellent review of the technical aspects of the development of the pill, of the individuals involved in that process, its side effects and adverse effects, and issues involved in its approval by the FDA.

Brezina, Paul R., and Yulian Zhao. 2012. "The Ethical, Legal, and Social Issues Impacted by Modern Assisted Reproductive Technologies." *Obstetrics and Gynecology International.* 2012. http://dx.doi.org/10.1155/2012/686253. Accessed on June 1, 2019.

This article provides an excellent overview of the ethical, legal, and social issues associated with the use of assisted reproductive technologies.

Cavedon, Matthew. 2019. "No Elephants: Women Who Have Abortions Won't Face Criminal Charges Under Georgia's New Law." Daily Report. https://www.law.com/dailyreporton line/2019/05/14/no-elephants-women-who-have-abortions-wont-face-criminal-charges-under-georgias-new-law/. Accessed on May 30, 2019.

> This author takes issue with commentators who have argued women who have abortions under a new 2019 Georgia law will *not* be subject to prosecution for murder. For the opposite side, see Stern 2019.

"Confidential Services and Private Time." 2019. American Academy of Pediatrics. https://www.aap.org/en-us/advocacy-and-policy/aap-health-initiatives/adolescent-sexual-health/Pages/Confidential-Services-and-Private-Time.aspx. Accessed on May 31, 2019.

> This web page lists some of the materials available from the Academy on confidentiality with regard to adolescents' sexual issues, along with other resources of value on this topic.

Doyle, Sadi. 2019. "Climate Change Is a Reproductive-Justice Issue." Dame. https://www.damemagazine.com/2019/03/07/climate-change-is-a-reproductive-justice-issue/. Accessed on June 1, 2019.

> This extended essay attempts to make a connection between a woman's right to reproductive freedom and decisions about having children that may have profound influence on the problem of climate change.

"Embryo Adoption." 2019. Office of Population Affairs. HHS. gov. https://www.hhs.gov/opa/about-opa/embryo-adoption/index.html. Accessed on May 26, 2019.

> The Office of Population Affairs sponsors a program by which frozen embryos that are no longer wanted by the sponsoring couple are made available for adoption by

members of the general public. This page describes the basic aspects of that program.

"Emergency Contraception." 2018. Women's Health Policy. Henry J. Kaiser Family Foundation. https://www.kff.org/womens-health-policy/fact-sheet/emergency-contraception/. Accessed on May 29, 2019.

This article provides a general introduction to emergency contraception, a review of the products available, women's knowledge and use of the product, and access, availability, and cost data.

"Facts about Sex Education." 2019. Future of Sex Education. http://www.futureofsexed.org/youthhealthrights.html

This excellent website provides detailed information on several issues relating to sex education; included are sections such as "Youth Health and Rights in Sex Education," "Reconnecting Science and Adolescent Sexual and Reproductive Health Policy Making," "Building a Foundation for Sexual Health Is a K–12 Endeavor," "Comprehensive Sex Education: Research and Results," "Comprehensive Sex Education and Academic Success," "Medical Organizations Support Comprehensive Sex Education," "Statistics and Profiles," "SIECUS State Profiles," and "Adolescent Sexual Health State Policies."

Gunter, Jen. 2016. "Dear Press, Stop Calling Them 'Heartbeat' Bills and Call Them 'Fetal Pole Cardiac Activity' Bills." Dr. Jen Gunter. https://drjengunter.com/2016/12/11/dear-press-stop-calling-them-heartbeat-bills-and-call-them-fetal-pole-cardiac-activity-bills/. Accessed on May 30, 2019.

This physician points out that the term "heartbeat" or "fetal heartbeat" in discussions of recent anti-abortion legislation is incorrect, since such an event does not occur at the embryonic stage proposed by such legislation. She notes that the electrical pulse to which these bills refer is more correctly called "fetal pole cardiac activity."

Haeger, Kristin O., Jacqueline Lamme, and Kelly Cleland. 2018. "State of Emergency Contraception in the U.S." *Contraception and Reproductive Medicine.* 3:20. https://contraceptionmedicine.biomedcentral.com/articles/10.1186/s40834-018-0067-8. Accessed on May 28, 2019.

This paper provides a comprehensive review of the status of emergency contraception in the United States in 2016, with data on its use, technical information about products, misconceptions about emergency contraception, and availability to various subpopulations.

"Here's What Really Happens When You Get Your Tubes Tied." 2018. Nameless Network. https://www.youtube.com/watch?v=o8NrYt3-TJ8. Accessed on June 1, 2019.

This very helpful video shows how tubal ligations are performed, how they can be reversed, and what some issues may be related to the procedure. An interesting comparison with vasectomies is included.

"The History of the Birth Control Pill." 2013. Planned Parenthood Advocates of Arizona. http://advocatesaz.org/2013/01/08/the-history-of-the-birth-control-pill-part-1-hormones-our-chemical-messengers/. Accessed on May 26, 2019.

This six-part series of articles traces the development of the oral contraceptive pill from earliest research on the nature and effects of hormones.

Hunt, Elle. 2019. "Birthstrikers: Meet the Women Who Refuse to Have Children until Climate Change Ends." *The Guardian.* https://www.theguardian.com/lifeandstyle/2019/mar/12/birthstrikers-meet-the-women-who-refuse-to-have-children-until-climate-change-ends. Accessed on June 1, 2019.

BirthStrike is an organization of women in the United Kingdom who have pledged not to have children until the world's ecosystem crises (such as climate change) have been solved. In addition to the stories told here, see the organization's website at https://birthstrike.tumblr.com/.

"In Vitro Fertilization." 2006. Discover Biology. http://www
.sumanasinc.com/webcontent/animations/content/invitrofer-
tilization.html. Accessed on June 1, 2019.
    This video provides a simple, complete description of the
    process of in vitro fertilization.

Jacobson, Heather. 2018. "A Limited Market: The Recruitment
of Gay Men as Surrogacy Clients by the Infertility Industry in
the USA." *Reproductive Biomedicine & Society Online.* 7: 14–23.
https://www.ncbi.nlm.nih.gov/pmc/articles/PMC6280596/.
Accessed on June 1, 2019.
    Surrogacy is essentially the only option for gay men who
    decide to have children join their families. This author
    explores the question as to how aggressively the surrogate
    industry in the United States recruits gay male clients and
    how that practice affects both potential clients and providers.

Khazan, Olga. 2018. "When the Religious Doctor Refuses to
Treat You." *The Atlantic.* https://www.theatlantic.com/health/
archive/2018/01/when-the-religious-doctor-refuses-to-treat-
you/551231/. Accessed on May 27, 2019.
    The administration of President Donald Trump has
    changed regulations on medical treatment that give
    greater opportunity for health care providers to decline
    to offer services about which they have religious or moral
    concerns. This article explores possible consequences of
    the new policy.

Knight, Nicole. 2018. "TRAP Laws Have Ensured 'Separate
and Unequal Treatment' for Abortion Care." Rewire. News.
https://rewire.news/article/2018/02/22/trap-laws-ensured-
separate-unequal-treatment-abortion-care/. Accessed on May
30, 2019.
    Most states have no laws regulating in-office surgeries such
    as liposuction, breast augmentation, and vasectomies but
    place severe restrictions on abortion, which is no more

dangerous than those procedures. The author reviews the current status to targeted regulation procedures in the United States.

Lewis, Ricki. 2013. "When Does a Human Life Begin? 17 Timepoints." DNA Science Blog. https://blogs.plos.org/dna science/2013/10/03/when-does-a-human-life-begins-17-time points/. Accessed on May 30, 2019.
    The author claims to be very knowledgeable about embryogenesis and suggests that there are 17 discrete points at which life can be said to begin. This analysis provides expert opinion that can be used in debates over so-called fetal heartbeat anti-abortion legislation.

Luna, Zakiya, and Kristin Luker. 2013. "Reproductive Justice." *Annual Review of Law and Social Science.* 9(1): 327–352.
    This article provides a good general overview of the Reproductive Justice movement and then focuses a discussion on legal issues related to the movement.

Martin, Nina. 2014. "This Alabama Judge Has Figured Out How to Dismantle Roe v. Wade." ProPublica. https://www.propublica.org/article/this-alabama-judge-has-figured-out-how-to-dismantle-roe-v-wade. Accessed on May 30, 2019.
    Some judicial authorities and legal scholars have developed a philosophy that can be used against the practice of abortion: personhood. This article explains how one Alabama judge has adopted this philosophy in approving new, severe bans against abortion in the state. Also see the associated web page on the timeline of the personhood concept at The Personhood Movement 2014.

Marty, Robin. 2014. "Is Life as Simple as a Beating Heart?" *Politico Magazine.* https://www.politico.com/magazine/story/2014/01/marlise-munozis-texas-life-as-simple-as-a-beat ing-heart-102634. Accessed on May 30, 2019.

The author raises the question as to the conflict between religion and science that may arise with the belief that "life begins at the first heartbeat."

Mazel, Sharon. 2019. "What Is a Surrogate Mother, and How Does Surrogacy Work?" What to Expect. https://www.whatto expect.com/getting-pregnant/adoption-and-surrogacy/using-a-surrogate-mother/. Accessed on June 1, 2019.
This website provides a good general introduction to the topic of surrogacy.

McWeeney, Clár, and Nicole Telfer. 2019. "Female (Internal) Condoms 101." Clue. https://helloclue.com/articles/sex/inter nal-condoms-101. Accessed on May 29, 2019.
This website provides a very nice general introduction to female condoms, how they are used, and their advantages and disadvantages.

"Museum of Contraception and Abortion." 2018. Museum of Contraception and Abortion. https://bib.muvs.org/en/. Accessed on May 29, 2019.
This website is an extraordinary resource on the topics of contraception and abortion, providing information on some subjects that is probably not conveniently available from other resource. Topics range from plights (criminal actions against providers) and pioneers to plants and literary quotes.

Oberman, Michelle, and W. David Ball. 2019. "When We Talk about Abortion, Let's Talk about Men. Since Women Don't Have Unwanted Pregnancies without Them." *The New York Times.* https://www.nytimes.com/2019/06/02/opinion/abortion-laws-men.html. Accessed on June 5, 2019.
The vast majority of discussions about birth control seems to be about women, since they are the ones who get pregnant. Yet, they don't get pregnant by themselves. And books, articles, online writing, and other sources rarely

mention the role of men in pregnancy and their birth control responsibilities. This editorial describes some of the ways in which men can become more involved in decisions about having or not having children.

Pérez, Miriam Zoila. 2010. "Surrogacy: The Next Frontier for Reproductive Justice." Rewire.News. https://rewire.news/arti cle/2010/02/23/surrogacy-next-frontier-reproductive-justice/. Accessed on June 1, 2019.

The author argues that the issue of surrogacy "involves many of the issues central to reproductive justice—bodily autonomy, a woman's right to abortion, definitions of parenthood, and custody of children." She goes on to define surrogacy and the ways in which these connections occur, along with recent developments in surrogacy case law.

"The Personhood Movement: Where It Came from and Where It Stands Today." ProPublica. https://www.propublica.org/arti cle/the-personhood-movement-timeline. Accessed on May 30, 2019.

This website provides a timeline of important events in the development of the so-called personhood movement among anti-abortionists. The web page is part of an article on the topic. See Martin 2014.

Robinson, Rachel Sullivan. 2018. "Sex Education Lessons from Mississippi and Nigeria." WTOP. https://wtop.com/edu cation/2018/07/sex-education-lessons-from-mississippi-and-nigeria/. Accessed on May 30, 2019.

Sex education policies and practices are remarkably similar in this U.S. state and African nation. The author explores the way in which these programs developed, blocks to their development, the consequences of inadequate sex education, and related issues in the two regions.

Russell, Camisha. 2018. "Rights-holders or Refugees? Do Gay Men Need Reproductive Justice?" *Reproductive Biomedicine*

and Society Online. 7: 131–140. https://www.ncbi.nlm.nih
.gov/pmc/articles/PMC6491715/. Accessed on June 1, 2019.

> The author outlines special considerations relating to the
> desire of gay men to have children and the biological limi-
> tations to achieving that result. She asks if gay men, there-
> fore, have common interests and goals with members of
> the Reproductive Justice movement and concludes that
> "yes, they do."

Samuels, Sarah E., and Mark D. Smith, eds. 1993. "Condoms
in the Schools." Henry J. Kaiser Family Foundation. https://
files.eric.ed.gov/fulltext/ED366882.pdf. Accessed on May 26,
2019.

> This collection of papers is of considerable historical
> interest with regard to the early years of free distribution
> of condoms for students of American schools.

Sanger-Katz, Margot. 2019. "Set It and Forget It: How Better
Contraception Could Be a Key to Reducing Poverty." *The New
York Times.* https://www.nytimes.com/2018/12/18/upshot/
set-it-and-forget-it-how-better-contraception-could-be-a-se
cret-to-reducing-poverty.html. Accessed on June 2, 2019.

> The state of Delaware has implemented a new type of
> birth control clinic, Upstream, that provides "one-stop
> shopping" for women looking for birth control solutions
> in their family planning. This article describes the pro-
> gram and explains how it can be helpful to women of
> limited financial means.

Sitruk-ware, Régine. 2018. "Getting Contraceptives for Men
to the Market Will Take Pharma's Help." Stat. https://www
.statnews.com/2018/05/11/contraceptives-for-men-pharma/.
Accessed on June 2, 2019.

> The author reviews the discussions on the development
> of a male contraceptive held at the Second International
> Congress on Male Contraception. She says that one reason

for the slow development of such a product is the lack of interest by pharmaceutical companies. For more information on this conference, see "Second International Congress on Male Contraception" under Reports.

Smith, Sharla, et al. 2019. "A State-Level Examination of School Nurses' Perceptions of Condom Availability Accompanied by Sex Education." *The Journal of School Nursing*. https://doi.org/10.1177/1059840518824728. Accessed on May 31, 2019.

A survey of school nurses in Kansas found that a large majority were comfortable with and approved programs of free condom distribution. Their participation was hindered to some degree, however, by a variety of factors, such as administration, parents, cost, community support, and policies.

Snider, Susannah. 2019. "The Cost of Birth Control." US News & World Report. https://money.usnews.com/money/personal-finance/family-finance/articles/the-cost-of-birth-control. Accessed on May 31, 2019.

Articles on birth control often fail to mention one of the most critical factors in the availability and type of device(s) discussed. This article points out that the cost of birth control devices can have a significant effect on the choices that women can and do make about those devices. She reviews economic factors associated with each of the most common birth control devices now generally available to women and men.

Sobel, Laurie, Alina Salganicoff, and Caroline Rosenzweig. 2018. "New Regulations Broadening Employer Exemptions to Contraceptive Coverage: Impact on Women." KFF. https://www.kff.org/health-reform/issue-brief/new-regulations-broadening-employer-exemptions-to-contraceptive-coverage-impact-on-women/. Accessed on May 27, 2019.

The authors offer a very detailed and somewhat technical explanation of the Trump administration's new regulations, contraceptive coverage, and religious exemptions.

Sobel, Laurie, Alina Salganicoff, and Ivette Gomez. 2018. "State and Federal Contraceptive Coverage Requirements: Implications for Women and Employers." KFF. https://www.kff.org/womens-health-policy/issue-brief/state-and-federal-contraceptive-coverage-requirements-implications-for-women-and-employers/. Accessed on May 31, 2019.

One of the most contentious issues with regard to contraception in recent years is the so-called *contraceptive mandate*, which requires employers to provide coverage for contraceptive materials in their health insurance plans. That mandate has, from the beginning, been the subject of acrimonious discussions among politicians, health care workers, and the general population. This article brings the situation up to date as of late 2019, although conditions will almost certainly change as time passes.

Stacey, Dawn. 2019. "The Today Sponge." Verywell Health. https://www.verywellhealth.com/the-today-sponge-906820. Accessed on May 29, 2019.

The vaginal sponge has gone through a troubled history in the United States since it was first introduced in 1983. This article reviews that history along with a complete review of current information on its latest reappearance on the market.

"State Law Approaches to Facility Regulation of Abortion and Other Office Interventions." 2018. Advancing New Standards in Reproductive Health. https://www.ansirh.org/sites/default/files/publications/files/trap_and_obs_laws_issue_brief.pdf. Accessed on May 30, 2019.

This organization conducted a survey of the number, location, and character of so-called targeted regulation of abortion providers (TRAP) laws in the United States.

Among their findings were that "laws do not bring abortion providing facilities in line with other health care facilities, but instead subject them to different and more stringent requirements" and that "differential treatment suggests a lack of health benefit from TRAP laws, indicating they reduce access without justification."

"State Personal Responsibility Education Program." 2017. Family & Youth Services Bureau. https://www.acf.hhs.gov/sites/default/files/fysb/state_prep_20170314.pdf. Accessed on May 30, 2019.

This pamphlet provides a general overview of the Personal Responsibility Education Program that was part of Title V of amendments to the Social Security Act, adopted in 2010.

Stern, Mark Joseph. 2019. "Georgia Just Criminalized Abortion: Women Who Terminate Their Pregnancies Would Receive Life in Prison." Slate. https://slate.com/news-and-politics/2019/05/hb-481-georgia-law-criminalizes-abortion-subjects-women-to-life-in-prison.html. Accessed on May 30, 2019.

One interpretation of the new Georgia anti-abortion law (2019) is that a woman who has an abortion can be convicted of murder, the murder of her unborn child, thus subject to a term of life in prison. (But for a different interpretation of this laws, see Cavedon 2019.)

Strang, Steven. 2019. "How One Woman Started the Heartbeat Bill Movement Sweeping America." Charisma. https://www.charismamag.com/blogs/the-strang-report/41509-how-one-woman-started-the-heartbeat-bill-movement-sweeping-america. Accessed on May 30, 2019.

This article describes a conversation between the author and Janet Porter, purportedly the person responsible for the idea behind so-called fetal heartbeat bills.

Strauss, Elissa. 2017. "When Does Life Begin? It's Not So Simple." Slate. https://slate.com/human-interest/2017/04/when-does-life-begin-outside-the-christian-right-the-answer-is-over-time.html. Accessed on May 30, 2019.

The author, whose own pregnancy included a fetal heartbeat one day, followed by a loss of heartbeat the next day, considers the variety of answers that have been given throughout the centuries by various individuals and religious groups. She points out how this variety of opinions is relevant to adoption of fetal heartbeat abortion bans.

"Surrogacy for Gay Men." n.d. Gays with Kids. https://www.gayswithkids.com/can-we-make-surrogacy-cheaper-2635661023.html. Accessed on June 1, 2019.

This website provides many articles on all aspects of surrogacy for gay men. Those articles cover almost every imaginable aspect of that issue.

"Targeted Regulation of Abortion Providers." 2019. Guttmacher Institute. https://www.guttmacher.org/state-policy/explore/targeted-regulation-abortion-providers. Accessed on May 30, 2019.

State laws specifically designed to shut down abortion-providing sites have become increasingly popular over the last decade. This study provides a review of the types of laws that have been passed and their influence on sources of birth control information in states.

Tarico, Valerie. 2014. "The Obvious Relationship Between Climate and Family Planning—and Why We Don't Talk about It." Grist. https://grist.org/climate-energy/the-obvious-relationship-between-climate-and-family-planning-and-why-we-don't-talk-about-it/. Accessed on June 1, 2019.

The author argues that there is an obvious and critical way for the world to deal with climate change: population control via birth control. She suggests that this solution would not be coercive or a burden on the world's women since well over 200 million women would already be open to the use of birth control (if it were available) for other reasons.

"Teen Pregnancy Prevention Program (TPP)." 2017. Office of Adolescent Health. HHS.gov. https://www.hhs.gov/ash/ oah/grant-programs/teen-pregnancy-prevention-program-tpp/ index.html. Accessed on May 30, 2019.

This website provides a comprehensive overview of the Teen Pregnancy Prevention Program, first passed by the U.S. Congress in 2010.

"Timeline of Abstinence-only Education in U.S. Classrooms." 2019. National Coalition against Censorship. https://ncac.org/ resource/timeline-of-abstinence-only-education-in-u-s-class rooms. Accessed on May 30, 2019.

This website provides a detailed review of the status and funding of abstinence-only-until-marriage sex education programs from 1981 to 2009.

"A Timeline of Contraception." 2019. American Experience. http://www.pbs.org/wgbh/americanexperience/features/pill-timeline/. Accessed on May 26, 2019.

This website provides an excellent survey of important events in the history of contraception in the United States from about 1920 onwards. Coverage of the development of the oral contraceptive pill is especially well done.

"Trump Administration Issues Rules Protecting the Conscience Rights of All Americans." 2017. HHS.gov. https://www.hhs .gov/about/news/2017/10/06/trump-administration-issues-rules-protecting-the-conscience-rights-of-all-americans.html. Accessed on May 31, 2019.

This press release announces the Trump administration's new rules on exceptions to the contraceptive mandate.

Links to the basic documents themselves, along with one to a helpful Fact Sheet, are available on the website.

"The Truth about Abstinence-Only Programs." 2007. Advocates for Youth. https://www.advocatesforyouth.org/wp-content/uploads/storage//advfy/documents/fsabstinenceonly.pdf. Accessed on May 26, 2019.

This report lists claims made for abstinence-only-until-marriage sex education and provides rebuttals for each of the claims made.

Van de Walle, Etienne. 2005. Birth Control in an Era of Natural Fertility: The Heritage of Dioscorides." https://iussp2005.princeton.edu/papers/50605. Accessed on May 28, 2019.

Dioscorides was a Roman physician who wrote extensively about contraceptive issues. This essays reports and comments on some of his most important teachings on the subject.

"Vasectomy." 2019. Mayo Clinic. https://www.mayoclinic.org/tests-procedures/vasectomy/about/pac-20384580. Accessed on June 1, 2019.

This website explains what a vasectomy is, why it might be performed, risks involved with the surgery, and steps in the procedure itself.

"Vasectomy Reversal." 2019. Mayo Clinic. https://www.mayoclinic.org/tests-procedures/vasectomy-reversal/about/pac-20384537. Accessed on June 1, 2019.

Men who have had, or plan to have, a vasectomy often ask whether the procedure can later be reversed. This website shows how such a procedure is done. An excellent animation provides the details of the process.

"What Is Sex Education?" 2019. Planned Parenthood. https://www.plannedparenthood.org/learn/for-educators/what-sex-education. Accessed on May 26, 2019.

This website provides an excellent general introduction to the topic of comprehensive sex education, with a list of topics most commonly included in such courses.

Wild, Chris. n.d. "400 BCE–1965. Vintage Contraceptives." Mashable. https://mashable.com/2015/06/07/early-birth-con trol/#Ys4K7i4PnZqT. Accessed on May 27, 2019.
This website is of special interest because of the illustrations it provides of early contraceptive devices and methods.

#HandsOffMyBC
NATIONAL WOMEN'S LAW CENTER
Coalition
for
Choice
Who Run the World
GIRLS
with
Birth Control Coverage
HANDSOFFMYBC
ESS
OL
yBC

Introduction

Contraception has been an issue of importance to women and men throughout human history. Research shows that individuals have been searching for substances and procedures by which they can avoid pregnancy for at least 5,000 years. No chronology of this long history can be complete, but this chapter provides an overview of some of the most important laws, court cases, discoveries, inventions, and other events in that story.

c. 26,000 BCE A device thought to be the earliest dildo ever discovered is found in the Hohle Fels Cave, in Ulm, Germany. Experts disagree about the object's purpose, but some suggest that it was used as a substitute for sexual intercourse.

c. 3000 BCE The first condom is said to have been invented for use by King Minos of Crete. The king's semen is thought to have contained serpents and scorpions that caused disease and death to his sexual partners, a consequence avoided by his wearing a condom.

c. 1825 BCE The Kahun Gynaecological Papyrus from Ancient Egypt describes a variety of methods for preventing

---

Pro-choice demonstrators appear outside of the Supreme Court as arguments were heard in a case in which religious organizations are challenging the Affordable Care Act's provision that requires employers to cover birth control in healthcare plans, March 23, 2016. (Tom Williams/CQ Roll Call)

pregnancy, including crocodile dung inserted into the vagina and honey spread on a woman's womb.

c. 1550 BCE   The Egyptian Ebers Papyrus contains directions for making a pessary out of acacia, dates, and honey, which is then smeared on wool and inserted into the vagina to prevent penetration of sperm.

c. 7th century BCE   Greek settlers in the North African region of Cyrene discover an herb, silphion, that they use as a contraceptive and abortifacient. The drug becomes so popular for these and other uses that it becomes extinct by about 100 CE.

c. 7th century BCE   Chinese master physician Tung-hsuan describes the methods of coitus interruptus and coitus reservatus. It is not clear if the methods are used for birth control or preservation of a man's *yang*.

c. 6th century BCE   Genesis 38:9 provides the story of Onan, who "spilled his seed upon the ground," an act for which God punished him with death.

70 CE   *The Didache* (*The Teaching of the Twelve Apostles*) lists the use of contraception and abortion as sins. The book is generally regarded as the earliest written catechism for Roman Catholic theology.

c. 70 CE   In his 37-volume *Natural History*, Roman natural philosopher Pliny the Elder lists several methods of contraception, including the use of two worms wrapped in deer hide inserted into the vagina.

c. 90 CE   Greek physician Pedanius Dioscorides produces *De Materia Medica* (*About Medical Materials*), which contains numerous substances and methods for preventing pregnancy and inducing abortions.

c. 100 CE   In his classic book, *Gynaecology*, Greek physician Soranus of Ephesus provides the most comprehensive treatment of birth control technology available at the time. His treatment of the topic reached a level said to have been "surpassed only in the last hundred years." (Hopkins, Keith. 1965.

"Contraception in the Roman Empire." *Comparative Studies in Society and History*. 8(1): 124–151. See page 131.)

306 CE   The Spanish Council of Elvira declares that "all bishops, priests, deacons, and all clerics engaged in the ministry are forbidden entirely to live with their wives and to beget children: whoever shall do so will be deposed from the clerical dignity." The ruling is the first of many such demands for clerical celibacy in the Roman Catholic Church. ("Why Does the Church Mandate the Priests Be Celibate?" 2019. Catholic Straight Answers. http://catholicstraightanswers .com/why-does-the-church-mandate-that-priests-be-celibate/. Accessed on May 25, 2019.)

388 CE   Christian theologian Augustine of Hippo teaches that women should refrain from sexual relations during the time each month when they are most likely to become pregnant. This admonition is among the earliest of all statements of the rhythm method of contraception.

c. 400 CE   St. Augustine declares that sexual intercourse that takes place "in an unlawful and shameful manner whenever the conception of offspring is avoided." (Hardon, John A. 1998. "The Catholic Tradition on the Morality of Contraception." The Real Presence Association. http://www.therealpresence .org/archives/Abortion_Euthanasia/Abortion_Euthana- sia_004.htm. Accessed on May 25, 2019.)

c. 400 CE   Indian philosopher Mallinaga Vatsayayana writes what some call the most complete encyclopedia of sex ever produced, the *Kama Sutra*, in which he specifies that erotic practices are one of the three primary aims of life.

476 CE   With the fall of the Roman Empire, the pursuit of secular knowledge in ancient Greece and Rome comes largely to a halt and centers of learning spring up in the young Islamic civilization. Among Islamic scholars who study and write about birth control technology are Al-Razi (Rhazes, 865–925), All ibn Abbas (619–687), and Avicenna (Ibn Sina, 980–1037).

1276   Portuguese physician and cleric Pedro Julião is elected to the papacy as Pope Paul XXI. He is probably best remembered today for a book he wrote prior to his election as pope, *Thesaurus Pauperum* (*Treasure of the Poor*), in which he described several contraceptive devices and methods. The book was reprinted in an Italian edition in 1485 and was later found to contain a number of efficacious methods of birth control.

c. 1630   English physician William Harvey expresses one of the fundamental principles of human reproduction, "omne vivum ex ovo," that is, everything ("all living things come from an egg").

1646   Archaeologists discover "the earliest definitive physical evidence for the use of animal-membrane condoms in post-medieval Europe" at Dudley Castle, in the West Midlands of England. (Gaimster, David, et al. 1996. "The Archaeology of Private Life: The Dudley Castle Condoms." *Post-Medieval Archaeology*. 30:1: 129–142. Available online at https://www.tandfonline.com/doi/abs/10.1179/pma.1996.003. Accessed on May 25, 2019.) There is no way of knowing whether these objects were used to prevent sexually transmitted infections or as contraceptives.

1677   Dutch microscopist Antonie van Leeuwenhoek is the first person to observe human sperm. In a formal report on his research, he describes sperm as "moving like a snake or like an eel swimming in water." (Kelly, Diane. 2015. "The First Person Who Ever Saw Sperm Cells Collected Them from His Wife." Gizmodo. https://gizmodo.com/the-first-time-anyone-saw-sperm-1708170526. Accessed on May 25, 2019.)

1734   In his memoirs, Italian adventurer Giacomo Girolamo Casanova tells of his use of condoms for the prevention of pregnancy. Although by no means the first description of such use, Casanova's reputation soon earns interest in the devices for birth control as well as prevention of sexual disease.

1821   The state of Connecticut adopts the first abortion law in the nation, banning the use of any type of chemical to produce an abortion.

1823 English physician James Blundell recommends tubal ligation as a way of sterilizing women. In a lecture, "The Principles and Practice of Midwifery," given at Guy's Hospital in London, he suggests that the procedure would "intercept the contact between the semen and the rudiments," thereby ensuring sterility in the women. (Siegler, Alvin M., and Amos Grenebaum. 1980. "The 100th Anniversary of Tubal Sterilization." *Fertility and Sterility*. 34(6): 610–613. Available online at https://www.fertstert.org/article/S0015-0282(16)45206-4/pdf. Accessed on May 25, 2019.)

1827 Estonian biologist Karl Ernst von Baer first describes the existence of a mammalian egg.

1832 American physician Charles Knowlton recommends douching after sexual intercourse as a dependable method of contraception. Although the method is later to be found largely ineffective as a birth control technique, it has continued to have some popularity among women.

1838 German gynecologist Friedrich Wilde invents the first modern cervical cap. He makes custom rubber molds of a woman's cervix to create the device.

1839 American inventor Charles Goodyear devises a technology for the vulcanization of rubber. The new technology is soon put to use in a variety of contraceptive devices, including rubber condoms, intrauterine devices, and diaphragms.

1844 British inventor Thomas Hancock receives a patent for his invention of a condom made out of rubber. Goodyear receives a similar patent in the United States about three weeks later.

1850 American physician Frederick Hollick publishes *The Marriage Guide*, a widely popular treatise on contraception. The book's 100th edition was printed in 1875.

1865 English polymath Sir Francis Galton publishes his first articles on the heritability of "talent and character," laying out the fundamental principles of the eugenics movement.

1873 The U.S. Congress passes the Comstock Law, a provision that defines any form of contraceptive to be "obscene" and "illicit." The law makes it illegal to transmit such devices by mail or across state lines.

1875   German embryologist Wilhelm August Oscar Hertwig discovers that fertilization occurs in a human when sperm penetrates an egg.

1880   American surgeon Samuel Smith Lungren conducts the first tubal ligation in the United States, using silver wire sutures to tie off the fallopian tubes.

1882   German physician Karl Hasse invents the diaphragm, a rubber-covered metal device designed to sit inside the vagina to exclude sperm from reaching the uterus. Hasse wrote under the pseudonym of "Wilhelm P. J. Mensinga" (sometimes given as *Mensinger*) to protect his professional reputation. (Authorities differ as to which name was his birth name and which his pseudonym.) The device later became widely known as the Mensinga diaphragm.

1883   Sir Richard Burton privately publishes the first English translation of the Indian sex classic the *Kama Sutra* (see c. 400 CE). The book is circulated secretly to members of the British Kama Sutra Society.

1883   Francis Galton coins the word *eugenics*.

1884   Philadelphia physician William Pancoast performs the first successful in vitro fertilization by inseminating a female patient who was infertile with semen from one of his students. Neither husband nor wife was informed about the procedure until many years later.

1885   English pharmacist Walter Rendell invents the first modern vaginal suppository. It is made of cocoa butter and quinine sulfate and is sold under the name of Rendell's Suppositories.

1885   The Women's Christian Temperance Union introduces a "social purity" campaign, one component of which involves a "white ribbon" commitment. Men who commit to remaining sexually abstinent until marriage wear a white small white banner indicating that promise.

1899   British physician Reginald Harrison performs the first vasectomy on a human. It is performed not for sterilization purposes but for treatment of atrophy of the prostate gland. A year later, he reports on the results of more than 100 such procedures, some for the purpose of sterilization.

1899   Dr. Harry Sharp, a surgeon at the Indiana State Reformatory, conducts the first vasectomy on a patient, as a way of dealing with the patient's problem of excessive masturbation. The procedure is declared to be a "complete success," when the patient is seen to develop a "sunny disposition," become "brighter of intellect" and "ceased to masturbate."

Over the next decade, Sharp conducts more than a hundred similar procedures, both as a method of dealing with sexual problems and as a method for sterilizing men thought to be "unfit" to reproduce as part of the eugenics movement. (Beatty, Dick. 2019. "The History of Vasectomy." The Vasectomist. https://thevasectomist.com.au/history-of-vasectomy/. Accessed on May 25, 2019.)

1905   Dutch gynecologist Theodoor Hendrik Van de Velde discovers that women ovulate only once during their menstrual cycle, thus providing a scientific basis for use of various kinds of natural birth control.

1907   The state of Indiana becomes the first state in the Union to adopt a compulsory, involuntary sterilization law permitting the sterilization of institutionalized persons thought to be unfit to reproduce. The law is declared to be unconstitutional by the state supreme court in 1921, by which time more than two dozen other states had passed similar laws.

1908   The British firm Excelsior markets the first female condom, called *Practice*. The device is not successful, and acceptable forms of the product are not available for at least two decades.

1909   German physician Richard Richter invents the first intrauterine contraceptive device (IUD). It is made out of silkworm gut with two protruding ends for insertion and removal.

The product is difficult to use and never becomes very popular as a contraceptive device.

1910 The American Federation for Sex Hygiene is formed in St. Louis by a group of interested parties. The purpose of the organization is to improve the public's knowledge of sexual health issues and to fight against sexually transmitted infections and prostitution.

1912 The first formal program of sex education in American schools is proposed for the city of Chicago by superintendent Ella Flagg Young. The program lasts only one semester, however, because of strong opposition from the Roman Catholic church and other groups.

1912 American psychologist Henry H. Goddard publishes a book, *The Kallikak Family: A Study in the Heredity of Feeble-Mindedness*, purporting to show that "feeble-mindedness" was a hereditary trait. The book went through multiple editions and was taken as the "bible" for many in the eugenics movement. The book was later found to be based on fictitious data.

1913 A group of organizations meet at a conference in Buffalo, New York, to form the American Sexual Hygiene Association. The group remains in existence today, focusing its efforts on information concerning contraceptive and sexually transmitted infections.

1914 The American Social Hygiene Association formed through the consolidation of two existing groups, the American Federation for Sex Hygiene and the American Vigilance Association. In 1960, the organization changed its name to the American Social Health Association.

1915 American birth control activists Mary Ware Dennett, Jesse Ashley, and Clara Gruening Stillman found the National Birth Control League. The organization is disbanded in 1919, after which Dennett founds the Voluntary Parenthood League.

1916 The first latex condoms are produced by American inventor Merle Leland Youngs. They are sold through his company, Fay and Youngs, later renamed Youngs Rubber Corporation in 1919.

1916   American nurse and sex education proponent Margaret Sanger, Ethel Byrne (Sanger's sister), and Fania Mindell open the first birth control clinic in the United States in Brooklyn, New York, on October 16. They are arrested on the same day for violating the Comstock Law. She is found guilty on February 2, 1917, and chooses a 30-day prison term over a $5,000 cash fine.

1917   Margaret Sanger begins to speak about the importance of "voluntary motherhood" for women. The concept includes the fundamental principle that women should be in control of their own bodies and make their own decisions as to whether and/or when they will become pregnant.

1919   American women's rights advocate Mary Ware Dennett resigns from the National Birth Control League and founds the Voluntary Parenthood League. The organization's primary goal was to fight for the removal of federal obscenity laws.

1920s   The British Reckitt Benckiser Company introduces the use of one of its products, Lysol, as a vaginal douche to be used for contraceptive purposes. Not only was it unsuccessful for that purpose but the product also caused a number of health problems for women who used it.

c. 1920   British physician Marie Stopes introduces a modified form of a French cervical cap to women in attendance at her London birth control clinic. The device is a modified version of a French cervical cap. American women do not have access to the device for another seven decades.

1921   Sanger founds the American Birth Control League, later to become Planned Parenthood.

1922   The U.S. Public Health Service publishes a booklet "High Schools and Sex Education," offering numerous suggestions for the content and methodology of sex education in U.S. high schools. (Gruenberg, Benjamin C., ed. 1922. *High*

Schools and Sex Education. United States Public Health Service. United States Bureau of Education. https://iiif.lib.harvard.edu/manifests/view/drs:2574361$1i. Accessed on May 25, 2019.)

1923   American embryologists Edward A. Doisy and Edgar Allen announce the discovery of a hormone crucial to the process of embryogenesis.

1927   In the case of *Buck v. Bell* (274 U.S. 200), the U.S. Supreme Court upholds the constitutionality of the state of Virginia's compulsory sterilization law for patients at the state's mental hospitals. In his written opinion, Justice Oliver Wendall Holmes writes that "three generations of imbeciles are enough." The court's decision has never been overturned and was cited in a court decision with regard to an Oklahoma sterilization law in 1942. (*Skinner v. State of Oklahoma* [316 U.S. 535]).

1930   In his encyclical *Casti Connubii* (*On Chaste Marriage*), Pope Pius XI teaches that all forms of artificial birth control are "intrinsically evil." He says that abstinence is the only approved method of birth control.

1930   American gynecologist Willard Myron Allen and his mentor, George W. Corner, announce the discovery of a hormone intimately involved in the early stages of pregnancy: progesterone.

1933   The German journal *The Birth Control Review* devoted its April issue entirely to eugenic sterilization. The article essentially lays out the theoretical rationale for the use of compulsory sterilization to produce a "pure Aryan race." By 1935, an estimated half million eugenic abortions have reportedly been completed.

1934   Embryologists Hermann Knaus (Austria) and Kyusaku Ogino (Japan) announce their discovery of a system for predicting the times at which a woman is most likely to become pregnant, a discovery that makes possible the use of a "rhythm method" of birth control.

1934   The concept of "wrongful pregnancy" first arises in a case heard by the Minnesota Supreme Court (*Christensen* *v. Thornby*, 255 N.W. 620). In that case, a woman files suit against her physician who had performed a sterilization procedure to prevent her from having more children. The operation failed, and she later had another child. Her husband sued for $5,000 to cover the costs of expenses and anxiety. The court ruled against the claim.

1936   American gynecologist John Rock opens a Rhythm Clinic in Boston, the first of its kind in the United States.

1936   In the case of *United States v. One Package of Japanese Pessaries*, the U.S. Court of Appeals for the Second District ruled that the federal government could not intercept shipments of a contraceptive (pessaries) from a doctor who lived in Japan.

1941   American chemist Russell Earl Marker develops a process for making progesterone synthetically, greatly decreasing the cost of making the product and increasing its availability for research and therapeutic applications.

1944   American obstetrician and gynecologist John Rock invents the rhythmeter, a device that women can use to calculate the times at which she is likely and not likely to become pregnant.

1951   Pope Pius XII approves periodic abstinence and the rhythm method of birth control for Catholics.

1951   Margaret Sanger meets American endocrinologist Gregory Pincus at a New York City cocktail party and convinces him to begin research on an oral contraceptive pill. In the same year, she founds the Worcester Foundation for Experimental Biology, for the purpose of conducting research on an oral contraceptive pill.

1953   American philanthropist Katharine McCormick makes a $40,000 contribution to Pinkus's research on an oral contraceptive pill. Her later contributions amounted to more than two million dollars (about $10 million in 2019 dollars).

1960   The U.S. Food and Drug Administration (FDA) approves the licensing and sale of Enovid as a contraceptive.

It is the first product of Gregory Pincus's research for an oral contraceptive pill. Because of dangerous side effects, the pill was never made available to the marketplace.

1960 The FDA approves the use of an intrauterine device called the Dalkon Shield for use as a contraceptive method. The product is subsequently found to cause a variety of medical problems, and more than 200,000 claims are filed against its manufacturer, A. H. Robbins. The company eventually spends more than $3 billion to settle these claims.

1963 John Rock, who played a major role in the development of the first oral contraceptive pill, publishes a book, *The Time Has Come: A Catholic Doctor's Proposals to End the Battle over Birth Control*, in which he argues that the Roman Catholic Church should accept the pill as an extension of the rhythm method of contraception and, therefore, a legitimate form of birth control.

1964 The Sexuality Information and Education Council of the United States is founded.

1964 Dutch physician Arie Haspels treats a 13-year-old rape victim with a massive dose of estrogen in a (successful) effort to end her pregnancy. The event is generally regarded as the earliest demonstration of sex hormones for the post-coital treatment of sexual intercourse.

1965 In the case of *Griswold v. Connecticut*, the U.S. Supreme Court rules that the state's ban on the use of contraceptives violates the right to marital privacy.

1966 American gynecologist John McLean Morris and biologist Gertrude Van Wagenen report on the successful use of high-dose estrogen pills as post-coital contraceptives in women and rhesus macaque monkeys, respectively.

1968 In his encyclical *Humane Vitae* (*Of Human Life*), Pope Paul VI reaffirms that every act of marital intimacy must acknowledge the "unitive" and "procreative" aspects of human sexuality and, therefore, that all artificial methods of birth control are unacceptable.

1968 The Mexican pharmaceutical company Syntex introduces the first progesterone-only birth control pill to the French market. It is withdrawn two years later because of safety concerns.

1970s The rise of genetic engineering provides scientists with mechanisms for making fundamental alterations in an individual's genetic composition, thus making possible, at least in theory, the rise of a new science of eugenics.

1970 The U.S. Congress passes the Family Planning Program, Title X of which is the Services and Public Research Act of 1970. The law is the only federal dedicated source of funding for family planning services in the United States.

1972 In the case of *Eisenstadt v. Baird* (405 US 438), the U.S. Supreme Court strikes down a Massachusetts law limiting the sale of contraceptives to married couples.

1973 In the case of *Roe v. Wade*, the U.S. Supreme Court establishes a federal policy for abortion services in the United States. It prohibits the banning of abortion during the first trimester of a woman's pregnancy but permits state legislation for actions in the second and third trimesters.

1973 A team of British researchers including Carl Wood, John Leeton, and Alan Trounson conducts the first successful in vitro fertilization procedure in modern history. The resulting pregnancy lasts only a few days.

1976 The U.S. Congress passes the Medical Device Amendments to the Federal Food, Drug and Cosmetic Act. The Act requires the FDA to require applicants to supply data on the testing of certain new medical devices, such as contraception. These requirements were not previously in place, meaning that most contraceptives had not been tested by standard methods for safety and efficacy before being released to the marketplace.

1976 American inventor Bruce Ward Vorhauer designs the Today vaginal sponge. It first becomes available on the marketplace in 1983 and rapidly becomes by far the most popular contraceptive used by American women. Whitehall Robins, manufacturer of the sponge, voluntarily ceased production of the sponge in 1995.

1977   In the case of *Doe v. Irwin* (441 F. Supp. 1247), the U.S. District Court for the Western District of Michigan rules that a person of any age is allowed to withhold information about her or his contraceptive experiences from parents.

1979   In the case of *Bellotti v. Baird* (443 US 622), the U.S. Supreme Court rules that women under the age of 18 are not required to notify their parents of an intent to have an abortion.

1980   French chemist Georges Teutsch develops mifepristone, an abortifacient that is effective for a period of about seven weeks following intercourse. The drug is later marketed commercially under the trade name of RU486.

1981   The U.S. Congress passes the Adolescent Family Life Act, one section of which provides for federal funding for "self discipline" (i.e., abstinence) methods of birth control programs in American schools.

1983   The U.S. District Court for the District of Utah rules on the confidentiality of minors' use of contraceptives, saying that "the state may not impose a blanket parental notification requirement on minors seeking to exercise their constitutionally protected right to decide whether to bear or to beget a child by using contraceptives." (*Planned Parenthood Ass'n of Utah v. Matheson*, 582 F. Supp. 1001 [D. Utah 1983].)

1983   In the case of *Bolger v. Youngs Drug Products Corporation* (463 US 60), the U.S. Supreme Court rules that it is unconstitutional to prohibit the sending of unsolicited mail dealing with contraceptives through the U.S. postal system.

1984   The administration of President Ronald Reagan implements the so-called Mexico City Policy, banning federal funding to any non-governmental organization anywhere in the world that provides abortion information, counseling, or services. That policy was later rescinded by Democratic presidents and reasserted by Republican presidents to the present day.

1984   Danish physician Lasse Hessel develops a prototype female condom. It does not become a commercial success.

1986   The term *outercourse* is first used in an article on teenage sexuality in the *Psychology Today* magazine.

1988   The FDA approves a copper IUD (Paragard) for use in the United States.

1988   RU486 is approved for use in France. Distribution is quickly halted, however, because of religious and moral arguments against its use as an abortifacient.

1988   The FDA approves use of the Prentif Cavity-Rim Cervical Cap for use in the United States. The action comes about 70 years after a similar device had been made available to women in England.

1988   The U.S. Supreme Court rejects arguments that the Adolescent Family Act is unconstitutional in that it violates the Establishment Clause of the First Amendment, which forbids Congress from passing laws "respecting an establishment of religion." The case is *Bowen v. Kendrick* (487 US 589).

1989   The FDA bans importation of RU486 into the United States.

1989   Austrian gynecologist Dr. Maria Hengstberger invents a method for estimating the times at which a women is most likely to be fertile, called *cyclebeads*. The device is especially useful in developing countries, where making such determinations may be a challenge for some women. Development of the device was later taken over by the Institute for Reproductive Health at Georgetown University.

1990   The FDA approves the first hormonal contraceptive implant, Norplant, produced in the United States by Wyeth Pharmaceuticals. The product is plagued by production issues and some serious side effects. Its use was discontinued in Great

Britain in 1999, in the United States in 2002, and the rest of the world by 2008.

1990   The New York City public school system creates a program for the free distribution of condoms to students who request them.

1991   The FDA approves the production and use of Depo Provera, an injectable contraceptive. It requires a notice that the drug is still being tested and may have deleterious effects on bone formation. In 2004, it changes its approval conditions to require a notice on the product's box stating that long-term use of the drug may contribute to the development of osteoporosis.

1993   In her book *Outercourse: The Bedazzling Voyage*, lesbian writer Mary Daly discusses a form of sexual contact that does not involve penetration.

1993   The FDA issues a premarket application approval for the first modern female condom, called the Reality Female Condom (later changed to FC1).

1994   A group of black women who feel that existing organizations do not adequately represent the special contraceptive needs of women of color form a new organization, Women of African Descent for Reproductive Justice, to remedy that situation. The group later expands to include women of all race, ethnicity, sexual orientation, income, and sexual identity to form the collaborative group SisterSong Women of Color Reproductive Justice Collective in 1997.

1994   The U.S. Congress passes the Freedom of Access to Clinic Entrances Act, which prohibits a number of actions attempting to prevent individuals from obtaining information and other services at clinics providing reproductive services and at various religious facilities. Such actions include blocking a person's access to the entrance of a facility, preventing cars from entering and/or exiting a facility, making it difficult or dangerous to get in and/or out of a facility, trespassing on the property of a facility, vandalism of a facility, stalking a clinic employee or reproductive health care provider, arson or threats of arson, and bombings or bomb threats.

1996   The Temporary Assistance for Needy Family Act of 1996 provides for funding of abstinence-only-until-marriage sex education in U.S. schools.

1998   Maryland becomes the first state to pass the so-called contraceptive mandate, requiring that insurance companies offer coverage for contraceptive services.

2000   The Special Projects of Regional and National Significance—Community-Based Abstinence Education (SPRANS) provides for funding of abstinence-only-until-marriage sex education in U.S. schools.

2000   The U.S. Equal Employment Opportunity Commission rules that any employer who provides insurance coverage for any prescription drug must also provide coverage for contraceptives.

2001   The Ortho-McNeil Pharmaceutical company receives approval from the FDA for its transdermal hormonal contraceptive patch, marketed under the trade name of Ortho Evra, or just Evra.

2001   The FDA approves the first hormonal IUD (Mirena) for sale in the United States.

2001   The FDA approves the first vaginal contraceptive ring, Nuva Ring, produced by the Merck company.

2003   In the case of *Chaffee v. Seslar* (786 N.E.2d 705), the Indiana Supreme Court rules on the legal indemnity of a surgeon who performs an unsuccessful sterilization operation of a women, who later becomes pregnant. The case is commonly referred to one of *wrongful pregnancy*.

2004   A report prepared for Representative Henry Waxman (D-OR) finds that "over 80% of the abstinence-only curricula, used by over two thirds of SPRANS grantees in 2003, contain false, misleading, or distorted information about reproductive health." ("The Content of Federally Funded Abstinence-only Education Programs." 2004. United States House of Representatives. Committee on Government Reform—Minority Staff. Special Investigations Division. https://spot.colorado.edu/~tooley/HenryWaxman.pdf. Accessed on May 25, 2019.)

2005   The Today vaginal sponge is once more made available in the marketplace under its new name of the Today Sponge.

2006   The FDA approves Implanon, a single rod contraceptive implant for use by injection under the skin.

2009   The FDA issues an approval notice for the Female Health Company's female condom, FC2. The product is a version of its FC1 but made of a different material. The agency begins to refer to such products as *internal condoms* rather than *female condoms*.

2010   The U.S. Congress passes the Patient Protection and Affordable Care Act (ACA; Obamacare). One provision of the Act is that, with few exceptions, all employers must provide contraceptive coverage as part of their health insurance programs.

2011   A group of interested individuals and organizations create the National Female Condom Coalition to encourage and support information about and research on the female condom.

2014   In the case of *Burwell v. Hobby Lobby Stores, Inc.*, the U.S. Supreme Court rules that closely held corporations need not provide contraceptive coverage in the health insurance plans if they present religious or moral reasons for opposing contraception.

2018   President Donald Trump's FY2018 budget calls for $277 million for the funding of abstinence-only-until-marriage sex education classes in US schools from 2018 to 2024.

2018   The U.S. Department of Health and Human Services announces the creation of a Conscience and Religious Freedom Division within the department. The purpose of the department is to ensure that a person's religious and moral beliefs are not violated by actions, among others, involving the prescription and use of contraceptive devices.

2018   The American College of Obstetricians and Gynecologists publishes a position statement in which it recommends that oral contraceptive pills be made available on an over-the-counter basis.

2018   Chinese biophysicist He Jiankui announces that a pair of twins with genes edited by the gene-editing tool CRISPR-Cas9 has been born. Some critics suggest that the research marks a new and more dangerous phase of the human eugenics movement.

2019   Several states, including Ohio, Alabama, Missouri, Louisiana, and Georgia, adopt new abortion legislation that, for all practical purposes, bans all or nearly all types of abortion. At the same time, other states, including New York, Virginia, and Vermont, pass laws guaranteeing the right of abortions within their borders.

Birth control is a topic in which many specialized terms are used. Understanding those terms is necessary to have a command of all aspects of many birth control issues. This chapter provides definitions of many such terms, some of which are used in this book and others of which may be encountered in one's future research in the field.

abortifacient   Any substance or other agent that causes an embryo or fetus to be expelled from the womb.

abstinence   The avoidance of sexual contact of any type.

amenorrhea   The absence of menstrual bleeding or suppression of the normal menstrual cycle for three or more consecutive months.

amniocentesis   A prenatal test that allows a healthcare practitioner to diagnose health concerns, genetic diseases, and chromosomal abnormalities in a developing fetus.

anovulation   The absence of ovulation, or release of an egg from the ovary, during the menstrual cycle.

artificial insemination (AI)   Introduction of sperm directly into the female genital tract, without sexual intercourse.

assisted reproductive technology (ART)   Any one of a variety of methods for increasing the likelihood of a woman's becoming pregnant and/or a couple's having children.

barrier methods (of birth control)   Any system that blocks a male's sperm from entering a female's uterus.

Caesarian section   A surgical procedure involving cuts in the abdomen and uterus as an alternative to natural childbirth. Also known simply as C-section.

celibacy   The state of abstaining from marriage and sexual activity.

cervical cap   A barrier method of birth control that consists of a silicone or rubber cut that fits securely on a woman's cervix. *Also see* **diaphragm**.

coition   *See* **sexual intercourse**.

coitus   *See* **sexual intercourse**.

coitus interruptus   A procedure in which a male withdraws his penis from a woman's vagina prior to ejaculation.

coitus reservatus   A procedure in which a man refrains from having climax during sex until a woman reaches organism.

condom   A thin sheath of rubber, plastic, or animal tissue that is worn on the penis during intercourse to prevent pregnancy and sexually transmitted diseases. *Also see* **female condom**.

contraceptive   A chemical, device, or procedure employed to prevent pregnancy.

copulation   *See* **sexual intercourse**.

cryopreservation   The process of storing cells, tissues, or organs at very low temperatures for possible future use.

diaphragm   A barrier method of birth control that covers the cervix and the area around it. Similar to a **cervical cap**. *q.v.*

dilation and curettage (or evacuation); also called D&C or D&E   The removal of tissue from the uterus with a sharp instrument (a currette) and suction.

ectopic pregnancy   Any pregnancy that occurs when an egg implants in any part of the body other than the uterus.

emergency contraception   Any form of contraception, but especially a pill, that can be taken to protect against pregnancy during some specific time period following intercourse.

ensoulment   The moment at which a person's soul is thought to enter her or his body, that is, at which he or she becomes a human being. Also known as **quickening**.

eugenics   The science of controlling the size and characteristics of a population by means of controlled breeding procedures, especially contraception and sterilization.

family planning   The practice of controlling the number of children in a family and the intervals between their births by means of artificial contraception or other means.

female condom   A device similar in appearance and function to the more traditional male condom, inserted into the vagina to prevent sperm from reaching the uterus.

fertility awareness   A contraceptive system that relies on measures such as ovulation times to determine appropriate times for engaging or not engaging in sexual relations.

frottage   A sexual act by which one receives satisfaction by rubbing against another person's body or against some physical object.

gamete intrafallopian transfer (GIFT)   A type of assisted reproductive technology in which eggs are removed from a woman's ovary, and sperm from a man, after which both samples are inserted into the woman's fallopian tube.

gestation period   The length of time between conception and birth, a period of about 266 days in humans.

implant (contraceptive)   A plastic rod about the size and shape of a matchstick containing hormones inserted underneath the skin of a woman's upper arm. Release of the hormones provides protection against pregnancy for extended periods of time.

implantation   The process in which a developing embryo comes into contact with and attaches to the uterine wall.

internal condom   The preferred name for a device formerly known as **female condom**, a version of the male condom intended for use by women.

intrauterine device (IUD)   A small device in the shape of a T made of plastic and placed in the uterus to prevent pregnancy. The device may also contain natural hormones and copper.

IUD   *See* **intrauterine device (IUD)**.

lactational amenorrhea method (LAM)   A form of natural birth control that relies on the new mother feeding her baby breastmilk only for up to six months after the child's birth.

lifestyle drug   A medication designed to improve a person's quality of life at least or as much as, and usually much more than, for the purpose of curing a disease. Other terms for such products are cosmetic, life-enhancing, recreational, or discretionary drugs.

long-acting reversible contraceptive (LARC)   Any method of birth control that provides effective contraception for an extended period without requiring user action. Some forms of LARC are injections, intrauterine devices, and contraceptive implants.

medical (or medication) abortion   An abortion brought about by the use of some chemical introduced into the body.

mini pill   Alternative name for a progesterone-only oral contraceptive pill.

miscarriage   *See* **spontaneous abortion**.

natural family planning   *See* **rhythm method**.

neonatal   The period from birth to 28 days of life.

non-penetrative sex   *See* **sexual outercourse**.

perinatal   The period just before or just after childbirth.

pessary   A device placed in the vagina to support the uterus or rectum or as a contraceptive device.

population control   The use of one or more variety of methods to increase or decrease the population of a geographical area. The most common method employed is birth control, although policies about death rate and immigration and emigration rates are also possible.

quickening   *See* **ensoulment**.

rhythm method   A birth control technique that involves the assignment of sexual relations to one or another part of a woman's menstrual cycle in order either to increase or to decrease the likelihood of pregnancy.

sexual intercourse   Any action that involves the penetration by one body part of one individual into one body part of a second individual, perhaps most commonly involving the penetration of a woman's vagina by a man's penis. Also called **coitus**, **coition**, and **copulation**.

sexual outercourse   Any form of sexual activity that does not involve the penetration of one person's body part into a second person's body part. Some examples include masturbation, mutual masturbation, kissing, cuddling, frottage, and cunnilingus. Also known as **non-penetrative sex**. The term is relatively recent and is still subject to a considerable variety of interpretations.

spermatocide   Any substance with the ability to kill sperm.

spontaneous abortion   Loss of an embryo or fetus as the result of natural conditions and not an intentional attempt to bring about this result. Also called a **miscarriage**.

sterile   Incapable of having children.

surrogate   A woman who agrees to carry an embryo/fetus and then give birth to a child for another woman or a couple.

telehealth   *See* **telemedicine**.

telemedicine   A system by which medical conditions can be diagnosed, explained, and treated by long-distance means, such as computer contact. Also called **telehealth**.

vaginal suppository   A thin sheet of material, about two inches square, that can be inserted into the vagina. At body temperature, it becomes liquid and can protect against infections and act as a contraceptive device.

vasectomy   The surgical cutting and/or blocking of all or part of the vas deferens ducts that deliver sperm from the testicles to the urethra. The procedure is used to make a male sterile.

womb veil   A type of barrier contraception used in 19th-century America consisting of a modified type of pessary.

Index

Page numbers followed by *t* indicate tables.

About the Author

David E. Newton holds an associate's degree in science from Grand Rapids (Michigan) Junior College, a BA in chemistry (with high distinction), an MA in education from the University of Michigan, and an EdD in science education from Harvard University. He is the author of more than 400 textbooks, encyclopedias, resource books, research manuals, laboratory manuals, trade books, and other educational materials. He taught mathematics, chemistry, and physical science in Grand Rapids, Michigan, for thirteen years; was professor of chemistry and physics at Salem State College in Massachusetts for fifteen years; and was adjunct professor in the College of Professional Studies at the University of San Francisco for ten years.

The author's previous books for ABC CLIO include *Global Warming* (1993), *Gay and Lesbian Rights: A Resource Handbook* (1994, 2009), *The Ozone Dilemma* (1995), *Violence and the Media* (1996), *Environmental Justice* (1996, 2009), *Encyclopedia of Cryptology* (1997), *Social Issues in Science and Technology: An Encyclopedia* (1999), *DNA Technology* (2009, 2016), *Sexual Health* (2010), *The Animal Experimentation Debate* (2013), *Marijuana* (2013, 2017), *World Energy Crisis* (2013), *Steroids and Doping in Sports* (2014, 2018), *GMO Food* (2014), *Science and Political Controversy* (2014), *Wind Energy* (2015), *Fracking* (2015), *Solar Energy* (2015), *Youth Substance Abuse* (2016), *Global Water Crisis* (2016), *Same-Sex Marriage* (2011, 2016), *Sex and Gender* (2017), *STDs in the United States* (2018), *Natural Disasters* (2019), *Vegetarianism and Veganism* (2019),

Spotlight on Current Events (editor, 2019), *Eating Disorders* (2019), and *Gender Inequality* (2019). His other recent books include *Physics: Oryx Frontiers of Science Series* (2000), *Sick!* (4 volumes) (2000), *Science, Technology, and Society: The Impact of Science in the 19th Century* (2 volumes, 2001), *Encyclopedia of Fire* (2002), *Molecular Nanotechnology: Oryx Frontiers of Science Series* (2002), *Encyclopedia of Water* (2003), *Encyclopedia of Air* (2004), *The New Chemistry* (6 volumes, 2007), *Nuclear Power* (2005), *Stem Cell Research* (2006), *Latinos in the Sciences, Math, and Professions* (2007), and *DNA Evidence and Forensic Science* (2008). He has also been an updating and consulting editor on a number of books and reference works, including *Chemical Compounds* (2005), *Chemical Elements* (2006), *Encyclopedia of Endangered Species* (2006), *World of Mathematics* (2006), *World of Chemistry* (2006), *World of Health* (2006), *UXL Encyclopedia of Science* (2007), *Alternative Medicine* (2008), *Grzimek's Animal Life Encyclopedia* (2009), *Community Health* (2009), *Genetic Medicine* (2009), *The Gale Encyclopedia of Medicine* (2010–2011), *The Gale Encyclopedia of Alternative Medicine* (2013), *Discoveries in Modern Science: Exploration, Invention, and Technology* (2013–2014), and *Science in Context* (2013–2014).